STEPHEN GUY-BRAY

Against Reproduction

Where Renaissance Texts Come From

UNIVERSITY OF TORONTO PRESS
Toronto Buffalo London

© University of Toronto Press Incorporated 2009
Toronto Buffalo London
www.utppublishing.com
Printed in Canada

ISNB 978-1-4426-4060-3

∞

Printed on acid-free, 100% post-consumer recycled paper with vegetable-based inks.

Library and Archives Canada Cataloguing in Publication

Guy-Bray, Stephen
  Against reproduction: where Renaissance texts come from / Stephen
Guy-Bray.

  Includes bibliographical references and index.
  ISBN 978-1-4426-4060-3

1. English drama – Early modern and Elizabethan, 1500–1600 – History
and criticism.   2. English drama – 17th century – History and criticism.
3. English poetry – Early modern, 1500–1700 – History and criticism.
4. Human reproduction in literature.   5. Marriage in literature.   6. Seduction
in literature.   7. Sex in literature.   8. Metaphor in literature.   I. Title.

PR418.T48G89 2009   820.9'353809031   C2009-903701-7

University of Toronto Press acknowledges the financial assistance to its publishing program of the Canada Council for the Arts and the Ontario Arts Council.

 Canada Council   **Conseil des Arts**   **ONTARIO ARTS COUNCIL**
for the Arts   **du Canada**   **CONSEIL DES ARTS DE L'ONTARIO**

University of Toronto Press acknowledges the financial support for its
publishing activities of the Government of Canada through the Book
Publishing Industry Development Program (BPIDP).

This book has been published with the help of a grant from the Canadian
Federation for the Humanities and Social Sciences, through the Aid to
Scholarly Publications Programme, using funds provided by the Social
Sciences and Humanities Research Council of Canada.

This book is for Julie Beebe

Contents

Preface

From the early 1970s on, scholars doing historical work in gay and lesbian studies in English (and other) departments were concerned chiefly with uncovering homosexuality in the past and with looking at and bringing to light gay lives and histories. In the late 1980s what is now called queer theory emerged, to a great extent in response to activism around AIDS. It dealt more with what homosexuality meant and how it was figured at any given time: as an intellectual movement – and it was much more as well – queer theory has drawn much of its vocabulary and theory from cultural studies and from semiotics. The emphasis was less on history in any traditional sense, that is, and more on representation (which is, of course, also true of much history done in the last thirty years or so). Many of the early writings that demonstrated this shift in focus were published in 1987 in an influential special issue of *October* called 'AIDS: Cultural Analysis / Cultural Activism.' The subtitle indicates that activism was still seen as a crucial aspect of this kind of intellectual work, and many of the most distinguished critics of this time were, in fact, also prominent in various kinds of AIDS activism). The repetition of the adjective *cultural* demonstrates the centrality of representation both to people's thinking about AIDS and to their ideas about what to do. While to a greater or lesser extent all the essays in this special issue count as required reading, I want to single out Leo Bersani's 'Is the Rectum a Grave?' as the piece that did most to inaugurate the kind of queer theory that I see myself as doing in this book, in which my concern is with the use of the reproductive metaphor to describe textual production. The reproductive metaphor that I discuss here inescapably sexualizes textual production, meaning that both homoeroticism and heteroeroticism come into play as ways of describing the connection between writers and other writers, writers and texts, and even between texts. I am interested in what is at stake in this attempt to understand both composition and finished texts within a heterosexual framework.

One of Bersani's aims in this article was to combat the idea that homosexuality was necessarily allied with a progressive politics: 'gay activist rhetoric has even managed at times to suggest that a lust for other men's bodies is a by-product or a decision consequent upon political radicalism rather than a given point of departure for a whole range of political sympathies. While it is indisputably true that sexuality is always being politicized, the ways in which *having sex* politicizes are highly problematical.'[1] To some extent, the conflation of homosexuality and progressive politics – a conflation that has by no means entirely disappeared – reflected the nature of the gay liberation movement in the early 1970s. Although there is much to be said for the association of transgressive sexuality and transgressive politics, both as a rhetorical strategy and as a desideratum, even a casual observer in the second half of the 1980s would have been aware that this association was no longer an accurate characterization of what was in any case no longer a coherent movement (if indeed it ever had been). But Bersani's point is not only a point about politics: in separating politics and sexuality, he crucially opens sexuality to a greater range of possible meanings in relation to and distinct from politics. Sexuality, he argues, is not something that has one political meaning but is rather part of a semiotic system that is capable of assuming multiple significations both in and of itself and in combination with other semiotic systems such as politics and culture. Both in the sense of a personal drive and in the sense of a series of actions, sexuality represents and is represented in a variety of ways.

In the second half of his essay, Bersani turns from the relation between sexuality and politics to a consideration of the ways in which the self is affected by sex. Rather than seeing sex as something that defines and supports the self, which could be said to have been one of the central tenets of gay liberation, Bersani argues that sex is instead potentially something that disrupts the secure identity on which our idea of selfhood is premised. Furthermore, he argues that the secure self – in this context, the well-adjusted male homosexual whose emergence as a subject was one of the chief aims of the gay liberation movement – is actually an indispensable part of the pernicious imbrication of masculinity and power and of power and sexuality more generally: 'the self which the sexual shatters provides the basis on which sexuality is associated with power.'[2] While a shattered self seems to be exactly the kind of thing that would require psychoanalytic treatment, something that is the result of the generalized and vicious homophobia of society, Bersani argues that the anality with which gay men are associated – always a source of abjection and now, with the advent of AIDS, strongly associated in the popular imaginary with danger, infection, and death – might provide a way out of always thinking sex through power: 'It may, finally, be in the gay man's rectum that he demolishes his own perhaps otherwise uncontrollable identification with a murderous judgment against him.'[3] In refusing the lure of the stable and well-adjusted self and in admitting the dark pleasures of anality (and even of an anal sexuality seen as a danger to society as a whole), gay men could perhaps represent both themselves and their sexualities in ways that might really be transgressive.

Bersani's approach opened up a number of questions that queer theory and queer cultural work has been asking ever since. In this highly selective survey, I want to identify the two possibilities that I see as most important. One is whether what is at issue, not just in sex but in any bodily activity, is not the exteriorization of the self but rather the performance of something that may or not be the self – an entity that may or not be real in any case – and that may or not be permanent. The most famous treatment of this subject is Judith Butler's *Gender Trouble: Feminism and the Subversion of Identity*. To some extent, Butler's critical project is continuous with Bersani's theories insofar as here, as well, the emphasis is on the self as something that is created through action, although her focus is on very different kinds of action. In her analysis, sexual activity does not have a privileged place as an agent of shattering; indeed, she has little to say about sex as such and concentrates instead on the performative aspects of everyday life. The discussions in which Butler participated have been very helpful for queer theory, perhaps most notably in that they have helped to show the extent to which it makes no sense to speak of real identities, or rather that such talk is the effect of discursively mediated power relations. While gay liberation sought to establish gay identity as valid and authentic (in other words, as just as good as straight identity), Butler challenges the idea that any sexual identity can really be valid and authentic. Rather than concentrate on what people were really like or on what form a fully enfranchised gay citizen would take, queer theorists could turn to examining the various acts (including speech acts) by which people constitute (and reconstitute) their identities. This line of inquiry also focuses on representation, although the representations in question are not necessarily literary or artistic.

Another set of questions has concentrated on Bersani's focus on abjection and on his concern with artistic strategies of representation. One of the best examples is D.A. Miller's 'Anal Rope,' an analysis of Alfred Hitchcock's 'Rope,' a film that is famous both for being shot in one take (or so we were led to believe) and for being a fictionalized version of the notorious Leopold and Loeb case, a story that associates homosexuality, intellectual elitism, and amorality in a way considered typical of homophobic discourse. Miller begins his discussion by connecting the focus in film criticism on the film's technical innovation with the inability to talk about the extent to which the film is about homosexuals or homosexuality. As he remarks, 'The heavy silence surrounding homosexuality requires explanation no less than the featherweight fussing over technique.' Pointing out that the censorship of the time prevented any explicit presentation of homosexuality, Miller asks about the film's two main characters: 'how do we think we know?' This question is at the heart of his brilliant analysis, and by way of answer he draws attention to the ways in which homosexuality was (and to a considerable degree still is) thought of as something that can be detected by signs and, ultimately, as something that consists primarily or even solely of signs. As Miller notes, 'if connotation, as the dominant signifying practice of homophobia, has the advantage of constructing an essentially insubstantial homosexuality, it has the corresponding inconvenience of tending to raise this ghost all over the place.'[4]

Miller's unfortunately rare combination of theoretical sophistication and formal expertise is shared by Lee Edelman, whose work has also been highly influential. In his book *Homographesis* (1994), Edelman turns his considerable talent for close reading and his knowledge of cultural and psychoanalytic theory to discussing a number of texts, perhaps most notably the film *Laura*. In a series of absorbing analyses, Edelman demonstrates a subtle awareness of how sexuality functions as a semiotic system in relation with other semiotic systems and how queerness is always bound up in issues of representation.[5] Like Bersani and Miller, Edelman has been very useful to me in a number of ways throughout this book. For one, these critics have explored abjection. Given the premium on 'positive role models' and 'positive representations' typical of much earlier work in gay studies, any association between homosexuality and abjection originally was taboo. More recently – and largely, I would argue, because of the critics I have cited – queer theory has begun to look at abjection and at what is now increasingly called gay shame. Among the many texts in this field I would single out Kathryn Bond Stockton's *Beautiful Bottom, Beautiful Shame*, Heather Love's *Feeling Backward*, and the essays in the very recent collection edited by David M. Halperin and Valerie Traub called *Gay Shame*.[6] Most directly, this focus on abjection has informed many of my discussions of textual production in this book. For instance, although we often think about writing as satisfying and even triumphant, I was struck by how often Renaissance writers identify writing with abjection of the body and of the spirit.

As well, these critics, and the many others like them, have helped to remove queer theory from an exclusive focus on the somatic and enabled it to concentrate on the semiotic aspect of queerness, an aspect that is central to *Against Reproduction*'s examination of queerness and textuality.[7] It was inevitable, of course, that a branch of scholarly inquiry that in many respects traces its origins to the gay liberation movement would focus on bodies and sexuality. And it is also inevitable that scholars growing up in times in which homosexuality could really be discussed only in medical, religious, or legal discourses would wish to point out how many gay people there are and always have been. And these things are not only inevitable but also advisable. Nevertheless, as one way of making the undeniably valuable points that the personal is political and also that the sexual is cultural, it is necessary to look at how sex and sexual identity are always discursive as well and at how sexuality, whether one's own or other people's, is often experienced in non-sexual ways. As one of our most important semiotic systems, sexuality inheres not only in people's sense of themselves or in their somatic activities but also in cultural texts and social relations more generally. These insights have been crucial for my own work. Queerness is still at issue, then, even if we are no longer speaking of real bodies or of what we would consider real sexual activity.

The final aspect of these critics that I want to mention as being useful to my own work is their opposition to teleology, including the teleology of the well-adjusted gay man. This opposition is especially prevalent in the work of Edelman, especially in his most recent publication, *No Future*. In this book, he attacks what he calls reproductive futurism, which he connects to the popular sense of history as a narrative that he calls 'the poor man's teleology.'[8] Edelman's argument is that both the past and the future are thought in narrative terms, and that the basis of this narrative is the elevation of the child (or, rather, the Child) to central status in our society. Reproduction within the framework of the nuclear family is thus established as what gives meaning both to us and to time. As a result, not only is time itself thought of teleologically inso- far as the purpose of the past is to lead to us and our purpose is to lead to our children, but sex itself is valued because of its teleology. The telos to which sex must lead is children, and sexual activity that does not lead to the conception of future citizens is wasteful and unvalued. In *Against Reproduction*, I connect this view of sex to literature, which I see as something else that is evaluated teleologically. Poetry, that is, must produce a result that is useful in a socially legible manner. Focusing on teleology has enabled me to discuss the ways in which poets deal with the requirement that their writing must lead to something and the sex- ualization inherent in the reproductive metaphor has enabled me to consider the extent to which many poets who use or misuse or abuse this metaphor also comment on ideas about sexual teleology. What is more, in associating textual production with abjection, some of the poets I discuss tacitly present their poems as objects that are perhaps incapable of being recuperated within a teleological framework.

I am aware, of course, that to write any account (however abbreviat- ed and tendentious) of one's intellectual influences lays one open to the charge of having constructed a teleological narrative with oneself as the happy ending, the product of one's own labours. However, this is not my intention. For one thing, the book that follows reveals many other intellectual influences and thus qualifies the status of this preface as a teleological statement. For another, queer theory's recent interest in time means that many other scholars are dealing with these subjects, and the passage of time itself means that many works appeared too late to be included in my book. Among these, I would like to single out Madhavi Menon's superb *Unhistorical Shakespeare*, a work that resists teleology both in its argument and in its arrangement. One thing that has struck both Menon and me is that many queer theorists, even ex- plicitly anti-teleological ones, often implicitly reproduce the standard historical teleology by seeing queer work on twentieth-century litera- ture as queer theory and queer work on the literature of earlier periods as historical scholarship: in effect, while scholars of Renaissance litera- ture may use queer theory, their work somehow does not qualify as real queer theory. Although from the beginning of this preface, I will seem to have been assenting to this view by tracing my intellectual develop- ment to works of queer theory concerned with twentieth-century texts, I end here by returning to a past that is not only queer in itself but also a site that produces queer theory.

Acknowledgments

To write a book about textual production is to become very self-conscious about the amount of other people's work that goes into one's own textual production. Throughout the writing of this book, I have relied on the intelligence, kindness, and patience of a large number of people. I have also relied on money, so I begin by gratefully the support of the Social Sciences and Research Council of Canada, which awarded me a Standard Research Grant. Part of chapter 2 appeared in somewhat different form in *Explorations in Renaissance Culture*. I thank the journal and its editor, Frances Malpezzi, for allowing me to reprint it here.

Much of the work that goes into producing a text is done by publishers. As always, Suzanne Rancourt has been helpful, efficient, and a pleasure to deal with. The two anonymous readers made many cogent suggestions that helped me to revise the book and make it stronger. Barb Porter and Catherine Frost handled the transition from manuscript to book with skill, efficiency, and tact.

My department has been a great source of support of all kinds. I thank my colleagues, especially Patricia Badir, Miranda Burgess, Barbara Dancygier, Dennis Danielson, Tony Dawson, Alex Dick, Siân Echard, Elizabeth Hodgson, Christina Lupton, Greg Mackie, Vin Nardizzi (whose acumen and good sense were invaluable throughout the writing of this book), Julia Staykova, Mark Vessey, and Gernot Wieland. I also thank the excellent staff of the department, especially Angela Kaija, Patricia Lackie, Donna Shanley, and Dominique Yupangco. They have made my work much easier. I am grateful to Craig Sabasch for his celerity. I benefited greatly from my participation in the NFBI: thanks to Meryn Cadell, Lisa Coulthard, and Kirsty Johnston.

I taught two versions of this book as graduate courses, and I also tried out many of the ideas and theories that are central to this book in undergraduate courses on gay fiction, on lyric subjectivity, and on Sir Philip Sidney. I thank the students in these courses for many helpful comments and many interesting discussions; I would like to single out Manuel Betancourt, Mono Brown, Jordana Greenblatt, Tom Hill, Eve Preus, Shaun Ross, Fenn Stewart, James Stevenson, and Paul Sutton, as well as Katie Calloway, my superb teaching assistant. Some of the preliminary research for this book was skilfully done by John Green and Rachel Kreuger, and I am happy to acknowledge their interest and efficiency. I also thank my doctoral student Ágnes MacDonald, who prepared the index: hálásan megköszönöm a kedves diákomnak, nyelv tanáromnak, és barátnémnek.

I gave versions of parts of this book as talks and conference papers, a way of doing research that I find indispensable. I thank the organizers and audience members at the following colloquia and conferences: in 2006, the Inside / Out Speakers Series at the University of Alberta, the Renaissance Society of America in San Francisco, Queer People III in Cambridge, and the Modern Language Association in Philadelphia; in 2007, the Group for Early Modern Studies at the University of Arizona; in 2008, the Marlowe Society of America in Canterbury and Queer People IV in Cambridge. In particular, I am grateful to Caroline Gonda and Chris Mounsey for organizing the Queer People conferences, which are a wonderful environment in which to present work; to Kristina Straub for a helpful suggestion; to Georgia Brown, for inviting me to the Marlowe Society conference; and, in Tucson, to Kari McBride for her hospitality and Cyndi Headley for her efficiency.

Going to conferences is also a wonderful way to meet interesting and congenial people. I thank all these people wholeheartedly. I am especially happy to mention how good it always is to see Rebecca Bach, Amanda Bailey, Bruce Boehrer, Gina Bloom, Will Fisher, Alexandra Halasz, Graham Hammill, Elizabeth Hanson, Jonathan Gil Harris, Natasha Korda, Joan Pong Linton, Joyce MacDonald, Jeff Masten, Steve Mentz, David Orvis, Rick Rambuss, Goran Stanivukovic, Will Stockton, Ayanna Thompson, Henry Turner, and Sue Wiseman, even if I don't see them nearly often enough. I am particularly grateful for both the friendship and the intellectual enlightenment generously given to me by Madhavi Menon. My friends Barb Morris and Craig Patterson have contributed more than they know. I am fortunate to have the inestimable benefit of Tom Kemple's understanding, support, wisdom, and critical acuity. It gives me enormous pleasure to dedicate this book to Julie Beebe, the best friend ever.

AGAINST REPRODUCTION:
WHERE RENAISSANCE TEXTS COME FROM

Introduction: The Work of Art in the Age of Human Reproduction

In her *Sociable Letters*, first published in 1664, the Duchess of Newcastle spoke of her literary productions as 'paper bodies,' a brilliantly memorable phrase that provides the title for a recent selection of her writing. As the editors of this selection note, Newcastle described her first book (*Poems and Fancies*, published in 1653) 'as a kind of substitute for physical offspring: "Condemne me not for making such a coyle / About my Book, alas it is my Childe."'[1] In these lines, Newcastle uses the familiar reproductive metaphor, according to which the author is the parent of the work and writing a text is like having a baby, but her use of the image of the paper body in its original context in *Sociable Letters* is more unusual. In Letter CXLIII, Newcastle tells her (imaginary) correspondent that she had heard that the ship carrying her plays to be printed has sunk, and that she would have been worried had it not been her practice to keep copies of all her manuscripts. Newcastle goes on to say that she keeps these copies until the books based on them are published and then she 'commit[s] the Originals to the Fire, like Parents, which are willing to Die, whenas they are sure of their Childrens Lives.'[2] It is only at this point that she speaks of her texts as paper bodies. In this metaphor, then, the author is not the parent of the text. It is the copies that are the parents and that act like parents. The papers themselves become the parents of the published books, here imagined as their offspring and, in an unusually extended version of the reproductive metaphor, as having bodies.

Newcastle's use of the metaphor in *Sociable Letters* does a number of interesting things. While in 1653 she wrote of her texts as children, in 1664, although she retained the reproductive metaphor, it was no longer she, as the work's author, who was doing the reproducing. Following the logical consequences of this figure of speech, Newcastle realizes that if texts are children, then they must have bodies – even if only paper ones – and that these bodies might be fertile. In other words, Newcastle's refashioning of the reproductive metaphor ascribes agency and sexuality to her texts: these paper bodies can have paper sex.[3] This agency might even be seen in the title *Sociable Letters*, which could be understood to mean that the book will contain letters that seek out the company of other letters. What is more, what assures the children's lives in this version of the metaphor is their transformation from the loose papers of manuscripts to the bound papers of books. When Newcastle came to write *Sociable Letters*, then, the reproductive metaphor was still useful, but she applied it to copying and printing rather than to writing. That is, the books may be still children, but they are not her children; in fact, by the time the paper bodies have paper sex and produce their own paper offspring, they are not children at all: Newcastle's use of the reproductive metaphor actually grants her texts autonomy rather than brings them further under her control.

However, Newcastle's version of the metaphor has not been the dominant one. The presentation of the author as a parent and the book as his or her child is so widespread as to have become a dead metaphor – or at least a zombie metaphor, as most uses of this figure of speech have been unreflective, or even mindless, and the idea that the author is the parent of his or her work has become so much a part of what everyone apparently knows. Newcastle's interrogation of the metaphor does not appear to have influenced other writers, whose use of it tends to stop at the idea that books are like children: there is almost never any consideration of what it would really mean to endow books with life. What is more, even critical discussions of the reproductive metaphor have tended not to challenge it but rather to seek to modify it so as to extend it to female authors. In a way, of course, this is a welcome development, since, as Eve Kosofsky Sedgwick remarks in *Epistemology of the Closet*, 'the language of sexuality not only intersects with but transforms the other languages and relations by which we know.'[4] As the popularity of the reproductive metaphor demonstrates, the 'relations by which we know' are literally or metaphorically familial relations. It is necessary to consider the ways in which this transformation occurs, the meanings of the resulting transformations, and the role that women play (or are made to play) in these relations, but the feminist intervention does not, as a rule, go far enough.

One interesting exception to this trend can be found in a recent book called *Literary Relations: Kinship and the Canon, 1660–1830* by Jane Spencer, who focuses on literary influence and on the possibility that the relationship between a male writer and a female predecessor could be re-imagined as a mother / son relationship. Here the family – perhaps our basic image of social control – is used to control not texts but male authors, and the heavily patriarchal model of literary history is rethought: it is the female author who is primary and the male author who is secondary. Spencer concludes her book by saying, 'New configurations of writers, different kinds of canons, will need other metaphors.'[5] One such metaphor was identified by Frances Teague in her article 'Early Modern Women and "the muses ffemall."' Teague argues that male authorities in the Renaissance feared that the muses – who are, after all, goddesses rather than gods – inspired female authors by having sex with them. Interestingly, at a time when male authors were not typically presented as having a sexual relationship with the muses, female authors were: an exception to the customary ignoring of female homoeroticism. However, it does not appear that the female authors themselves used this trope, nor does it appear to have been taken up by recent authors, although it would certainly be a welcome addition to our stock of metaphors.

New tropes of textual production are welcome, but sometimes a transformation of the same old metaphor might be useful in transforming our thinking. For instance, in the acknowledgments to her novel *Stone Butch Blues*, first published in 1993, Leslie Feinberg thanks one of her femmes by speaking of her 'commitment to this book – from planting the seed to midwifing its birth ("Push, push!").'[6] Here, the reproductive metaphor is used in a way that complicates its relation to sexual reproduction. As a female author, Feinberg imagines herself giving birth to the book, but her femme acts as a man in planting the seed. The question of how the metaphor is to be mapped onto the women's bodies is complicated by the fact that a midwife can be male or female and further complicated, as Feinberg is the butch in this relationship; that she assumes the feminine role of childbirth while her femme takes a masculine role reminds us that the tendency to understand the butch / femme dynamic as corresponding to or mimicking (or reproducing) male / female relations points to a lack of subtlety in thinking about gender and an insistence on seeing heterosexuality as real, original, and primary. Feinberg is thus able to use the reproductive metaphor without being caught up in the network of socio-political ideas about gender and sexuality that usually accompanies it and against which this book seeks to work.[7]

Spencer's call for new metaphors and Feinberg's refashioning of the metaphor have been the exception rather than the rule, however, as many feminist critics have sought merely to extend the metaphor so that women, as well as men, can be the parents of their texts, and they have argued that women have a right to the reproductive metaphor that men do not. Susan Stanford Friedman, one of the first critics to write on this subject, said, for instance, that in the case of a text by a woman writer 'the reader knows that the author has the biological capacity men lack to birth both books and babies.'[8] Without denying that men and women have very different roles in the reproductive process, I feel that I should point out that women do not, as it happens, have the biological capacity to birth books. More recently, Patricia Dienstfrey and Brenda Hillman, the editors of an anthology called *The Grand Permission: New Writings on Poetics and Motherhood*, comment in their introduction, 'Most of our great literary "mothers" of recent history were childless.'[9] At least Dienstfrey and Hillman put quotation marks around the word *mother*; still, their awareness that these women writers had no children should lead them to add a second set: not "mother" but ""mother.""" One of the things that interests me in this debate is to ask in whose interest this propping-up of a very old metaphor is done. Why, to use the examples in this paragraph, is the metaphor maintained by creating new (and surely unwelcome) uses for the uterus or by giving children to dead authors who never reproduced?

A good recent example of the desire to read the metaphor literally can be found in an essay by Jennifer Wynne Hellwarth. In a discussion of Anne Bradstreet, Hellwarth suggests that 'Bradstreet's use of the birth metaphor might seem initially to us more apt or "natural"' than it does coming from male writers. Hellwarth goes on to say that the poet 'was herself a mother of eight, so in some sense the metaphor can be read *literally* as well as symbolically' and adds that Bradstreet's 'tactical use of the birth metaphor is an example of what Judith Rose refers to as a "re-appropriation of female procreative ability."'[10] Perhaps the best way to begin analysing this passage is with the statement that Bradstreet's use of the metaphor can be read literally 'in some sense.' As women cannot literally give birth to books, the only possible meaning of 'in some sense' in this passage is 'metaphorically.'[11] That is, the reproductive metaphor is, in fact, a metaphor, even when used by a woman who has literally given birth. As it happens, Newcastle was a woman who could not give birth, a fact that must have been empha- sized because noblemen's wives were expected to have babies and their fertility was never a private matter and by the fact that her husband had children by his first marriage. Are we to believe that Newcastle's infertility should disqualify her from using the reproductive metaphor? And for that matter, is Bradstreet four times more entitled to the meta- phor than a woman who had only two children?

I am not seriously suggesting that either Friedman or Hellwarth would answer yes to either of these questions. What I do want to sug- gest here is that feminist objections to the use of the reproductive meta- phor by male writers on the grounds that men do not give birth are beside the point. After all, a metaphor is by definition a statement that is not meant to be taken literally. The carrying over indicated by the word *metaphor* is a transfer from the realm of the literal (my book is my book) to the realm of the resemblance (my book is like my child). Unless one were to argue that either masculinity or infertility should deny a writer access to a group of metaphors, the main objection to the femin- ist objection I have identified is that these criticisms posit an essentialist and biological femaleness. It appears that for these critics a woman writer is importantly – and even perhaps most importantly – a human being who has a uterus; the unfortunate effect of this is that the woman writer becomes the only too familiar figure of woman as container for the womb, in this case a womb that comes furnished with metaphorical possibilities. Ironically, while feminist critics typically interrogate vari- ous aspects of patriarchy, they frequently do not question the society that reduces women to this one-use value. Furthermore, the approach seems to me to be particularly unjust in the case of Newcastle, a woman who fought publicly and valiantly against such reductive views of what women are and what women should do.

Of course, it must be admitted that the desire to assign a text to a mother rather than to a father is an understandable response to the power of the author's name in our literary system. As Michel Foucault points out in his highly influential essay on authorship, 'an author's name is not simply an element in a discourse ... it performs a certain role with regard to narrative discourse, assuring a classificatory func tion. Such a name permits one to group together a certain number of texts, define them, differentiate them from and contrast them to others. In addition, it establishes a relationship among the texts.'[12] As Foucault's wording suggests (whether unintentionally or intentionally), for us the reproductive metaphor is built into the very concept of authorship, and part of that concept is that the author is male.[13] Still, it is important to stress the metaphoricity of the metaphor. In a fascinating discussion of Renaissance technologies that worked by making (literal) impressions – the signet ring, the printing press, and so on – Margreta de Grazia says that 'it was not simply that these reproductive machines generated reproductive metaphors. Reproductive metaphors structured reproductive machines.'[14] Discussions of the use of the metaphor tend to assume that this figure of speech arises naturally. De Grazia draws our attention to the possibility that the figure of speech is not caused by, for instance, mechanical reproduction, but may, in fact, be responsible for the forms that mechanical reproduction takes. The relationship among texts of which Foucault writes is then from the very beginning forced to be a family relationship, which is to say, a power structure that is part of a larger apparatus of social control.

Thus, the reproductive metaphor is not simply one metaphor for textual production among many possible ones, but rather is one that has been carefully aligned with our sense of how human sexual relationships should be organized. Judith Roof has suggested that it may even be the case that reproduction itself has a special relationship to metaphor: 'Reproduction is the literalized, material figuration (if any such oxymoron is possible) of metaphor, epitomizing its processes of substitution, condensation, and signification ... the layered substitutions of metaphor produce history, tradition, narrative, and order in the guise of the law which functions ... to impose order on an otherwise chaotic body politic.'[15] We could say, then, that reproduction is always inherently metaphoric and that 'history, tradition, narrative, and order' are always reproduced along with children. The most serious objection to the use of the reproductive metaphor to describe textual reproduction thus is not that the metaphor is hackneyed or that only male authors get to be the figurative parents of their texts or even that the metaphor ignores women's physical experiences of childbirth, but rather that the metaphor brings both the 'otherwise chaotic' writing body and the 'otherwise chaotic' desiring body (and, for that matter, the 'otherwise chaotic' reproducing body) under the rule of law. Furthermore, our contemporary thinking about writing, desiring, and reproducing is exactly that: contemporary. For that reason, I want now to look briefly at literal reproduction in Renaissance England.[16]

I

A great deal of what we now know about how biological reproduction works was discovered in the Renaissance. In an interesting recent book, Eve Keller points out, 'Early modern texts speak of "generation" rather than "reproduction" ... the latter term becomes current only after the physiological processes from conception through birth came to be understood within the context of mechanism.'[17] The shift to a mechanistic view of conception is important, but I propose to continue referring to the reproductive metaphor, as by the end of the sixteenth century the discourses of both social and sexual reproduction were in place and, as the article by de Grazia that I cited earlier suggests, ideas about sexual reproduction were already intertwined with various mechanical forms of reproduction. In any case, conception and birth had always been embedded in larger social discourses, partly because reproduction was seen as one of the basic human duties. In her discussion of Renaissance Italy, for instance, Valeria Finucci argues that at that time 'what makes a man a man [was] not a penis ... but testicles; that is, not phallic potency, but the power to make progeny for society's sake.'[18] Finucci also identifies in the writings of this time 'a fantasy of birth without alterity ... a non-genealogical birth' and discusses at some length popular stories of women conceiving without men, men conceiving without women, and human generation from putrefaction.[19]

The belief that all living things – higher animals (including humans) as well as insects and plants – were capable of various methods of reproduction was not confined to Italy. In a recent article on the famous passage in *Religio Medici* in which Sir Thomas Browne wishes that humans could reproduce like trees without the foolishness of the sex act itself (Browne refers to it as 'this triviall and vulgar way of coition' and 'the foolishest act a wise man commits in all his life'),[20] Marjorie Swann discusses the plethora of beliefs about reproduction in seventeenth-century England. As she points out, 'Browne and his contemporaries believed that God the Creator had devised more than one "method for Generation," establishing nonsexual processes of biological origin as well as the sexual "conjunction" by which Adam and Eve begat humanity.'[21] This sexual conjunction was felt to be only one option among many, and while it was the most common one for humans, even there folk belief, in England as in Italy, suggested that humans could reproduce in other ways. The prevalence of beliefs such as those examined by Finucci and Swann should remind us that Renaissance ideas about the relation between gender and generation worked differently than ours do, and, as a result, that people in the Renaissance would have had a different view of the reproductive metaphor.

For my purposes in this book, these views of reproduction are obviously crucial. If people in the Renaissance could imagine conception and birth without sexual activity or sexual difference, then the reproductive metaphor for textual production appears much less odd – much less metaphoric, we could say, especially given Renaissance beliefs about monstrous births and about the extent to which the fetus was influenced by the mother's thoughts during pregnancy.[22] My argument is that, as it cannot be shown that a male author's claim to have given birth to his text would have appeared ridiculous either on the grounds that humans give birth only to other humans or on the grounds that only women could give birth, the reproductive metaphor in its Renaissance context would appear less strange and would also be less suitable for adaptation to contemporary knowledges and discourses of gender; what is more, I feel that the problematic nature of this adaptation has been insufficiently discussed. In a society in which, as Finucci suggests, there was a fantasy of birth without alterity, then the mechanical reproduction of texts afforded by the printing press, for instance, might seem not just something like reproduction – the source for a metaphor – but actually a version of it.[23] And in a society in which it was believed that pregnancy could occur without sex or that the sex that leads to pregnancy could be between women or between men, it is less credible to speak of appropriating the language of childbirth in the sense of the violation of gender norms.

On the other hand, I am concerned with a certain kind of appropriation of reproduction in the Renaissance: the increasing concern with pregnancy and birth, both in metaphor and in reality, on the part of governments. Always ruled by religious law, reproduction in the English Renaissance was increasingly influenced by and indispensable to civil law as well. This connection has most famously been adumbrated by Foucault in *The History of Sexuality*. After saying that 'a power bent on generating forces, making them grow, and ordering them' has been typical of the West since the Renaissance and characterizing governments as increasingly concerned with the power over life, Foucault argues that 'starting in the seventeenth century, this power over life evolved in two basic forms ... One of these poles ... centred on the body as a machine: its disciplining ... the extortion of its forces ... its integration into systems of efficient and economic controls ... The second ... focused on the species body, the body imbued with the mechanics of life and serving as the basis of the biological processes.'[24] It is the second of these forms, which Foucault calls a bio-politics of the population and which he sees as the first of these forms to appear, that is my chief concern here, although the two forms are obviously closely related. Over the course of the Renaissance in England, the reproductive and reproducing body became not merely a source of religious concern and control but a vital part of the economic and cultural life of the country.

In a recent book, David Glimp argues, 'Biological reproduction requires practices of cultural reproduction' and that in the English population boom during the Renaissance (from approximately 3 million to approximately 5 million between 1550 and 1650) the link between these kinds of reproduction became crucial to government.[25] As Glimp points out, throughout this period reproduction acquired an ever larger discursive presence:

> The frequent attribution of generative effects to the acts of a sovereign, a military leader, a colonial administrator, a pastor, a teacher, or to a poem or play, constitutes an evocative way of imagining the person's or thing's future impact on the community, parish, nation, or faith. Characterizing any endeavor as reproductive likewise calls people to task for their actions, insists that they are obligated to conduct themselves and others in a responsible manner so that what they do will stabilize rather than disrupt families, communities, the church or the polity.[26]

As this passage indicates, both literal and metaphorical reproduction become aspects of the total regulation aimed at by governments.

Under such a regime, reproduction becomes (or becomes to a greater extent) an instrument of social control, and what we think of as the public sphere grows bigger. Seth Lerer has written that one of the typical features of early Tudor literature was 'a poetics of the body: a conception of the act of writing as trespassing in the space between the private and the public.'[27] We might now think of children as the typical inhabitants of this space, but Glimp's argument could be taken to imply that such a space effectively ceased to exist over the course of the Renaissance; this change had important consequences for literature. Once everything is to some extent public, texts have to follow the same rules as people: a poem, like a person, should be a good citizen and contribute to stability. I am suggesting not that there was no censorship before the Renaissance, but rather that because texts were seen as having not only a public existence but also a public role (like children), they became increasingly subject to social regulation throughout the period. Thus, it can be argued that to call human procreation reproduction is already metaphoric, as it suggests that what is desired is a knowable and controllable result. However, the reality of even printing is different. In a recent essay, Stephen Orgel writes, 'What the Renaissance wanted from books was not exact replication, it was dissemination.'[28] He thereby draws a useful parallel between increasing the number of citizens and increasing the number of books and acts as a corrective to our tendency to associate print with absolute textual fixity.[29] With both children and books, some deviation from the originals is permitted, but the fact of dissemination means that the questions of purpose and use become more important and more carefully policed, as do questions of good or bad traits.

One way to characterize my comments on the status of reproduction in the English Renaissance is to say that Renaissance humanism anticipated the 'posthumanity' about which N. Katherine Hayles has written. Here is part of her definition:

> the posthuman privileges informational pattern over material instantiation, so that embodiment in a biological substrate is seen as an accident of history rather than an inevitability of life ... the posthuman view thinks of the body as the original prosthesis we all learn to manipulate, so that extending or replacing the body with other prostheses becomes a continuation of a process that began before we were born ... the posthuman view configures human being so that it can be seamlessly articulated with intelligent machines.[30]

Hayles is concerned chiefly with the effect of computers and other new technologies on ideas about what it means to be human, but I think that we can also see her comments as applying to questions about reproduction in the Renaissance. The importance of human reproduction to social and political reproduction that is Glimp's topic requires a strongly teleological view of both the individual human and the sexual activity that he or she engages in. That is, to put it baldly, people are valued insofar as they will have reproductive sex. Their individual humanity – their 'material instantiations,' as Hayles would say – matters less than the 'informational pattern' they can convey through reproduction: the family name or the inheritance, to name only two examples.

My point is not that in the Renaissance humans were 'articulated with intelligent machines,' as there were as yet no such machines, but rather that in a society in which the most important thing is reproduction, humans themselves become intelligent machines and their sexual activity is evaluated in terms of its use to a society dedicated to self-propagation. The result, as Hayles suggests, is 'a teleology of disembodiment,'[31] since to have a body that can reproduce means, in effect, that it is never your body that is important but only the bodies that will be produced from it. In this economy, sex itself is only a means to an end and never the end in itself. Here, I think, Hayles is building on the work of Gilles Deleuze and Félix Guattari, and specifically on their discussion of the reduction of humans to mechanized adjuncts of the social process. After writing that 'the subject is produced as a mere residuum alongside the desiring-machines,' Deleuze and Guattari expand on this point by arguing that the 'subject itself is not at the center, which is occupied by the machine, but on the periphery, with no fixed identity, forever decentered, *defined* by the states through which it passes.'[32] They are talking not about reproduction here, but rather about a state of affairs in which the need to be productive in a way that is useful to society as a whole comes to be the single most important evaluative criterion. I would argue that for Deleuze and Guattari reproduction is only one of the many ways in which humans are subjected to mechanistic thinking.[33]

The posthuman may seem a depressing concept, and I think this is how it has typically been received, but the idea of intelligent machines can also offer possibilities for thinking in new ways about what texts are and what they can do. Perhaps texts rather than human bodies could be intelligent machines. Here, I am drawing on the work of Henry S. Turner. In his new book on *A Midsummer Night's Dream* and DNA (among other things), Turner discusses Plato's theory of language in the *Cratylus* and concludes, 'Under the cover of a dialogue about the origin of language, we have found a philosophy of action and of acting, including in a theatrical sense, and I will indulge in an act of onomatopoietics and call this philosophy of language-as-action and action-as-language a "dramatology."'[34] For Turner, a play is an intelligent machine, and *A Midsummer Night's Dream* is an especially good example 'of the theater's ability to create life through artificial means, from the smallest unit to the largest: vocable, syllable, word, metaphor, image, line, sentence, phrase, speech, character, prop, group, "scene," "plot," to play itself – the component cells, as we could call them, of a self-replicating organism that lived through artifice and grew through assemblage.'[35] The argument is obviously easier to make about plays than about poems, but poems too, I think, can usefully be thought as this kind of organism: artificial, artful, alive. Turner's 'dramatology' gives us a way to look at texts outside the reproductive paradigm.

I also want to make the point that mechanistic thinking about the body is not unknown in English Renaissance writing. Perhaps the best-known example comes from the very beginning of Thomas Hobbes's *Leviathan*. While *Leviathan*'s famous frontispiece would seem to present the state as a humanoid organism, Hobbes does not actually argue that this is the case. Indeed, as Leonard Barkan points out, 'far from viewing the state as animate, Hobbes barely sees man as an organic being. Man is above all a mechanism.'[36] Hobbes opens the introduction by saying:

> Nature (the art whereby God hath made and governs the world) is by the art of man, as in many other things, so in this also imitated, that it can make an artificial animal. For seeing life is but a motion of limbs, the beginning whereof is in some principal part within, why may we not say that all *automata* (engines that move themselves by springs and wheels as doth a watch) have an artificial life? For what is the *heart*, but a *spring*; and the *nerves*, but as many *strings*; and the *joints*, but so many *wheels*, giving motion to the whole body, such as was intended by the Artificer?[37]

Hobbes presents nature as a form of art and then goes on to present the body as a work of art, and his emphasis is on what is made rather than on what is generated or grown. Indeed, this passage will turn out to be typical of Hobbes's attitude to nature in the book, as in chapter XX when he distinguishes between dominion by generation and dominion by conquest. While the former kind of dominion arises from some sort of family structure, the latter depends on individual action. When Hobbes writes of babies, for instance, he says that 'dominion is in him that nourisheth it': he subordinates the ties of blood to contractual ties based on human agency.[38] Hobbes's stress on the contractual basis of human relationships (both personal and political ones) can offer a way out of understanding human relationships through the family.[39]

Hobbes's emphasis on the individual rather than the family draws attention to the human body itself, even if that body is understood as a kind of machine, and thus to some extent he guards against the disembodiment Hayles mentions. In the context of my discussion, it is important to note that what happens to humans also happens to texts:

they are disembodied (or perhaps we should say 'detextualized') insofar as they lose what Newcastle called their 'paper bodies.' Like sex,
that is, texts are subjected to the calculus of profit and loss and are
expected to lead to something, to be productive – not, indeed, to produce pleasure, since textual pleasure, like sexual pleasure, can only
ever be a by-product of this process. The real reason to object to the
reproductive metaphor is perhaps that it forces textuality into a teleological and heterosexual narrative, one that is no better for women –
or, for that matter, for men – than it is for texts. In her study of motherhood in nineteenth-century American literature, Stephanie A. Smith
writes, 'Reproduction is a heterosexual norm, compulsory, middle-
class, nostalgic, even simplistic.'[40] Her concern is with nineteenth-
century American literature, and the terms might have to be altered to
apply to the Renaissance, but I think that Smith's point is indispensable: to produce a child is to reproduce a particular vision of society.
Later in this introduction I shall consider in greater detail what I consider to be some of the most cogent objections to teleological views of
sexuality and of textuality, but now I want to turn to two recent critical
discussions in which the reproductive metaphor is not only used but
also interrogated. Looking at these discussions will help me to make a
point about the durability and power of the reproductive metaphor and
about the ways in which it has adapted to new technologies.

II

My first example is the metaphors used in the description of Artificial
Life, or A-Life and, to a lesser extent, of recent technologies more generally. A-Life is a practice that crosses (or perhaps ignores) the boundary
between science and art, one in which people create environments,
which may be either computer programs or networks of machines;
these environments change over the course of their existence. To some
extent, A-Life is a response to the quest to create artificial intelligence,
one that starts from the opposite end of definitions of what is human. In
both, the idea is to create life through mechanical means. Crucial to
A-Life – and to its claims to be the creation of a life form – is the fact that
the environments change by responding to internal or to external stimuli or to both and thus fulfil one of the basic definitions of life. As the art
historian Mitchell Whitelaw has observed in the first book-length study
of this practice, 'the processes ... are never simply computational but
are elements in a discursive process.'[41] In some of the works, humans

are brought into this discursive process. For example, in his discussion of Rodney Brooks's *Cog*, a work in which the machines respond to human movement within their environment, Whitelaw says that this sort of A-Life should be understood as 'an attempt to build an artificial infant, a collection of complex embodied sensing and acting processes which is socialized into subjectivity through its interaction with human beings.'[42]

This is a large claim, but then the discourse of A-Life is full of similarly large claims.[43] At the beginning of his book, for instance, Whitelaw attempts simultaneously to sum up and to interrogate what A-Life is doing: 'this practice entails an expansive, godlike creative sweep, bringing whole worlds into being, populating them with virtual creatures. Ingenious, certainly, but is this also an extreme form of artistic hubris? ... conventions of creative agency are stretched to breaking point: much of the work is made in such a way that it makes itself – it is somehow autonomous. Is this an abdication of creative will or its ultimate fulfillment?'[44] One thing to note here is that this passage (and it is typical of much of the book) demonstrates that metaphors are prevalent, and perhaps even inescapable, in writing about making art: the 'discursive processes' mentioned by Whitelaw are both the processes of the A-Life works themselves and the larger discourses of art and nature in which these works make an intervention and through which they are discussed. But my main concern here is to follow up Whitelaw's interest in the relation of these artworks to the sorts of issues I have raised to this point. We could say that it is not so much that artists working in A-Life give us a new perspective on the reproductive metaphor as that they seek to make the metaphor literal or, at least, to narrow the gap between the metaphor (my artwork resembles a living being) and the literal (my artwork is a living being). As a result, the appropriate metaphor for the A-Life artist may well be theological rather than reproductive (as the beginning of the passage I have just quoted suggests).

The theological metaphor is, of course, the largest claim of all. It may well seem odd that, while the appropriation of divine labour has not been extensively criticized (although it is, as Whitelaw points out, hubris), the reproductive metaphor has been. In her feminist analysis of the discourse of electronic communication, for instance, Tiziana Terranova comments on 'the stunning silence about issues of physical reproduction out of other human (female) bodies – reproduction in genes is totally sexless. It is reproductive of the Same. It has become, by now, the tiresome duty of feminist criticism to point out this incorrigible re-enactment of the masculinist act of erasure of the female body (among others) and its obsession with immaculate fatherhood.'[45] This duty must indeed be tiresome. What Terranova does not appear to realize is that in the reproductive metaphor the male body is erased as well. The reproduction in this metaphor is not only totally sexless, as she remarks, but also totally bodiless. The male is the sole creator, but not through his body, and the result is what Hayles calls the 'teleology of disembodiment.' I said earlier that A-Life could be said to make the reproductive metaphor literal; similarly, I would argue that discussions of A-Life (and, especially, attempts to account for the motivation of A-Life artists) tend to expose what is behind the reproductive metaphor, which is what Finucci describes as the fantasy of birth without alterity.

Thus, instead of the messiness of actual reproduction with its almost infinite potential for disaster and disruption – its tendency to become the dissemination of different versions, to return to Orgel's point, rather than the generation of exact copies – society seeks, as Terranova suggests, to reproduce sameness. What she and many other critics do not sufficiently acknowledge, I think, is that from the point of view of the regulation of what Foucault calls the bio-politics of population the presence of the female body would make no difference. As well, by focusing on real reproduction and by insisting that metaphors be assessed on the grounds of their real-life feasibility, these critics continue to situate difference in the heterosexual couple and in the heterosexual family and thus re-enact the same reductive and atomizing analysis of the world that legitimates the bio-political regime. Difference is enshrined as one of the central facts about the family; sameness operates in the society in which the family lives. One of the few commentators on A-Life to look at the topic from this standpoint is the anthropologist Stefan Helmreich, who did a study of the scientists who work in this area. Helmreich's awareness of the importance of finding new metaphors is apparent as early as the acknowledgments to his book, in which he speaks of his 'first webs of gratitude.'[46] He is also unusual in that he discusses the race, class, gender, and sexual orientation of the researchers at the institute where he conducted his fieldwork.[47] Helmreich's discussion of the scientist (or artist, or creator) insists on the embodiment of that figure, and his understanding of embodiment is more nuanced than the simple male / female dichotomy.

Although he depends at times on the reproductive metaphor and seems to see it as a logical point of reference for his work, Helmreich is at least able to draw attention to the heterosexualization at work in the discourses he studies. At one point in his book, for instance, Helmreich says that 'the metaphor of productive heterosex is gleefully emphasised by most authors.'[48] He means most authors who write about A-Life, but the comment certainly has a wider application. My second example of recent critical discussions that employ the reproductive metaphor is the recent collection *Printing and Parenting in Early Modern England*, edited by Douglas A. Brooks. As the title indicates, the book as a whole is devoted to exploring the connections between printing and parenting – although there is not much discussion of actual parenting – but it also exemplifies the insistence on the heterosexual character of both.[49] In one of the best essays in the collection, for instance, Katharine Eisaman Maus says of feminist critics that they 'share the important assumption that writers naturally imagine their creativity in terms of their own bodies, their own genders.'[50] Drawing attention to this assumption is certainly one of the most valuable tasks performed by feminist criticism, but it is important to note that neither Maus nor the critics of whom she writes seem to consider sexual orientation as one of the factors determining how writers imagine their creativity – and how critics approach the topic. And as Maus's use of 'naturally' indicates, our discussions of this point have tended to blur the distinction between nature and culture. As so often in discussions of the reproductive metaphor, and even in discussions that seek to interrogate the metaphor, the result is in part a reproduction of heterosexuality.

A particularly good example of what Helmreich characterized as the gleeful emphasis on productive heterosex is provided by the opening anecdote in the editor's introduction. Here, Brooks cites a posting that appeared under the heading 'Second Edition' on the listserve for the Society for the History of Authorship, Reading, and Publishing. The posting, which began with 'NEW PUBLICATION,' followed the pattern for book announcements except that the title was the name of the poster's new baby, the publisher was the hospital, the publication's dimensions were the child's birth weight; as books are not free, readers will be happy to know that the stated price was 'priceless.'[51] Without commenting on the vulgarity and mawkishness of the posting, I would like to look at how the poster deals with the question of authorship. The author of the publication is the baby's mother, and its father is credited with 'minor editorial assistance.' So far, then, the writer appears to be inverting the reproductive metaphor and emphasizing the often erased female body. Yet although the mother and father have different surnames, the entry under 'title' reveals that the baby has the father's surname. Thus, even a writer who is determined to interrogate the reproductive metaphor feels obliged to follow the patriarchal practices that ensure the domination (and reproduction) of the name of the father. Strikingly, neither Brooks nor, apparently, any of the later posters to the listserve quoted by him comments on this aspect of the posting, and the anecdote as a whole serves to illustrate how incomplete most challenges to the reproductive metaphor really are.

If Brooks's example shows that challenges to the reproductive metaphor may actually perpetuate it, Laurie Maguire's contribution to the collection demonstrates that to extend the reproductive metaphor may serve to extend a heterosexualized and heterosexualizing understanding of the world. This essay, entitled 'How Many Children Had Alice Walker?' is a fascinating study of the works and influence of the great British textual scholar. In Maguire's presentation of Walker's life, both her texts and the students she trained are metaphorically presented as her children. Recognition of Walker's achievement is overdue and Maguire's tribute is timely and often moving, but her reliance on the reproductive metaphor to speak of the life and work of a woman who never reproduced is problematic. It becomes especially problematic towards the end of Maguire's essay, when she summarizes Walker's personal life, primarily by talking about her will. The bulk of Walker's estate went 'to the National Trust for the upkeep of its gardens in memory of her parents and of Miss Janet Ruth Bacon. (Bacon, former principal of Royal Holloway College, was the friend with whom Walker shared houses in Devon, Cornwall, and Oxford from 1944–65).'[52] As it turns out, Bacon is a significant figure in her own right: while principal of Royal Holloway, an institution that at one point explicitly preferred to hire women over equally qualified men, she fought an unsuccessful battle to keep the college all female.[53]

In Maguire's version of Walker's life, Bacon's existence is literally and metaphorically parenthetical, buried in the middle of the essay's antepenultimate paragraph in a discussion of Walker's will that is introduced by this rather terse sentence: 'She never married; her will names no surviving family.'[54] Maguire seems to feel that she has given us the essential information about Walker's private life by stating that she was unmarried and had no living family, but surely most people will feel that the crucial information on this subject can be found in Maguire's parenthesis. Walker and Bacon lived together, moving together more than once, for over twenty years; they stopped living together only because Bacon died – a fact that Maguire omits. It appears that the heteronormative imperative of the reproductive metaphor does not allow the recognition of affective relationships other than the traditional ones. In her will, Walker was more flexible and clearly assigns Bacon a position equal to that of her parents. Based on the available facts, there is absolutely no reason not to conclude that Walker's primary emotional commitment was to the woman with whom she lived for over twenty years and that this relationship was centrally important to her life. The answer to the question 'How Many Children Had Alice Walker?' is 'zero.' There are, it turns out, more important questions to ask about Walker's life and work.

The examples I have briefly discussed here could be said to show how the reproductive metaphor reproduces itself. My point in this section has been not that writers who use this metaphor are actively seeking to promote a narrow and conservative view of human sexuality, although such a possibility cannot be ruled out, but rather that this narrowness is to some extent built into the metaphor. When a writer uses the reproductive metaphor, certain statements are possible and certain ones are impossible, or at least less likely.[55] In an essay entitled 'Is Kinship Always Already Heterosexual?' on recent appropriations of the term 'kinship' by queer people, Judith Butler makes this point with reference to the discursive framework of normalcy: 'once we enter that framework we are to some degree defined by its terms.'[56] Throughout the essay, Butler is clearly aware of the power of language to shape thought, especially the power of the language of heterosexuality. She starts her discussion by separating kinship from marriage and the nuclear family, for instance, and argues that the figure of the child 'raises the question of whether there will be a sure transmission of culture through heterosexual procreation ... whether the culture will be defined, in part, as the prerogative of heterosexuality itself.'[57] Butler even says, 'One may wish for another lexicon altogether.'[58] Still, Butler's hypothetical wish for another lexicon is a reference to the use of the terms 'legitimate' and 'illegitimate,' not to the term 'kinship' itself. Her discussion of the possibilities of queer kinship is vitiated by the fact that the answer to the question 'Is Kinship Always Already Heterosexual?' is 'yes.' Perhaps queers should come up with their own terminology to describe their relationships, even in the case of blood relationships.

III

In the influential essay whose title I have adapted for this introduction, Walter Benjamin says that 'to an ever greater degree, the work of art reproduced becomes the work of art designed for reproducibility.'[59] While Benjamin was writing specifically of technologies that were new in the first decades of the last century, I propose to understand his point as akin to Hayles's comments on the posthuman, which is to say that what is important about texts and about humans is the extent to which they can lead to something. Benjamin himself displays a version of this kind of thinking in another essay when he says, 'Rather than ask, "What is the *attitude* of a work to the relations of production of its time?" I should like to ask, "What is its *position* in them?"'[60] Benjamin's instrumental thinking here is in the service of his movingly optimistic discussion of the intersection of artistic and political change, but one effect of the reproductive metaphor can be to enlist texts in the service of artistic and political continuity. Like sexuality, textuality is supposed to lead to or contribute to something, and that something is chiefly the maintenance of the society in which the text was produced. The work of art, that is, does not reproduce itself: it reproduces social relations, a point implicit in Glimp's discussion. This is the equivalent on the textual level for both the human capacity for reproduction and the mechanical reproducibility that is Benjamin's topic; in both cases the guiding principle is teleology.

As I noted in the preface, teleology has been one of the major subjects of an important kind of queer theory. For instance, Lee Edelman has recently argued that 'politics is a name for the temporalization of desire, for its translation into a narrative, for its teleological determination.'[61] In this formulation, a teleological view of desire becomes the basis for politics and, as Edelman, goes on to point out, the Child is its symbol:

> the fantasy subtending the image of the Child invariably shapes the logic within which the political must be thought. That logic compels us, to the extent that we would register as politically responsible, to submit to the framing of political debate – and, indeed, of the political field – as defined by the terms of what this book describes as reproductive futurism: terms that impose an ideological limit on political discourse as such, preserving in the process the absolute privilege of heternormativity by rendering unthinkable, by casting outside the political domain, the possibility of a queer resistance to this organizing principle of communal relations.[62]

A few years before Edelman, Lauren Berlant and Michael Warner suggested that reproduction's centrality to the political imaginary is to some extent a mistake: 'A complex cluster of sexual practices gets confused, in heterosexual culture, with the love plot of intimacy and familialism that signifies belonging to society in a deep and normal way. Community is imagined through scenes of intimacy, coupling, and kinship. And a historical relation to futurity is restricted to generational narrative and reproduction.'[63] In this reading, the familial metaphor as a whole shapes our political lives, as Butler's use of 'kinship' demonstrates.

In these passages, Edelman and Berlant and Warner demonstrate the extent to which we are always thinking reproductively. The reproductive metaphor is thus not only a way of describing textual production (although that is my main concern in this book), but also a way of describing the individual's relation to the society in which he or she lives, as well as the very structures that make that society possible. Perhaps we could see this as the political equivalent of Benjamin's mechanical reproducibility. When Edelman says that 'futurism thus generates generational succession, temporality, and narrative sequence, not toward the end of enabling change, but, instead, of perpetuating sameness, of turning back time to assure repetition,' he identifies what I see as the main danger of the reproductive metaphor in all its forms and in all the purposes to which it is put.[64] That is, reproduction is, among other things, a way of harnessing sexuality in the service of society. In this model, sexuality can be read as only part of a narrative: sex leads to children born within a marriage, or perhaps we should rather say to citizens. As Edelman suggests, this teleological narrative is one that can never end and what appears as the difference of narrative – each narrative deals with individuals doing individual things – is really the sameness on which social relations depend.

The sharpest and most entertaining critic of this state of affairs has been the chronically underappreciated Raoul Vaneigem, who was a member of the Situationist International.[65] In *The Book of Pleasures*, he takes as his starting position that 'the system governing history has operated on the social need to transform our sexual potential into the energy for work.'[66] In this respect, his point resembles that of Foucault in *The History of Sexuality*, but Vaneigem's work is much more of a furious polemic. For instance, he describes the mother as 'a virtual State official whose task it is to integrate a piece of raw flesh into society. Mother kills both the woman and the child.'[67] I think that this statement – and Vaneigem's blistering attack on the contemporary discourses of maternity as a whole – should be required reading for critics who seek to bring women into the reproductive metaphor without addressing the position of women in the state-sanctioned regime of maternity. Throughout the book Vaneigem argues against the co-option of our pleasures in the maintenance of order and of the status quo, and his statement that 'all pleasure is creative if it avoids exchange' is one of the best anti-teleological slogans.[68] As I see it, this is the dream: a pleasure and a creativity that exist without exchange, without circulation, and without use value.

One of the few writers to take Vaneigem seriously is the American philosopher Karmen MacKendrick. In her remarkable book *Counterpleasures* she develops many of his points in a more philosophical and literary way. Her starting point is Freud's theory of the 'forepleasure' from *Three Essays on the Theory of Sexuality*. According to Freud, a pleasure becomes a forepleasure (and thus perverse) when it is lingered over instead of serving as an introduction to penetrative sex.[69] MacKendrick says that 'the counterpleasures ... are ... pleasures that tend away from all sorts of teleologies.'[70] For instance, they may be 'so absurdly difficult in attainment that we must sometimes suspect that the pleasure comes in the intensity of the challenge itself.'[71] In her illuminating discussions of sadism, masochism, and asceticism (both as bodily practices and as literary subjects), MacKendrick argues that these things represent ways of having a body and of responding to the bodies of others that are not teleological, not directed either towards use or towards narrative. At one point she makes a comparison that has been crucial to my own thinking on this subject: 'language and art are important, and all the more so if they refuse to be reduced to the useful.'[72] With this statement I would place Vaneigem's reference to 'the convolutions of language prised from the grip of trade.'[73] For him, trade, by which he means financial considerations in general, restricts language's freedom of movement. Thus, in their different ways, both writers are concerned to uphold the idea of a language that is not purely instrumental, one that may take various forms, perhaps any form it wishes.

One important aspect of the work of both Vaneigem and MacKendrick is their critique of the orgasm. In *The Book of Pleasures*, Vaneigem discusses orgasm in the context of his attack on the reduction of sexuality to genitality, which, he argues, 'has promoted orgasm to the rank of universal model of satisfaction and frustration. And what better reproduction of the mechanisms governing us: a charge-discharge reducing erotic tensions to zero.'[74] Here, orgasm itself is social reproduction. Similarly, for MacKendrick, orgasm would be one of the teleologies from which the counterpleasures diverge. She also sees the orgasm as having at least potentially a role in the regulation of sexuality: 'If we turn this teleological discipline to the organization of the force of desire, we come to value most a quick, efficient gratification ... or else a productive channeling in which desire is directed to ends that uphold the established order and secure it in its functioning.'[75] We could say that for MacKendrick, there is little to choose between the orgasm as the *telos* of a specific sexual act and the child as the *telos* of sexual acts in general. The movement to give up the orgasm may not win many adherents, but decentring the orgasm is a different idea altogether. Perhaps we should invoke the title of Valerie Traub's brilliant analysis of Shakespeare's sonnets: 'Sex Without Issue.'[76] Issue is both the semen produced by the male orgasm and the child produced, under certain conditions, by that semen. Sex without issue could be sex between women, sex that does not lead to orgasm, sex that does not lead to children, and, of course, all the above. It could also be – and this may be the most important way to take the phrase – sex in which whatever issue may ensue is not at issue.

The term 'counterpleasure' is new, but the phenomenon of language enjoyed for its own sake, without consideration of its use value, is not. The argument that poetic language, which we tend to see as a form of communication, may sometimes communicate only pleasure can arguably be seen in a very wide variety of texts from all periods. Here, however, I want simply to suggest some of the ways in which MacKendrick's argument is anticipated by Plato. Plato is often cited in discussions of the reproductive metaphor because of the passage in the *Symposium* in which poems are compared to children. The speaker in this passage adds, 'every man would rather have for himself those children than human ones, and looking at Homer and Hesiod and the other good poets would desire the offspring they left behind, who gave them immortal glory and renown because they are such [sc., immortal].'[77] But Plato also wrote the *Phaidrus*, which begins with a discussion of speeches used for seduction. The character Lysias 'wrote some things about the attempted seduction of beautiful men, by one who is not in love, and that is the refinement.'[78] Similarly, we are told a little later of a man 'who is crazy about hearing speeches.'[79] In both cases, the desired end is not a real-world result, such as sex, but the language itself: the rhetoric leads nowhere but to itself, and in this sense both Lysias and the other man could be said to be interested in the resistance to teleology afforded by the counterpleasures.

But despite Plato's gesturing in the *Phaidrus* towards the possibility of a pleasure in language (and, specifically, in rhetoric) that would be separate from a consideration of its effects and despite the text's focus on male beauty, the text ultimately affirms the reproductive metaphor. For example, Lysias is referred to 'as the father of the speech' and, even more significantly, Socrates (here, as so often in Plato, clearly the person to be followed) insists throughout the text on the teleological aspect of speech.[80] Thus, the idea of highly ordered language as a counterpleasure is eventually foreclosed. Still, the possibility that people might take a completely unproductive pleasure in language is raised: the rhetoric of seduction is supposed to lead to sexual pleasure, but if, as in the example from the *Phaidrus* of the seduction speech directed at a man to whom one is not attracted, one does not want the speech to lead to sex, the result can be only textual pleasure. I would identify this idea as textually productive. After all, the foreclosure I have mentioned occurs only within the narrative of the *Phaidrus*: as habitual – perhaps inveterate – readers of complex philosophical narratives (and of complex texts in general), we ourselves may be 'crazy about hearing speeches.'[81] And even independently of our own textual counterpleasures, texts in which poetry is celebrated for its own sake, not for what it might lead to, are one important medium for poets to protest the implications of the reproductive metaphor.

The tension between instrumental language and language for its own sake becomes especially important and poetically productive in the Renaissance, a period in which, as Richard Halpern has reminded us, classical rhetoric was central to humanist pedagogy and 'rhetorical education tried to evolve a mode of indoctrination based on hegemony and consent rather than force and coercion; it aimed to produce an active embrace of ideology rather than a passive acceptance.'[82] As part of his important discussion of rhetoric, Halpern makes the point that the aims of poetry and the aims of rhetoric are in some ways inherently opposed; he even suggests that poetry 'actualizes or manifests what is latently disturbing about rhetoric as well.'[83] This statement would come as a surprise to many Renaissance poets, who, I think, saw their poetry and their rhetoric as working together. But the danger is always that the energy of rhetoric – and, in particular, of highly elaborate rhetorical passages aimed to persuade – will fail to be recuperated by the end to which they are designed. As Halpern remarks, 'Persuasion can free itself from "true" or dominant values or ... it can devolve into linguistic pleasure without direction or purpose';[84] he goes on to suggest,

'poetry ... embodied the ideological instabilities of rhetoric by representing a textual decoding without limits, a persuasiveness without
truth, and a discursive pleasure without aim.'[85] For the rhetoricians,
this was a danger, but for at least some poets, rhetoric's tendency to
exceed its aim could function as a pointer to other kinds of excess
and other non-teleological pleasures. Poetry itself, that is, could be a
counterpleasure, and one of my interests in this book is the ways in
which writers create a non-teleological poetry.

IV

As well as focusing on language for its own sake, texts may exhibit an
explicit resistance to the narrativization of sexuality: in order to be an
instrument, after all, sex has to be part of a narrative. The discourses of
reproduction are probably the commonest example of sexual narratives. Slavoj Žižek recently suggested that reproduction may be bound
up in narrative itself when he asked, 'Is narrative not ultimately a narrative about what Hölderlin called the "law of succession," the paternal
symbolic order which keeps the chaotic abyss of the Sacred at a proper
distance?'[86] Žižek is interested primarily in psychoanalysis and politics
here, but if we make the happy change from 'Sacred' to 'Sexual' the
question is also good for the texts I shall discuss in this book. I would
say that the twentieth-century writer most interested in the desire to
understand language instrumentally and most concerned to combat it
is Roland Barthes. His thinking on this subject is clearly expressed when
he says of himself, writing in the third person, that his 'work is not anti-
historical ... but always, persistently, anti-genetic, for Origin is a pernicious figure of Nature'; Barthes goes on to say that his strategy is to
make everything – including Nature – into a culture that is 'restored to
the infinite movement of various discourses, set up one against the
other (and not engendered).'[87] Narratives tend to have a highly restricted movement towards a goal that is only too easy to guess; in Barthes's
plan, discourses (rather than narratives) would collide endlessly, and it
is notable that at the end of the passage I have quoted he explicitly rejects the reproductive metaphor.

   Barthes's most famous work on this subject is, of course, *The Pleasure
of the Text*. In that text, I see the 'infinite movement' of discourses in his
comment that textual pleasure 'is a drift, something both revolutionary
and asocial' and that it 'is scandalous, not because it is immoral but
because it is *atopic*.'[88] In not having a place, this pleasure cannot be

narrativized , as there is no possibility of getting to the place, whether metaphorical or – in, for instance, the case of the wedding altar – real, that is the *telos* of the standard narrative. As Barthes points out, the movement from place to place promised by narratives is illusory: 'encratic language (the language produced and spread under the protection of power) is statutorily a language of repetition; all official institutions of language are repeating machines.'[89] I see Barthes's 'repeating machines' as the equivalent of the repetition of heterosexuality I mentioned in my discussion of Edelman (I would also note that the repeating machines recall Deleuze and Guattari's focus on most of human life as mechanistic). Among the repeating machines that are linguistic institutions I would place both the standard heterosexual (and heterosexualizing) narrative and the reproductive metaphor that is a part of this narrative. In this book, I shall be concerned both with texts that seek not to be repeating machines and with texts that make this repetition their subject; the latter texts may well end with marriages. Thus, my concern is to some extent with the resistance to 'encratic' language.

The question of how to resist the official institutions of language is central to Barthes's thinking in *The Neutral*, a collection of lectures he gave at the Collège de France in 1978, although they were not collected and published until 2002.[90] For Barthes, the Neutral was a way out of binary oppositions. In his discussion of affirmation, he outlines a task: 'in order ... to preserve the discourse from affirmation, in order to nuance it (toward negation, doubt, interrogation, suspension), one must ceaselessly fight against speech, raw material, "law of discourse."'[91] His main weapon in this fight is the Neutral, which he defines as 'like a language without predication.'[92] Later, he says, 'The Neutral is not an objective, a target: it's a passage. In a famous apologue, Zen makes fun of people who mistake the pointing finger for the moon it points to – I'm interested in the finger, not in the moon.'[93] In this sense, we could say that the Neutral is queer. As Graham Hammill suggests in a discussion of Leo Bersani and Ulysse Dutoit's *Caravaggio*, 'If homosexual desire is "reaching out toward an other sameness," as Bersani and Dutoit contend, then queer art is not the representation of that other sameness but the sensual enjoyment of this reaching out.'[94] For Barthes, just as the pleasure of the text is atopic, so the Neutral is not a way to get anywhere: it is a linguistic practice that rejects linguistic instrumentality and forsakes destinations and uses for what might be a momentary pleasure. And if queer art is more about enjoyment than representation, then it is freed even from the responsibility to represent queerness. It is in this sense that most of the works I discuss in this book can be described as queer: that is, these texts are queer in their attitude towards representation rather than in what they represent.

In *The Neutral*, Barthes sees writing as 'the very discourse that unfailingly baffles the arrogance of discourse' and adds that one of the ways in which it does this is 'to take on the arrogance of language as a specific lure: neither an individual lure (that of the subject who says "in my humble opinion"), nor a referential lure (science – truth), but the lure of writing insofar as it is the origin of its own violence instead of receiving it by proxy from another power.'[95] One of the ways to understand this statement is to say that Barthes is trying to circumvent two kinds of authority. One is the authority of the individual who speaks from a certain position and has therefore, however tenuously, some authority, however qualified that may be either by the mock humility of a statement such as 'in my humble opinion' or by the relative powerlessness of the individual. The other kind of authority is authority itself, in the sense of a discourse that identifies itself with the truth and therefore has or seems to have the power to make statements that oppose it untrue – we could say unconceivable (and the word would for once have almost its literal meaning) or even ungrammatical. The writing Barthes is referring to here is a writing that does not depend on the authority of a source: no paternity, no maternity, no validation from the outside, no validation other than what can be provided by writing itself.

The texts done in this writing would be truly free. I see this as connected to Theodor Adorno's comments on lyric poetry. Adorno famously argues that lyric poetry, often considered purely private and even perhaps trivial, has both power and force. He says that the lyric poem's 'detachment from naked existence,' often considered to make such poetry politically irrelevant, actually 'becomes the measure of the world's falsity and meanness. Protesting against these conditions, the poem proclaims the dream of a world in which things would be different.'[96] A similar statement has been made more recently by the American poet and critic James Longenbach. In *The Resistance to Poetry*, Longenbach says that 'because we don't necessarily expect a poem to be useful in obvious or immediate ways, the language of poetry is liberated to create this potential space, hovering between the literal and the figurative.'[97] Both Adorno and Longenbach are writing in a time in which it is often feared that poetry has become irrelevant, while in this book, I shall be chiefly concerned with poets who wrote in a time in which poetry was seen as more vital and more central and was consequently expected to do more work and make more sense, to be more obviously useful. As a result, it was harder for Renaissance poets to focus on poetry's ability to make things different, and their struggle to imagine difference often ended in defeat. Nevertheless, for them, as for Barthes and Adorno and Longenbach, poetry could be less a way to reproduce what was than to produce something new – which is exactly what Sidney praised about the best poets in his *Defence of Poesie*.

We are not necessarily going to be happy with the textual worlds we encounter or, to use Barthes's phrasing, with the violence originated by writing. These worlds will often turn out to be depressingly like our own, and the violence will also seem only too familiar. So will the omissions, and this is the most serious aspect of the feminist objection to the male use of the reproductive metaphor. As Harry Berger Jr remarks, many of these uses are motivated by what he calls 'the fantasy of modes of production and reproduction dominated by androgenesis or male parthenogenesis.'[98] Insofar as male use of the reproductive metaphor seeks to relegate women to a lower status or to downplay specifically female forms of work, we should certainly object to it, but what is most striking to me about Berger's formulation is the telltale slippage from production to reproduction. While human reproduction does require a woman (although, as I showed earlier, this was not universally believed in the Renaissance), production obviously does not. At the same time as Berger argues that reproduction should not be used metaphorically, then, he applies it to a kind of work in which it can be only metaphoric. Although my starting position in this book is to show that both poetry and sexuality are figured as sources of socially dangerous excess and that reproduction (both metaphorical and real) provides a way to recuperate them for social profit, what interests me is the issue of the metaphoricity of our vocabulary that is raised by Berger's terminology.

Berger's use of 'androgenesis' is noteworthy, as most writers use 'parthenogenesis' to refer to male uses of the reproductive metaphor even though the Greek 'parthenos' means a maiden or girl.[99] Either 'androgenesis' or 'poetogenesis' would be preferable, although there is a further point to make in this connection. In Liddell and Short, the standard Ancient Greek dictionary, the word *genesis* has the primary meaning of 'origin, source, productive cause'; meanings associated with birth are given a second place. In other words, when we use 'genesis' or any of its compounds to refer to birth, we are already speaking metaphorically. Thus, Ancient Greek vocabulary connects production and reproduction, but sees the former as primary and the latter (which is for us the very sign of authenticity and origin) as a metaphorical extension. We could then argue that the whole issue has been a confusion of tenor and vehicle all along, but in a sense parthenogenesis is the right word, not indeed in its Ancient Greek meaning but in its modern scientific meaning of asexual reproduction. My point is that the reproductive regime that governs sexuality and that reduces both men and women to mere containers of genetic information tends towards asexuality, as its ideal is the 'birth without alterity' or 'non-genealogical birth' discussed by Finucci and Swann.[100] The problem is with the system itself, not with attempts to see reproduction as purely masculine (or as purely feminine), and in this book I aim to show that many Renaissance writers were aware of this problem. In section V, I want to look at Virgil's account of textual production, an account that rules out reproduction altogether (as well as sex), and then at an essay by Montaigne that I see as in some ways a response to Virgil.

V

Virgil is one of the most self-conscious poets in our literary tradition and also one of the most influential. His poetry contains many meta-poetic moments in which he writes about his poetic plans, hopes, and fears, and perhaps the most famous of these comes near the beginning of the third book of the *Georgics* when he says, 'temptanda uia est, qua me quoque possim / tollere humo uictorque uirum uolitare per ora' (a way must be found by which I too may lift myself from the ground and fly as a victor through the mouths of men).[101] The metaphor for poetic success that concludes these lines is taken from Ennius, one of the earliest Latin poets, but Virgil's reference to lifting himself from the ground is less usual, although it is certainly appropriate for the *Georgics*, whose first two books were about crops and trees, respectively.[102] In fact, 'tollere humo' has a triple signification: it refers to the literal raising from the ground of both agriculture and arboriculture, to the metaphorical raising of his theme from the plants that are the subject of the first two books to the animals that are the subject of the third and fourth books and to the metaphorical raising of his poetic career from the pastoral to the georgic to the (at this point still unwritten) epic, a progression that is underlined by Virgil's depiction of himself as not only flying through the mouths of men, but flying as a victor.

Each book of the *Georgics* begins with an invocation, but the beginning of the fourth approaches epic elevation. Virgil begins by speaking

of honey as heavenly – 'Protinus aërii mellis caelestia dona / exsequar'
(Now I shall pursue the celestial gifts of honey sent from the air; 1–2) –
and then suggests that, although bees are small, the poetic renown he
hopes to gain from them might not be: 'in tenui labor; at tenuis non
gloria, si quem / numina laeua sinunt auditque uocatus Apollo' (I work
in miniature, but the glory will not be small if hostile gods permit it and
invoked Apollo hears; 6–7). As readers would expect, Virgil praises the
bees' social organization and industry; what may seem odd is that he
also praises them for their asexual reproduction:

> neque concubitu indulgent, nec corpora segnes
> in Venerem soluunt aut fetus nixibus edunt;
> uerum ipsae e foliis natos, e suauibus herbis
> ore legunt.

> they do not indulge in sexual intercourse, nor relax their sluggish bodies
> in love or bring forth their young in childbirth; but by themselves they
> gather their young in their mouths from leaves and sweet herbs. (198–9)

The idea that bees reproduce asexually was apparently widespread in
the classical period. Virgil's use of 'ore' (in their mouths) could be said
to link this account of apian generation with his picture in Book III of
the *Georgics* of the famous poet as someone who flies through the
mouths – 'ora' – of men. In the context of this introduction, it is striking
that Virgil relies on the same opposition between sexuality and work –
an opposition underlined by his use of the adjective 'segnes' (sluggish)
– that we have seen in some of the writers I have discussed . As well, his
insistence on the asexual reproduction of bees obviates even the possibility of the reproductive metaphor.

The first half of Book IV deals with bees in a manner that recalls the
agricultural discussions in the first three books of the *Georgics*. In the
second half, however, Virgil changes the subject and tells the story of
Orpheus and Aristaeus, the former's rival for the love of Eurydice. Bees
are important to this story as well, and I would also argue that the introduction of Orpheus points to the implicit play on words between 'mel'
(honey) and 'melos' (song). The transition from the first half of the book
to the second is signalled by Virgil's description of the *bugonia* (a Greek
compound of the word for cow and a cognate of the word 'genesis'), a
practice that he recommends to apiculturists when every other remedy
to preserve the hives has failed. In the *bugonia*, a putrid cow carcass was

used to generate a new swarm of bees; it was believed that the bees arose spontaneously from the rotting animal. Virgil has now given us two examples of asexual reproduction among bees, a fact whose importance becomes clear when Aristaeus learns from the god Proteus that all his bees have died, which is a punishment for his attempted rape of Eurydice. According to Virgil (and this version of the story is unique to him) it was while Eurydice was fleeing Aristaeus that she was bitten by the snake. The contrast between the orderly and asexual (and perhaps orderly because asexual) conduct of bees and the disorderly and fatal lusts of humans, for which the bees themselves must suffer, is strong, if implicit. The condemnation of disorderly lust is emphasised by the famous story of Orpheus that follows.

Book IV has two endings: first the narrative of Aristaeus is brought to a close and then Virgil, speaking *in propria persona*, ends the poem as a whole. In the first ending, Proteus gives Aristaeus remarkably detailed advice on how to perform the *bugonia*. Virgil tells us, in one of his most vivid descriptions, that the advice works:

aspiciunt, liquefacta boum per uiscera toto
stridere apes utero et ruptis efferuere costis,
immensaque trahi nubes, iamque arbore summa
confluere et lentis uuam demittere ramis.

throughout the liquefied entrails of the cows, throughout all the guts they see the bees hiss and bubble up from the ruptured sides; the bees are drawn together into a vast cloud and now they swarm together to the top of the tree and hang down like a cluster of grapes from the yielding branches. (555–8)

The story of Aristaeus and the apicultural advice of Book IV as a whole end with the horrifying picture of the vast swarm of bees bubbling up out of the putrefied carcass. The sound they make is intended, I think, to link this picture of sounds emerging from a dead body with the description only thirty lines earlier of the disembodied head of Orpheus crying out as it floats downstream: 'Eurydicen uox ipsa et frigida lingua, / a miseram Eurydicen! anima fugiente uocabat' (the voice itself and the cold tongue called out Eurydice, o wretched Eurydice as the soul [of Orpheus] fled; 525–6).

In the last eight lines of the *Georgics* Virgil speaks of himself, of the composition of the poem, and of his poetic career. This is the famous *sphragis*, or seal, and it represents the most self-conscious passage by this most self-conscious of poets. In these lines, Virgil situates his composition of this agricultural poem in a political context:

Haec super aruorum cultu pecorumque canebam
et super arboribus, Caesar dum magnus ad altum
fulminat Euphraten bello uictorque uolentis
per populos dat iura iamque adfecta Olympo.

I sang these things about the cultivation of fields and flocks, and about trees, while great Caesar thundered down war from on high on the Euphrates and as a victor gives laws to a willing people and now seeks the way to Olympus. (560–2)

As I see it, the most important aspect of the contrast between Virgil and Caesar is the contrast between 'uictorque' here, when it is used in its literal sense to refer to the actual military triumphs of Caesar, and 'uictorque' in Book III, when it refers metaphorically to the potential poetic triumph of Virgil. He goes on to underline the contrast when he uses 'lusi' (I played; 566) to describe the composition of his pastoral and georgic poetry. Poetry, it appears, is not serious work.

A further contrast in this passage is evident when Virgil describes what he was doing while Caesar was conquering Mesopotamia: 'illo Vergilium me tempore dulcis alebat / Parthenope studiis florentem ignobilis oti' (in that time sweet Parthenope [sc., Naples] nourished me, Virgil, flowering at my studies, ignoble in leisure; 563–4). In the last line of the poem Virgil addresses one of the characters from his first eclogue: 'Tityre, te patulae cecini sub tegmine fagi' (Tityrus, I sang you under the shelter of a spreading beech; 566). The return to the first poem Virgil wrote is underscored by the fact that the last line of the *Georgics* is a slight rewriting of the first line of the eclogues: 'Tityre, tu patulae recubans sub tegmine fagi' (Tityrus, reclining under the shelter of a spreading beech you; I.1).[103] The effect of Virgil's auto-allusion is to present his entire poetic output at this point as circular. Instead of the progression for which Virgil's poetic career has been famous for so many centuries, we have only repetition: the poet as one of Barthes's 'repeating machines.' Furthermore, the poet cuts a noticeably unheroic figure, lying in the shade singing about shepherds and trees while Caesar extends Roman control to the bounds of the known world. At the beginning of the fourth book, Virgil argues that bees should be taken seriously, proposes to sing of their civilization, and concludes his preamble grandly with 'proelia dicam' (I shall speak of wars; 5). At the end of the poem, however, Caesar's real 'proelia' might be said to expose the hollowness of the metaphor when applied to apian unrest.

However, the position of the poet at the end of the *Georgics* is not as bad as the comparison with Caesar might suggest. In his very abjection, lying under a tree, Virgil recalls the abject carcass of the cow, also lying under a tree. This comparison might seem even less flattering, but recall that the putrefaction of the cow led to the return of the bees – which is, after all, the highest good in the world of the fourth book. What is more, there is an unstated comparison between the bees and Caesar: not only does the description of each end with a clause beginning with 'iamque' (and now; 557, 562), but the hissing of the bees ('stridere') is echoed on an appropriately larger scale by Caesar's thundering ('fulminat'), and each passage concludes with an ascent – the bees' to the top of the tree and Caesar's to Olympus. I believe that both of the sounds in these passages are versions of the 'melos' or song of Orpheus, who is also reduced to a carcass, not even to an intact one, and of Virgil himself. Furthermore, if there is a parallel between the cow and Virgil, then Caesar is not present in the poem solely as an example of someone who is doing real work but is also in a sense produced by the poet just as the bees are produced by the cow. Insofar as Virgil presents his leisure as giving rise both to poetry and to empire, then, the conclusion of the *Georgics* could be read as the first announcement of the *Aeneid* and as a claim for the importance of poetry in the real world.

For my purposes in this book, one important thing about this metaphor is that it suggests that abjection – the dismemberment of Orpheus, the rotting of the cow, the ignoble ease of Virgil – may give rise to poetry. As we shall see with Montaigne and with other Renaissance writers, writing is often presented as arising from abjection. What is more, as the cow's carcass fortunately leads to a swarm of bees rather than to a swarm of cows or a swarm of entrails, Virgil has described production rather than reproduction. I want to point out once again that, from the classical period on, European ideas about where animals – even humans – come from included many methods that cannot properly be described as reproduction. As Marjorie Swann points out, for instance, Renaissance writers made a 'distinction between the mutability of identity characteristic of spontaneous generation and the transference of stable form through "seminall production."'[104] The importance of this distinction cannot be overemphasized. To think about textual production through sexual reproduction is to expect texts to display sameness, to promote continuity rather than change, but while beliefs such as the *bugonia* still usefully associate production of various sorts – including, metaphorically, textual production – with the body, they do so in a way that allows for the possibility of discontinuity. As well, this model fits better with what Stephen Orgel, in a passage I have already quoted, sees as 'what the Renaissance wanted from books': 'not exact replication ... [but] dissemination.'[105]

My argument about the ending of Book IV is thus that we can read it as affording a metaphor for textual production, one that is very different from the reproductive metaphor. In Virgil's metaphor, poetry comes from abjection, both from those things felt to inspire universal disgust such as dishonoured corpses (the scattered limbs of Orpheus, the decaying cow) and from shame (the poet who withdraws from the world in a time of crucial activity in his nation).[106] I think that this metaphor offers real possibilities for queer theory, particularly given discussions of queer shame such as Eve Kosofsky Sedgwick's or the generally antihumanist strain in queer theory probably originally associated with Leo Bersani.[107] I would add that the metaphor also offers real possibilities for poetry itself. In Virgil's account, textual production is not heterosexualized and the resulting text is not infantilized, wrapped in a blue blanket (if it is an epic) or a pink one (if it is a lyric). Instead, although poetry does come from abjection, the poetry itself is something crucial, as Virgil suggests when the result is either the bees on which so much agriculture depends or the mighty Caesar himself. The metaphor thus suggests that something that is abject or peripheral or marginal may become not only central but actually indispensable. This suggestion could open up new avenues both for thinking about queer people and for thinking about poetry, which I think itself is now increasingly marginal.

Nevertheless, perhaps admitting that one has been idle while others have worked (let alone comparing oneself to a putrefying animal carcass) will always have a limited appeal. Most poets have preferred the reproductive metaphor with its built-in implication that the text is not only welcome but also socially useful, and by the Renaissance the metaphor was firmly entrenched, although, as I shall argue, many writers interrogated the metaphor or used it only to reject it. I now want to look at one particularly interesting Renaissance version of the metaphor, a version that draws on Virgil as well.[108] This is Montaigne's 'De l'Oysiveté,' ('Of Idlenesse,' in John Florio's translation), the eighth essay in his first book of essays. The critic who has written most interestingly on this essay and on Montaigne's use of the reproductive metaphor is Richard L. Regosin.[109] But while Regosin is consistently stimulating and perceptive, he, like many of the critics I have discussed is unable to think outside the reproductive metaphor. For instance, he says that 'Montaigne apparently appropriates the female prerogative, but we might choose to recognize the admission that writing is always even in spite of itself, "pere et mere ensemble."'[110] In this formulation, textual production is heterosexualized. As well, Regosin says that the standard male use of the reproductive metaphor is 'an act that eliminates and ignores the engendering function that is properly, and literally, the province of women.'[111] Here, we see the same kind of confusion as in the passage from Friedman that I quoted earlier: if 'engendering' is used to mean having children, then it is literally the province of both men and women; if 'engendering' is used to mean writing, then it is in most cases literally the province either of a man by himself or a woman by herself.

With this in mind, we could say that one function of the reproductive metaphor is to turn the autoerotic associations of the solitary act of writing into the more acceptable heterosexual associations of the husband and wife dyad. In 'De l'Oysiveté,' however, Montaigne chooses instead both to stress textual production's solitary nature and to present it as the result of a monstrous heterosexuality. The essay opens with an extended simile; the tenor here is the mind, although that is not clear at first. The first comparison is to 'terres oisives';[112] Florio translates the adjective twice, saying that the grounds are 'idle fallow' (14). The French adjective 'oisives' is derived from the Latin 'otium,' a form of which appears in Virgil's phrase 'ignobilis oti.' Montaigne's simile is a version of – or, rather, a rewriting of – Virgil's *sphragis*, one in which leisure is apparently only bad, as it produces 'wilde and vnprofitable weedes' (14). The second simile is stronger: 'as wee see some women, though single and alone, often to bring foorth lumps of shapelesse flesh, whereas to produce a perfect and naturall generation, they must be manured with another kinde of seede' (14).[113] The idea that women need control is certainly familiar (and, as I have already pointed out, the belief in spontaneous reproduction was common in the Renaissance), but I would argue that by describing the desired and artificially produced result as 'naturall,' Montaigne raises the possibility that our ideas of nature and culture may be at fault. Many of the attacks on the reproductive metaphor that I have cited have relied on the concept of the natural; as I see it, Montaigne's point is that the natural is not something that should be taken as a standard, perhaps especially not in the case of something as artificial as textual production.

In both of these similes, for instance, we are told that natural fertility must be regulated or it will produce something that is useless, something that is neither food to eat nor people to eat it. Montaigne goes on to tell us that the same is true of minds: 'except they be busied about some subject, that may bridle and keep them vnder, they will here and there wildely scatter themselves through the vaste field of imaginations' (14). The conclusion may seem orthodox, but it is remarkable that the mind is both female, insofar as it is something that must be brought under control and is thus equivalent to the women of the second simile, and male, insofar as it is a kind of seed, although a bad one; it is also both artificial and natural. In both similes Montaigne stresses the importance of having the proper seed, and in the comparison as a whole we can see both the reproductive metaphor (as it is clear that Montaigne is speaking of his own essays) and the metaphorical equivalence of agriculture and reproductive heterosexuality, but it is worth remarking that he refuses to be bound by the gendered terms of reproduction. Furthermore, and crucially, if the mind is both male and female, how will the comparison be plotted against the facts of human reproduction? That is, what is the thing that will produce the 'perfect and naturall generation' (even leaving aside the question of whether we are to see the thing in question as the right kind of seed or as the right kind of womb)?

For me, the answer is provided by what comes next: a quotation from Virgil, the first and longest of the four Latin quotations crammed into this short essay. In this passage (*Aeneid* VIII.22–5), Virgil compares the perturbation of Aeneas's mind to light in water, but I think that the original context of these lines (however apt they may be at this point in Montaigne's essay) is more important than their content. At this point in the poem, Aeneas has just begun the war that he must win in order to fulfil his destiny; dreading the combat, he cannot sleep. Tiberinus, the god of the river that flows through Rome, appears to Aeneas to reassure him and to tell him that he is about to enter what will one day be the capital of his empire. The next day Aeneas and his men reach this site. Virgil speaks dismissively of the settlement that existed at that time under the rule of Evander:

muros arcemque procul ac rara domorum
tecta uident, quae nunc Romana potentia caelo
aequauit, tum res inopes.

far away they see the walls and the fortress and the roofs of a few houses, which now Roman power has equalled with heaven – then it was a poor thing. (98–100)

The contrast between Evander's humble capital and the imperial capital that will replace it is a version of the contrast between the cow's carcass and the bees and between the lazy poet and the conquering Caesar: in each of these cases, something high comes from something low, and these adjectives should be taken both literally and metaphorically.

There is a further important contrast in the scene from the *Aeneid*. Evander and his people, who will, of course, eventually have to be displaced or absorbed by Aeneas or his descendants, were originally Greeks from Arcadia, the region most associated with pastoral poetry – that is, with the genre Virgil left behind in order to become an epic poet. Here as well, but now in a literary sense, something low produces something high. This returns us to the 'terres oisives' with which Montaigne began his essay and that we can now read as an allusion both to the idle poet of the conclusion of the *Georgics* and to the setting of pastoral and georgic poetry. The difference is that while Virgil hoped to write something in a higher mode, Montaigne disclaims ambition altogether:

> I retired my selfe unto mine owne house, with full purpose, as much as lay in me, not to trouble my selfe with any businesse, but solitarily, and quietly to weare out the remainder of my well-nigh-spent life, where me thought I could doe my Spirit no greater favour, than to give him the full scope of idlenesse, and entertaine him as he best pleased, and withall, so settle himselfe as he best liked: which I hoped he might now, being by this time become more setled and ripe, accomplish very easily. (15)

Unlike Virgil, flowering in his youth, Montaigne, nearing the end of his life, hopes for an unproductive idleness.

The hope is disappointed, however. Montaigne began by externalizing and personifying his spirit, which we should take in the sense of creative mind, and planned a quiet retirement for them both. We soon learn that his spirit is not a person but a horse, a horse that has taken control of and raped its master:

> contrariwise playing the skittish and loose-broken jade, he takes a hundred times more cariere and libertie unto himselfe, than hee did for others, and begets in me so many extravagant *Chimeraes*, and fantasticall monsters, so

orderlesse, and without any reason, one hudling upon an other, that at-leasure to view the foolishnesse and monstrous strangenesse of them, I have begun to keep a register of them, hoping, if I live, one day to make him ashamed, and blush at himselfe. (15)

As was the case with Virgil, idleness turns out to be productive after all, but the mode of textual production in this case is very different. In Montaigne's essay, the spirit (the part of man that is or should be high-er) brings forth lower things: monstrous, disorderly, foolish.[114] What is more, in this metaphor Montaigne becomes simultaneously the 'idle fallow grounds' of the first simile and the woman 'though single and alone' of the second. Producing short essays rather than a serious work of philosophy or an epic is presented as something that debases the writer and that will eventually cause shame. Like the cow's carcass and the lazy poet, Montaigne is abject, but his abjection is equated with a passive and fecund femininity.

For my purposes, Montaigne's (mock?) humility does a number of important things: for one, it connects the abjection of Virgil's metaphor for textual production with the reproductive metaphor that provides a more popular way to talk about textual production and to make it so-cially intelligible. In his stress on the productive nature of his abjection Montaigne could be said to anticipate Kathryn Bond Stockton's recent discussion of shame, in which she speaks of 'its beautiful, generative, sorrowful debasements that make bottom pleasures so dark and so strange.'[115] Stockton's brilliant book explores the connections between blackness and queerness as sites of abjection in contemporary (mainly American) society; the 'bottom' is her general term for a category that includes, most saliently for her, both anality and race. Montaigne's con-cerns in 'De l'Oysiveté' may seem very different, but the image of rape he uses to describe his writing is and has been for some time, as Stockton points out, an important part of the racial imaginary, both insofar as it is male-on-male and insofar as it is interspecies and could thus be said to anticipate the racist discourse of non-white bestiality. Perhaps the features of Stockton's phrasing that are most apposite to Montaigne are the association of shame and beauty and the insight that shame is pro-ductive. Virgil's abjection at the end of the Georgics is also productive, but it is a kind of production that he must leave behind as he moves from minor to major poetry. In his rural retirement, however, Montaigne gives himself permission to embrace both the beauty and the genera-tive power of abjection.[116]

As well, Montaigne's essay might remind us of something that recent arguments about which gender may legitimately use the reproductive metaphor tend to obscure. At their crudest, these arguments depend on a literal reading of the metaphor: since men cannot literally have children, men are not entitled to use images of reproduction to describe their textual production. But if books are like children, we should ask, in a version of the question popular with children, 'where do poems come from'? Where or what, that is, is the sexual act that leads to the offspring? At the beginning of this introduction I showed that Newcastle's image could be taken to suggest that paper texts have paper sex, so perhaps we could say that texts come from intercourse between texts. What is most significant, however, is that the discussions of reproductive metaphor are willing to take literalism only so far: sexual activity has no place in their accounts of the metaphor. As I suggested earlier, asexual reproduction is in many ways the ideal of a social regime for which sex will always be a distraction from work, and I feel that to use the reproductive metaphor without thinking about all the facts of reproduction amounts to approval of this ideal. Part of the value of Montaigne's essay is that it forces us to consider the sexual aspect of the reproductive metaphor.

Montaigne's association of pregnancy and abjection might seem to be especially misogynistic, and I am certainly not denying the misogyny of much of his essay. 'Of Idlenesse' could even be said to identify not only pregnancy but femininity itself with abjection. In a culture in which the mind is prized over the body, which is seen as both literally and metaphorically dirty, to be made of flesh and to produce another being made of flesh will always appear abject to some degree. But I think that there is something to be gained from this abjection. Julia Kristeva's famous definition of the abject as 'something rejected from which one does not part' could describe many things: two of them are children and texts.[117] Both begin in the body and are subsequently externalized. What distinguishes children and texts from other bodily products, of course, is that both are seen as good, indeed – although in very different ways – as necessary to civilization. And this, I think, is precisely the problem: for textual production, for having babies, and for the metaphoric equivalence of the two. Our culture's willingness to overlook the messiness of both personal and literary origins in the interests of social utility depends to a considerable extent on the elision of the reproducing, writing, and desiring body. I think that some Renaissance writers felt that to use the reproductive metaphor was a way to bring the body in all its messiness, in all its potential for abjection, back into the centre of our stories of where things come from.

VI

In this book I shall consider both interrogations of the reproductive metaphor and more general discussions of the connections between sexual and linguistic activity in terms of what is licit or illicit. To some extent, my aims in this book are similar to those Jeffrey Masten announced at the beginning of *Textual Intercourse*, his superb study of Renaissance ideas about collaboration and authorship: 'This project ... traces the correspondences between, on the one hand, models and rhetorics of sexual relations, intercourse, and reproduction and, on the other, notions of textual production and property.'[118] I do not cite Masten here because I feel that the reader will be ignorant of my aims by this point in the introduction, but because I want to pay tribute to one of the major influences on my thinking about these subjects before I move on to the specific analyses with which the rest of the book is concerned. In keeping with my generally anti-teleologic stance, my chapters will follow a familiar narrative in reverse: first a chapter on marriages, then one on seductions, then one on beginnings. I begin with marriage, as it is generally seen as the *telos* for texts and as the device that legitimizes sexual activity. And while the subtitle of this book is 'Where Renaissance Texts Come From,' I begin with plays, as Renaissance drama is often seen as the crowning glory of Renaissance literature (and sometimes even of English literature in general). The importance of Renaissance drama to a teleological literary history is thus a useful analogue to the role of reproduction in more general teleological narratives. As a result of this view of literary history, the movement from drama (in the first chapter) to poetry (in the next two) could be said to echo the book's movement backwards from marriage. The reproduction to which both sex and texts must lead has to pass through marriage in order to provide a recognized and recognizable (and reproducible) result.

There is no shortage of texts on marriage from the Renaissance – or, indeed, from most other periods. I have chosen three texts that simultaneously interrogate their own concern with marrying and highlight issues of creation. The first is John Lyly's *The Woman in the Moone*. In this play, Nature herself is a character, and we see her as a powerful creative force. When she creates a woman for the loveless shepherds of Utopia, the marriage plot begins, but as there are four shepherds and only one woman, marriage can never be the answer. Thomas Middleton and Thomas Dekker's *The Roaring Girl* is set in a London in which the institutions on which society is built – marriage, the family, gender, the rule of law – seem to be on the verge of failing altogether. While the marriage plot that is the ostensible subject of the play is concluded satisfactorily, the play works to undermine both marriage and language as signifying mechanisms. John Fletcher and William Shakespeare's *The Two Noble Kinsmen* dramatizes the difficulty of forming mixed-sex couples out of same-sex ones; it is also a work that tries to find suitable metaphors for its own creation out of a famous earlier text. To return to my comments on Hammill and on Barthes's *The Neutral*, the queerness of these works – and I would say that all are queer – lies not in what they represent, since that, after all, is primarily mixed – sex marriage, but rather in the way in which they focus on strategies of representation (and, in particular, on linguistic representation) rather than on the end of the process. To some extent, this claim could be made for most Renaissance plays that focus on the marriage plot, but I feel that the focus on the process is especially marked in these plays.

In chapter 2 I look at poems that focus on seduction. As the main purpose of rhetoric is to persuade, seduction scenes are central to rhetoric; as the main purpose of sex is to produce children, seduction is also central to the marriage plot. All the poems that I consider here demonstrate an awareness of these beliefs while making them problematic. Christopher Marlowe's *Hero and Leander* features extended, prominent, and memorable seduction speeches, but the rhetoric is beside the point, as Hero is already eager to have sex with Leander. Incapable of being recuperated teleologically, these speeches must be valued for their own sake, for their linguistic variety, invention, and elaboration. As *Hero and Leander* as a whole can be read as an attack on the sexual system of his day, I feel that Marlowe seeks in this poem to gesture towards a sexuality liberated from use. The reverse is true of my second example in this chapter, John Marston's *The Metamorphosis of Pigmalions Image*. Marston retells what is arguably the most famous story of artistic creation in literature in order to seduce a woman. In Ovid, Pygmalion produces a human being through art without resorting to sex; for Marston, art is chiefly important, at least in this poem, as a way to get sex. The poem I discuss first in this chapter is somewhat different from both of these works. In his first book of original poetry, Samuel Daniel also looks at the rhetoric of seduction. My concern is with the first half of this book, the sonnet sequence *Delia*, in which the poet attempts to use poetry to obtain the favour of the women he loves and, to a lesser degree, the sympathy of fellow lovers. Daniel considers the purpose of poetry, its effect in both the private and the public spheres, and the extent to which poetry's rhetorical power can be reconciled with sexual morality; for him, being a poet is at once produced by abjection and serves to produce it.

Appropriately, chapter 3 is called 'Beginnings.' Here, I look at how poets actually present their textual production.[119] My two primary examples are Sir Philip Sidney's *Astrophil and Stella* and Milton's *Paradise Lost*. In each, the poet uses the reproductive metaphor, but only as one possible way to write about writing. Producing a text may be like having a baby, but it is like many other things as well. Both poems are remarkable for beginning more than once, and each time the poet makes a new beginning, he calls our attention to it and to the process that led to the poem we are now reading. One way to understand this beginning again (and again) is as a form of the resistance to narrativization that I discussed above. In these sections of this chapter, I am particularly interested in Sidney's and Milton's concern with abjection and with the relationship between abjection and writing. My final example is John Bunyan's *Pilgrim's Progress*, or rather 'The Author's Apology for his Book,' the enchanting doggerel with which he begins his text. Here, Bunyan tells the story of how he wrote the book and why he wrote it the way he did. 'The Author's Apology for his Book' makes extensive use of metaphors for textual production, and despite its generally happy tone, it too presents abjection as part of textual production.

1 Marriages

The three plays I discuss in this chapter are in some ways very different. For instance, while both Lyly's *The Woman in the Moone* and Middleton and Dekker's *The Roaring Girl* are comedies, Shakespeare and Fletcher's *The Two Noble Kinsmen* barely makes the transition from tragedy to tragicomedy – if indeed it ever does. As well, *The Woman in the Moone* is set in a pastoral land called Utopia, *The Roaring Girl* in early seventeenth-century London, and *The Two Noble Kinsmen* in ancient Athens. And while Shakespeare and Fletcher's play is the latest version of a story that can be traced through Chaucer to classical literature, Lyly's play, although it draws on the pastoral genre and on one of the most famous of all Greek myths, has no obvious source, and Middleton and Dekker's play is a city comedy, a genre that was only about ten years old when the play was written. The plays thus seem to differ not only in theme and subject, but also in any literary classification beyond the general one of drama. Nevertheless, they have some important similarities. For one, each of these plays can be read as an exploration of dramatic teleology and of the extent to which marriage is a social and literary necessity. What is more, each draws attention to the construction of stage characters through language, which is never a transparent medium in these plays. The same is true of the plots, which are never primarily ways to produce the required dramatic ending–indeed, all three endings are notably odd and, in many ways, unsatisfactory. In all three plays, then, we could say that plot and language serve as counterpleasures that prevent the endings from functioning, as Vaneigem said of orgasms, as 'a charge-discharge reducing erotic tensions to zero.'[1]

Another feature common to these plays is that to some extent they all present marriage as work (real work, that is). One of the best discussions of marriage as work is Laura Kipnis's article 'Adultery.' Drawing on the work of Herbert Marcuse, Kipnis argues that we are increasingly unable to disentangle marital life from economic life. Early on in the essay, she points out the significance of the metaphors we use: 'Yes, we all know that Good Marriages Take Work. But, then, work takes work, too. Wage labor, intimacy labor – are you ever not on the clock? If you're working at monogamy, you've already entered a system of exchange: an economy of intimacy governed – as such economies are – by scarcity, threat, and internalized prohibitions; secured ideologically – as such economies are – by incessant assurances that there are no viable alternatives.'[2] Kipnis's analysis recalls the writings of MacKendrick and Vaneigem, as all three writers protest the assignation of a use value to pleasure, or rather to what should be pleasure. In emphasizing the significance of the metaphors we use to talk about marriage – and, of course, about relationships in general – Kipnis makes the same kind of point that I want to make about the reproductive metaphor, which is that the danger of metaphors is that they could become real and that they cannot be context free. In the context of the marriage plot, all the playwrights I discuss here could be said to emphasize the extent to which not only marriage but also art is work. Writing plays appears less like responding to inspiration and more like the painstaking labour of a craftsman, a point that has recently been made by Henry S. Turner of Renaissance theatre in general.[3] It could be said that in these plays art is another form of labour rather than something removed from labour.

The plays I discuss in this chapter do succeed in producing marriages, and in that sense their labour is successful, but as I have already remarked, each play focuses on language to an unusual extent and encourages spectators to consider the ways in which language is often not an instrument of signification. With reference to *The Woman in the Moone*, I would argue not only that language is already highly marked, as this is Lyly's only play in blank verse, but also that, owing to the plot of the play, in which the main character undergoes several radical changes in personality in succession, the audience is forced to reflect on the extent to which dramatic language conveys character. As a result, the illusion that the characters on stage are real is undermined. As well, the play begins with a focus on art, when the prologue tells us that 'all is but a Poets dream.'[4] The language of *The Roaring Girl* is marked for contemporary audiences because of the profusion of puns, most of which are now explicable only by footnotes, but what is perhaps most unusual about the play's language is the famous scene in which some of the characters use the canting slang of thieves; in the discussion that follows, the audience is forced to reflect on the extent to which language conveys character. Finally, although the language of *The Two Noble Kinsmen* may not appear unusual in the context of other tragicomedies of the period, I see it as unusual in that it is not the Middle English couplets of Chaucer's *Knight's Tale*, the famous medieval poem that is its source. As the play begins with a prologue in which the question of the writers' debt to Chaucer is raised (if not answered), the comparison, which is partly a linguistic comparison, is crucial to our experience of the play that follows.

An important part of what interests me in these plays is that it could be argued that none of them is really a play about marriage. This statement will probably seem counterintuitive, as *The Woman in the Moone* chiefly documents the almost immediate collapse of a marriage (and of the first marriage in the world) and the narratives of *The Roaring Girl* and *The Two Noble Kinsmen* are primarily and explicitly taken up by the relentless motion of the marriage plot, but in fact it would be more accurate to say that each focuses on dramatic contrivance. For the most part, the marriages are the ostensible reason for all the contrivance, but the frequently elaborate plotting that characterizes these plays is only ever partially recuperated by the marriages. To a greater or lesser extent, all the playwrights repeatedly draw our attention to the sheer amount of work they and their characters perform in the name of the marriage plot. One valuable effect of this is to denaturalize marriage: it becomes impossible to argue that marriage is inevitable or even that it arises naturally from the love between two young people. I have suggested that all three plays are concerned with language as a system of signification; a parallel concern shared by all three plays is the extent to which marriage signifies. Although marriage often appears to be not only the primary subject of these plays but, in fact, their only subject, I would argue that the centrality of marriage (whether to plays or to life in general) is never taken for granted and that the marriages produced by the plots can never be said to sum up the plays as a whole.

The way in which these playwrights treat both language and marriage is what makes the plays queer in our modern sense. It may seem strange to label as queer three plays in which romantic and erotic relations between the sexes are so clearly paramount – indeed, of the three only *The Two Noble Kinsmen* deals in any extended fashion with same-sex relations – but this may well be because our definitions of queerness are unduly restricted. In his recent book on Oscar Wilde, Jeff Nunokawa has suggested that what often appears to us in Wilde's works as transgressive desire is not entirely assimilable to contemporary ideas of transgression. As he points out, 'Wilde's light passion becomes unfamiliar ... when we consider that this performance of desire works not to subvert heterosexual normativity, but rather to cooperate with it.'[5] The comment could also be applied to the plays I discuss here, in which it seems that all the work in the play goes to bringing about marriages rather than to creating new forms of relationship. Rather than come up with an alternative, these playwrights are concerned more to look at the existing way of life through what Pierre Bourdieu has called the 'effect of parody': the playwrights '"get beyond" [dépassent] the dominant mode of thought and expression not by explicitly denouncing it but by repeating and reproducing it in a sociologically non-congruent context, which has the effect of rendering it incongruous or even absurd, simply by making it perceptible as the arbitrary convention it is.'[6] In the plays I discuss below, the 'dominant mode of thought and expression' is marriage and specifically the marriage plot.

Of course, this means that all the plays I discuss in this chapter are to a greater or lesser extent, and for more or less time, involved in cooperating with heterosexual normativity, just as Wilde's plays are, but I would still argue that they are queer, not only because they expose marriage as an arbitrary convention rather than as the natural goal of lives and narrative, but also because they are concerned more with process than with results. In the introduction, I cited Barthes's comment, 'The Neutral is not an objective, a target: it's a passage. In a famous apologue, Zen makes fun of people who mistake the pointing finger for the moon it points to–I'm interested in the finger, not in the moon.'[7] I suggested that in this sense the Neutral is queer, and I would extend the comment to include the plays I discuss in this chapter. While marriage is usually presumed to be an objective and a target both in drama and in real life, these plays focus on what Barthes calls a passage – in these plays, a passage that looks like very hard work indeed. In other words, these playwrights cooperate with the marriage plots that give them their ostensible reason for being, but they consistently draw attention to the cooperation at the expense of what it is intended to produce. It is the interest of these playwrights in the finger rather than in the moon that makes their plays so queer.

I

The Woman in the Moone is generally thought to be Lyly's last play and to date from the early 1590s.[8] There has always been a certain amount of criticism on *Euphues*, and in recent years the court comedies (especially *Gallathea*) have been the subject of a great deal of analysis, but very few critics have written on *The Woman in the Moone*. Perhaps this is due to the play's oddness: as it is largely in blank verse, it is certainly odd in the context of Lyly's works, but the play, which is set in Utopia and tells the story of the creation of Pandora by Nature and the disasters that ensue, is odd in many other ways as well. Despite its peculiarities, however, *The Woman in the Moone* is in some ways typical of Lyly; for me it is most crucially so in that it demonstrates, to a very high degree what Jacqueline Vanhoutte has recently called 'Lyly's unusually sceptical attitude towards marriage.'[9] Although many Renaissance playwrights show some ambivalence about the marriages to which their plays inexorably tend, Lyly does seem to be particularly uncomfortable with the marriage plot, and his plays often subvert this plot in various ways, sometimes going so far as to suggest that marriage is not, after all, desirable. What is especially interesting to me about *The Woman in the Moone* is that the play does not lead to marriage: the marriage – and it is the first marriage ever in Utopia – happens early on and most of the play demonstrates what a bad idea this marriage is. As well, Lyly emphasizes creation and artificiality throughout in a way that draws attention to his own authorial strategies.

I want to begin my discussion of the play by situating it in the context of how Lyly deals with resolution and the marriage plot in some of his other plays. Most famously, for instance, in *Gallathea* the plot reaches an impasse early on, when the two girls disguised as boys fall in love with each other.[10] Thus, they are unable to form a dramatically viable couple in either of what are, in the context of the narrative, their natural or disguised states, although this fact does not seem to trouble them unduly. At the end of one scene, for instance, one of the girls says, 'Come let vs into the Groue, and make much one of another, that cannot tel what to think one of another' (III.ii.58–9). The parallelism of the phrases sets up a contrast between making much of someone, an expression that could refer to a range of activities including, of course, sexual activity, and thinking of someone, an expression that could mean holding someone in (affectionate) regard but that could also refer to a more rational assessment. In the latter sense, the girl's point is that neither can fit the other into a familiar category, such as potential friend or potential love object. But even before it was made, Lyly's parallel has been rendered irrelevant by the invitation to go into the grove: the girls may be perplexed by each other and by their situation, but the exploration of the natural world (an exploration that may extend to their bodies) is a pleasure that transcends the need for classification.

Tellingly, however, these pleasures can take place only between scenes: they cannot be represented dramatically. Vanhoutte wrote of *Gallathea* that 'forgoing "compulsory heterosexuality," the play renders explicit the superiority of equitable (and homosocial) relationships left implicit in Lyly's other plays,' but while this comment is true of much of the play, the narrative of *Gallathea* does end with heterosexuality, at least to a certain extent.[11] The two girls remain together throughout the play, even after their gender is revealed, but at last Venus proposes to resolve this unresolvable dilemma: 'What is to Loue or the Mistrisse of Loue vnpossible? Was it not *Venus* that did the like to *Iphis* and *Ianthe*? howe say yee? are ye agreed? one to bee a boy presently?' (V.iii.142–4) Venus proposes to create heterosexuality out of homosexuality, a mixed-sex couple out of a same-sex one. At this, the girls' fathers complain, both swearing that they want daughters not sons. Venus's solution is to make the specific nature of the resolution a surprise: 'neither of them shall know whose lot it shal be til they come to the Church-dore. One shall be: doth it suffise?' (V.iii.170–2). It appears that the answer is yes, as this is the last we see of the girls. Thanks to the intercession of Venus, *Gallathea* ends with a couple proceeding to the altar and comes to resemble other Renaissance comedies more closely than might have seemed possible earlier.

However, three factors vitiate what might appear to be the triumph of heterosexuality in this play. The first is that we do not learn which girl will become a boy, and our ignorance of this fact is emphasized by Venus' allusion to the story of Iphis and Ianthe from Ovid's *Metamorphoses*. In this famous story, Ovid tells us that the father of Iphis wanted a son and his wife deceived him and pretended that her baby was a boy. Iphis is raised as a boy; when she grows up she falls in love with Ianthe and the result is the same sort of impasse that occurs at the end of *Gallathea*. Here as well, of course, Venus solves everything, and once Iphis has been turned into a man, she is able to marry Ianthe; the happy couple places an inscription on the temple of Isis, at which Iphis had made offerings, that reads: 'DONA PUER SOLVIT QUAE FEMINA VOVERAT IPHIS' (the gifts promised by Iphis as a girl are fulfilled by Iphis as a boy).[12] In this story, the change only completes the practice begun by the girl's mother, and the girl who is now a boy has in any case lived as a boy all along. In Lyly's play, both Gallathea and Phyllida have lived almost all of their lives as the girls they are and have only recently been disguised as boys. Heterosexuality, then, is not something the two girls have been playing at all along, as is the case with Ovid's characters, but rather something that is imposed by Venus as a way of ending both the problem and the play.

Another way to characterize the ending of *Gallathea* would be to say that the change Venus proposes makes the love between the girls socially legible, but in this connection it is important to point out that Lyly does not endorse this social legibility with dramatic representation, as Gallathea and Phyllida still are girls when we last see them. That both the change of one of the girls into a boy and their resulting marriage take place offstage connects these events and the play's conclusion as a whole to the girls' earlier withdrawal to the grove to 'make much one of another.' This, I think, is the second factor vitiating the triumph of heterosexuality. Ultimately, neither what we would now call homosexuality nor what we would now call heterosexuality can be represented, which means that both are literally obscene. Lyly follows convention to the extent of providing a heterosexual ending to his play, but he refuses to dramatize it. Our ignorance of which girl becomes a boy continues the suspense that a conclusion is intended to resolve past the ending of *Gallathea*. I would argue that this has the effect of separating the energies of the plotting from the recuperation of those energies in matrimonial closure. Finally, the third of these factors can be found in the important subplot of the play, in which three young men attempt to find a trade, which sets up an implicit parallel between the world of labour, even of manual labour, and the efforts of the playwright: the main plot's equivalent for the subplot's stress on labour is Lyly's dramatic contrivance. We could say that throughout *Gallathea* forms of work predominate and, in a way that Kipnis would appreciate, that getting married is presented primarily as work.

Another way to put this is to say that when Venus appears onstage to solve problems, she could be described as a *dea ex machina*, but it is the machine, not the goddess, that predominates, a fact that is emphasized by the objections of the fathers to her proposal. The conclusion of *Gallathea* could be summarized in such a way as to make the play resemble more conventional Renaissance dramas that feature crossdressing, such as *Twelfth Night* or *As You Like It*, but unlike Shakespeare, Lyly does not restore order but imposes it by force. Nor is *Gallathea* unusual among his plays in this respect. In *Mother Bombie*, for instance, the plot becomes gradually more complex and the problems faced by the characters (once again, the obstacles to the successful conclusion of the marriage plot) seem gradually more hopeless. The play's eponymous character is an old woman who makes a number of cryptic comments throughout before resolving all the problems at the end. In this play, it is familial relationships that must be changed in order to lead the characters to the altar: the revelation of a baby swap years earlier makes the marriage possible. But perhaps the most extreme example of Lyly's calling attention to his dramatic contrivance is provided by *Endimion*, in which Bagoa, who has been turned into a tree, is turned back into a woman just so that Sir Tophas may have a lover: 'I cannot handsomly goe to bed without *Bagoa*' (V.iii.274). As Sir Tophas has been exceptionally unlikeable throughout the play, there is no reason for the goddess (Cynthia, in this play) to make him happy except to swell the number of happy couples, or at least of couples.

When Cynthia grants Tophas's request, she says, 'I will trie whether I can turne this tree againe to thy true loue' (V.iii.277–8), to which Tophas replies, 'Turne her to a true loue or false, so shee be a wench I care not' (V.iii.279–80).[13] The modesty of his requirements may seem entirely suitable to the wretchedness of his character, but I think Lyly's point is that our own requirements are similarly modest. At the theatre, for instance, as long as the romantic intrigues end in a marriage, we are satisfied. Lyly's emphasis on the artificiality of the contrivances of the characters such as Venus, Cynthia, and Mother Bombie sets up an implicit critique of the teleology of dramatic narratives. While many playwrights try to make their artifice seem natural, both for aesthetic reasons and because events dictated by ideological concerns are typically disguised as both natural and inevitable, Lyly focuses attention on his artifice. His work is not precisely anti-teleological, as the plays do end in familiar ways, but I think that he does force us to consider the extent to which outcomes that we might otherwise be inclined to think of as natural or desirable or inevitable take a great deal of work and sometimes even, as is the case with *Gallathea*, work that can be accomplished only by supernatural means. As we shall see, this characterization of Lyly's work is particularly true of *The Woman in the Moone*, a play whose subject could be said to be the artificiality of marriage and of the marriage plot, a comment that could also be made of *The Roaring Girl* and *The Two Noble Kinsmen*.

Indeed, *The Woman in the Moone* is characterized by artificiality throughout, and to an even greater extent than Lyly's other plays. Lyly's focus on artifice here may explain the work's relative unpopularity with critics, although it has had its admirers. For instance, Joseph W.

Houppert says, 'Along with *Mother Bombie*, *The Woman in the Moon* is Lyly's most unusual play; it is perhaps his best.'[14] The play's supporters – and, to a considerable extent, the supporters of Lyly's work as whole – have defended his artificiality and have seen his work as the triumph of style over substance.[15] G.K. Hunter makes the point that Lyly is at an unfair disadvantage because 'Shakespeare has made an integrated humanity seem to modern readers to be the key virtue of Elizabethan drama.'[16] It is certainly true that Lyly shows no interest in the illusion of depth and three-dimensionality that is one of Shakespeare's hallmarks, something that can perhaps be better demonstrated by *The Woman in the Moone* than by any of Lyly's other plays. Houppert describes this play as 'Lyly's most cerebral comedy in that it tends towards abstraction more than the others do. Of the twenty characters, all but six are abstractions. Even though they are given human form, they are far too simplistic to approximate men and women; they are without complexity in either action or motivation.'[17] In his discussion, Hunter compares the play's characters to chess pieces and says that they 'have only one or two moves open to them; the mastery of the playwright lies in the skill with which these moves are combined, and the surprising and piquant new patterns of movement produced.'[18]

The point these critics make is valuable, as Lyly's interests clearly are not in realistic drama either on the level of plotting or on the level of characterization. Arguments such as those made by Hunter and Houppert are a useful corrective to narrow standards of evaluation, although it must be admitted that unfortunately they have not had much effect in the years since they were published (1962 and 1975, respectively). Nevertheless, I feel that in focusing on 'the mastery of the playwright' in technical matters, these critics underrate the extent to which *The Woman in the Moone* might be considered not merely a tour de force or an interesting work of meta-theatre but also a serious critique of marriage as a system. For instance, when Houppert says that the characters 'are without complexity in either action or motivation' or when Hunter says that the characters 'have only one or two moves open to them,' they do not appear to have taken into account the possibility that this is not because Lyly was not interested in characters as such but rather because he was. The play can be seen to suggest that the limitations of the characters, the extent to which they seem to have only a very few options, are typical of humans in general. Lyly's control over the play, of which these critics have written, can be seen within the play in the power of Nature and the gods; the resulting powerlessness of the play's characters can be read allegorically as indicating our own powerlessness in the grip of the marriage plot, whether that plot is understood as something within literature or as something that affects real people.

The play opens with Nature attended by Concord and Discord in Utopia. Nature tells us that she has come 'from farre aboue the spheeres, / To frolicke heere in fayre Vtopia' (I.i.1–2). Nature, then, is not only the creator of all but also the highest force in the universe, even above the gods and goddesses who will appear later in this first scene. The land to which Nature has descended is not Thomas More's Utopia, but a place where her 'chief workes do florish in their prime, / And wanton in their first simplicitie' (I.i.3–4). This world, which is not exactly our world, inspires great self-satisfaction in Nature: 'Heere I suruey, and glory in my selfe' (I.i.14). The only problem for her is the complaint of Discord, whose 'sorrowes clowde eclips[es] our delights' (I.i.16). Discord is unhappy because as quickly as she creates opposites –

good and bad, or light and darke,
Pleasant and sad, moouing and fixed things,
Fraile and immortall, or like contraries –   (I.i.20–2)

Concord unites them. The speech is significant because it leads Nature to reveal her thoughts:

in your selues though you be different,
Yet in my seruice must you well agree.
For *Nature* workes her will from contraries.   (I.i.27–9)

The picture of Nature creating everything from the union of opposites dates back at least to the Pre-Socratic philosophers; what is significant about Lyly's use of this idea in this context is that we are invited to consider the extent to which this idea is either a theory of personality or a theory of marriage, both of which are important to the play that follows.

It is at this point that Nature is visited by the four Utopian shepherds and the plot begins. These shepherds are not merely the only four shepherds in Utopia but, in fact, the only four people of any kind in Utopia – with the exception of Pandora's servant Gunophilus, although it is possible that he was created after Pandora; most important, there are no women. Stesias, the first to speak, asks Nature 'To finish vp the heape of thy great gifts' (I.i.33). The shepherds see themselves as incomplete, and Iphicles, the next to speak, reveals why. They want what

> euery other creature hath,
> A sure and certaine meanes among our selues,
> To propagate the issue of our kinde.   (I.i.40–2)

Iphicles adds that this would be a 'comfort to our sole estate' (I.i.43) and points out that all the fish, birds, and beasts

> Haue mates of pleasure to vpholde their broode;
> But thy Vtopians, poore and simple men,
> As yet bewaile their want of female sex.   (I.ii.48–50)

These three ways of phrasing the request are significant: first, Iphicles asks for a way to continue their kind, then for 'mates of pleasure,' and then, most generally, for the female sex. In other words, he passes from reproduction to companionship and finally to a particular kind of human being.

Indeed, it is not entirely clear what sort of reproduction Iphicles has in mind here. We might be inclined to understand 'our kinde' as meaning humankind, but it is entirely possible that it means men (or perhaps even shepherds), and when he says that they want to find the means to reproduce 'among our selues' he could refer to androgenesis. As the belief that reproduction could occur in many ways was current in the Renaissance, the reference to other animals cannot be taken to prove that Iphicles has heterosexual reproduction in mind. He could even be saying that they already have means of propagation, but that these are unsure or uncertain. While the phrase 'mates of pleasure' indicates a desire for companionship, it should be remarked that these mates are intended 'to vpholde' the shepherds' issue. That is, it is not clear that Iphicles is making any connection between sex (as one of the pleasures they will have with their mates) and the children these mates will help to raise. His final reference to the 'female sex' that he and his fellow shepherds lack might seem to name a kind of person who will provide both reproduction and companionship, but this cannot be proved from what he says. In any case, it is certainly clear that the shepherds are not asking for marriage in the sense that the institution would have been known to Lyly and his audience (or, for that matter, to us). I would argue that, if we do assume that the shepherds want wives, then we have fallen into Lyly's trap insofar as it is then we, rather than Lyly, who begin the marriage plot.

I suggested above that *The Woman in the Moone* begins with a focus on art and, what is more, with a focus of Nature's art as a kind of work; in conjunction with my idea that Lyly wants us to realize that the marriage plot of the play – a feature we usually consider essential to most narratives – is largely our doing, I might be understood as arguing that the play is, at least at this point, meta-theatrical. This is not a new insight: in 1982 Anne Lancashire wrote of *The Woman in the Moone* that its 'total effect is ceremonial, episodic, masque-like: a triumph of obvious dramatic craftsmanship.'[19] Nor would I restrict Lyly's self-reflexivity to theatrical concerns. One way to understand the beginning of the play is to see it as a dramatization of the shift in literary history from the predominance of the all-male pastoral and epic genres to the rise of genres such as romantic comedy and prose fiction that concentrate on relations between the sexes.[20] In this reading, the four shepherds inaugurate an important moment in literary history; what is more, Lyly's version of literary history would then present an artistic change as a natural one. This reading is appealing, but for now I want only to point out that part of Lyly's purpose here is not merely to display his own dramaturgical skills but also, as I have said before, to hint that our own lives are similarly stage-managed. Although he is not explicit on this point here or elsewhere in *The Woman in the Moone*, I think that the discrepancy between what the shepherds ask for and the marriage that ends up ruining everything is telling. Lyly gives us the materials to consider how unnatural and unsatisfactory marriage really is.

This point is underlined by what follows in the first scene. Although the shepherds support their request with evidence from nature and although their request is made to Nature herself, what we see in the rest of the scene is an emphasis on construction and artifice. Once the shepherds go, the workshop of Nature is revealed: Concord and Discord 'draw the Curtins from before NATURES shop, where stands an Image clad and some vnclad, they bring forth the cloathed image' (I.i.56, S.D.). This is hardly 'Natura naturans'; instead, nature turns out to be art after all. That the image chosen to be the first woman is the 'cloathed' image emphasizes the artificiality of the situation. What is more, Nature speaks of having 'arayde this lifelesse Image' (I.i.57), which raises the possibility that she did not create it: first, we see her as a sculptor rather than as a creator of life and then not even as a sculptor but rather as a dressmaker. As the speech progresses, however, Nature stresses her

creative power. She tells us that she was prompted by her 'deepe prou-
idence, / To make it such as our Vtopians craue' (I.i.58–9) and that 'The
matter first when it was voyde of forme, / Was purest water, earth, and
ayre, and fyre' (I.i.61–2). The creation of this first woman recalls the
creation of the world itself from the chaos of the four elements.

Interestingly, at some point the making of the image became a natural process, since while at first Nature 'shapt it in a matchlesse mould'
(I.i.63), the image subsequently 'grew to this impression that you see'
(I.i.65). This is the second time that Lyly has used the word *mould*: when
Nature promised to fulfil the shepherds' request, she said that she
would give them a woman who would be 'Like to your selues, but of a
purer moulde' (I.i.52). Lyly is playing here on the two meanings of
mould: first, earth and, metaphorically, human flesh and also character
or quality; second, the pattern by which things are made. The result is a
confusion in our sense of what exactly the status of Pandora is. She appears to be simultaneously a natural thing and a work of art; what is
more, if we take mould to mean a pattern, she becomes not so much a
work of art as something mass-produced. In this reading of mould, and
in conjunction with the word 'impression,' Pandora could be compared
to a book or a coin or, conceivably, a printed picture, an illustration of
some kind. Nature's theory of artistic production thus recalls not simply Renaissance debates about art and nature but also Renaissance
theories of textual production and debates about the status of texts
themselves and of their producers. The artist could be someone who
usurps the function of God (of course, in *The Woman in the Moone*,
Nature is above the gods) or an artisan; the artwork itself could be a
natural thing (and conceivably something even better than nature) or
a way to make money or merely a consumer good intended for the
widest possible distribution. Nature's presentation of herself sets her
up as a parallel for Lyly, and in the context of my book as a whole it is
remarkable that, while the desire for a woman was connected with reproduction, reproduction plays no part in this account of artistic production. The passage inverts our sense of which is the tenor and which
the vehicle in the reproductive metaphor.

A further look at artistic production is provided by Nature's first
speech to the newly animated Pandora: 'Now art thou *Natures* glory
and delight, / Compact of euery heauenly excellence' (I.i.93–4). The
statement might seem like the hyperbolic praise of feminine beauty
typical of much Renaissance poetry, but in context it is strictly literal.
Nature begins by explaining that Pandora is 'indowd with *Saturns*

deepe conceit' (I.i.95) and works her way through all seven planets, summarizing, 'Thus haue I robd the Planets for thy sake' (I.i.102), and then adding that she has given Pandora '*Iunoes* armes, / *Auroraes* hands, and louely *Thetis* foote' (I.i.103–4). Nature's comments are instantly proved true when the seven planets enter and identify the specific features that have been copied. This part of the scene presents the artist as plagiarist. In this case, the accusation is not especially serious, since when Nature says that she has 'robd' the gods, she has, in fact, only taken what she gave them, as she makes clear when she answers their accusations by asking, 'Ordeynd not I your motions, and your selues? / And dare you check the author of your liues' (I.i.121–2). Still, plagiarism is evidently the rule rather than the exception for all artists since Nature's original creation; we should perhaps read the passage allegorically as indicating the indebtedness of poets not only to Nature or nature but also to earlier authors in general.

This idea of the individual character as a kind of dictionary of quotations has important consequences in the play both for the action and for the point Lyly is making. When Nature leaves, Saturn incites the gods to 'to shew our Emperie: / And bend our forces gainst this earthy starre' (I.i.133–4). His plan is that each of the gods will rule Pandora in turn, 'that she may feele the influence of our beames' (I.i.136), which means that she will successively exhibit the salient characteristic of each god: Saturn's melancholy, Jupiter's pride, Mars's fury, and so on. From this point, the play has, in effect, a double plot: one part is concerned with Pandora's relations to the four shepherds and to her servant Gunophilus, while the other shows how these relations are affected by her changing character. That is, Lyly simultaneously demonstrates and mocks an entirely deterministic theory of human character (in this case the theory is astrology, perhaps the most popular example of this sort of theory in his own time; I think the satire applies equally well to other theories such as the humours or indeed DNA or neuroscience). He also demonstrates and mocks his own craft as a playwright, as we could see the relentless combining and recombining of characters as an only slightly exaggerated version of the normal plot twists of a romantic comedy.

In romantic comedies, the list of dramatis personae is usually carefully constructed to result in the formation of as many couples as possible, but such an outcome is impossible in *The Woman in the Moone*, where there is only one woman for four men – and once Gunophilus begins to exceed his role as servant, there are, in fact, five men. But if Nature's decision to make only one woman in answer to the shepherds' plea seems inexplicable, that is because we are blind to the possibilities. Nature tells Pandora, 'I make thee for a solace vnto men' (I.i.91): it is not her idea to invent marriage. Instead, it is the shepherds and Pandora who construct a marriage plot that is bound to lead to trouble. There is no reason why Pandora could not be a solace unto all the Utopian men nor, for that matter, is there any reason why the men could not solace each other. After all, there is certainly no talk of reproduction after the first act and, as I have shown, it is not entirely clear from the first scene that what the shepherds really want is children. In the Renaissance, of course, the alternative sexual behaviour I have mentioned was typically presented in poetry as the province of the gods and as forbidden to humans; by beginning the play with a scene that informs us that Pandora is constructed out of divine attributes, Lyly draws our attention to another divine attribute (unfettered sexuality) that Pandora does appear to possess but that the shepherds emphatically do not.[21]

One way to read the play is as a misogynist fantasy: in this reading, the sign that the original setting was really utopian in the popular sense of the word would be that it was peopled solely by men. The ending of *The Woman in the Moone* certainly seems to support such a reading. After Pandora has worked her way through all five men with admirable thoroughness, Nature intervenes to restore order and allows Pandora to choose her future planet of residence. She chooses Cynthia and explains that she does so because 'change is my felicity, / And ficklenesse *Pandoraes* proper forme' (V.i.301–2). Nature grants her wish and sentences all women to be like Pandora:

> Raigne thou at womens nuptials, and their birth;
> Let them be mutable in all their loues,
> Fantasticall, childish, and folish, in their desires,
> Demaunding toyes:
> And starke madde when they cannot haue their will.   (V.i.322–6)

This is recognizable as an efficient summary of the sort of misogynist rhetoric familiar from much Renaissance literature, but in its context in *The Woman in the Moone* the scene as a whole is also more than this, and I want to look at some of the ways in which the passage signifies.

First, Pandora's statement that fickleness is the right 'forme' for her could be said to be a contradiction in terms, as fickleness could be defined as the absence of a fixed form. Pandora is saying that she has a real self but that is it is unfixed and always being remade: to use the terms of a famous recent debate, Pandora has an essence, but it is constructed (and deconstructed and reconstructed). Furthermore, a 'forme' is normally the shape or appearance of something, and since we see Pandora as a mere image before we see her as a woman with a series of wildly contrasting personalities, we should logically associate her physical form with stability, as it is the only constant thing about her. Secondly, Nature's speech reveals that the proverbial fickleness of women is actually not their fault, or even Pandora's fault. All women are to be punished because of the sins of the first woman: this is called Genesis. Lyly's play can thus be seen as an allegory of the story of Adam and Eve, or perhaps as a radical new version of it, one in which divine power is clearly at fault. My point here is not that *The Woman in the Moone* should be read as an attempt to rewrite the book of Genesis or even that the ending is not misogynist after all, but rather that Lyly wishes, in an essentially satiric way, to criticize the gods and to do so with reference to human sexuality.

Pandora does not go off to the moon alone, however, as Stesias is forced to accompany her and there is thus both a woman and a man in the moon. By this point in the play, the other shepherds have melted away. They were not really needed for the plot, as what could have been the story of a sexual free-for-all settles down into the much more conventional story of a man, his wife, and her lovers. The crucial moment for the emergence of this plot is Pandora's statement to the shepherds, not quite halfway through *The Woman in the Moone*, 'One of you foure shalbe my wedlocke mate' (III.i.40). She chooses Stesias and for that reason; he must accompany Pandora at the end of the play, although he is extremely unwilling to do so: 'Ile rather dye then beare her company' (V.i.313). It is clear, then, that Lyly's satire is not only focused on the gods but also extends to humans. It is the human insistence on marriage, on an exclusive and socially intelligible sexual relation, that really causes the trouble. While marriage often closes narratives and solves the tensions created during the movement of the plot, here it is marriage itself that is the obstacle. What is more, the marriage is nearer the play's beginning than its end. The presence on stage at the beginning of *The Woman in the Moone* of a woman and four suitors might seem to indicate that what will follow is a romantic comedy, but that is not what we get. Instead, the story becomes to a great extent the story of adultery, of a serial non-monogamist. It turns out that Pandora's lasting legacy to us is to have simultaneously invented marriage and adultery. Without allowing the play to become a serious or even tragic story of a woman's infidelity, Lyly suggests that sexual transgression is the norm rather than the exception.

In the context of this book, what interests me most about *The Woman in the Moone* is how Lyly deals both with a theory of artistic production and with the marriage plot. As I have shown, Nature is presented (initially, at least) as an artist who proposes a theory of artistic production; what is more, she creates something perfect. Nature's creation and her theory of it have no connection to the reproductive metaphor at all. In fact, after Iphicles has stated the shepherds' desires – 'A sure and certaine meanes among our selues, / To propagate the issue of our kinde' – no more is heard about reproduction, and although the play ends with a married couple prominently displayed, there is still no suggestion that the marriage will produce children. Tacitly, at least, the reproductive metaphor for artistic production is ruled out altogether. At the beginning of my discussion of *The Woman in the Moone* I commented on Lyly's focus on art; I would identify this as his central concern in the play. One way to characterize the play as a whole, in fact, would be to say that it is about how a perfect work of art is ruined both by the gods and by humans. The gods ruin the perfect character that Nature gave to Pandora, and by insisting that marriage should be accompanied by sexual exclusivity – after all, it is not clear that Pandora's idea of marriage includes monogamy – the shepherds ruin the solution to their loneliness that Nature gave to them. The human insistence on use value turns out to be inimical to the work of art. To an even greater extent than Lyly's other plays, *The Woman in the Moone* registers a protest against the social use of both artistic production and sexuality.

It may seem most reasonable to describe *The Woman in the Moone* as a play about marriage, and certainly the love intrigues of the main human characters occupy most of the action, but the conclusion reveals that this has also been a play that purports to explain a natural phenomenon. Read retrospectively, then, the play explains the origins of the markings on the moon. But this explanation comes only at the very end and, as the conclusion reveals that there is both a woman and a man in the moon, it is not an entirely satisfactory explanation. As I see it, Lyly has replaced marriage with an explanation of a natural phenomenon as the play's *telos*. In making this replacement only at the very end of the last scene and in not really connecting the explanation to the events of the play's narrative, Lyly makes this new *telos* seem inadequate – or, at least, he emphasizes that, although the placing of Pandora and Stesias in the moon may seem to explain the play's title, it cannot be said to arise logically from the narrative. My suggestion is that we should read Lyly's conclusion allegorically as a comment on the inadequacy of marriage as a dramatic conclusion. Read in this way, *The Woman in the Moone* more closely resembles Lyly's other plays, which tend to present the inevitable marriages with which they conclude as either unsatisfactory or arbitrary or both.

II

While the meaning of Lyly's title is not clear until the end of the play, the title of Middleton and Dekker's play is obviously important from the beginning. In fact, as Stephen Orgel explains, *The Roaring Girl* as a title is more significant than has usually been thought: 'Middleton and Dekker's titular epithet was designed as an oxymoron, transgressing a variety of boundaries, not merely those of gender. As the term was initially used, roaring boys were characteristically upper class or gentry, their riotous behaviour an assertion of aristocratic privilege.'[22] Moll Cutpurse, then, is in drag not only as a man but also as a member of the upper classes. In fact, the title indicates a third kind of drag, as roaring boys were actually men and Moll is actually a woman rather than a girl. This third kind of drag is not particularly important, perhaps, but it is worth remembering that entering into marriage is often taken to be one of the necessary signs of mental and social maturity. Moll could be said to be other than what she seems to be in gender, in class, and in age. She is also different in a number of ways from the real Moll Cutpurse, who was a figure of some fame in Jacobean London and would have been known to the play's contemporary audience – and, in fact, would presumably have been one of the play's main attractions.[23] I shall return to the question of the relation between the real Moll and the play's Moll at the end of my discussion of *The Roaring Girl*; for now, I shall only suggest that we can see the play as providing a dramatically acceptable and manageable drag for a notorious woman.

Of all these kinds of drag it is the first (Moll's dressing as a man) that has received most commentary, especially in the last twenty years or so. *The Roaring Girl* has been seen as a play primarily concerned with what Kathryn Bond Stockton in a discussion of *The Well of Loneliness* calls '"clothemes" (to coin a comic word from Roland Barthes's "mythemes"): ... myths surrounding clothes.'[24] Moll's cross-dressing is usually seen as the single most important fact about her, and much of the criticism of the play has concentrated on the question of the extent to which her subversion of gender norms is merely sartorial.[25] As Valerie Forman suggests, this discussion is probably beside the point: 'the question of whether or not Moll is subversive is not a particularly useful one, precisely because Moll is not a coherent character who is the source of action, but is instead a locus of cultural fantasies, an embodiment of the culture's contradictions.'[26] What I have called the play's 'clothemes' are only part of its myths, and it is not only cross-dressing that is important but also cross-talking, a term proposed by Jodi Mikalachki in her article on the play; Mikalachki points out that Moll's 'role as intermediary comprehends both linguistic and monetary transactions.'[27] The connection is crucial, as language and money are the two things that drive the plot of *The Roaring Girl* and both are connected through Moll.

Moll's ostensible function in the play is to bring about the marriage of Sebastian Wengrave and Mary Fitzallard, but she clearly does a great deal more, and it is surprising how little space the marriage plot takes up in *The Roaring Girl*. Indeed, Forman goes so far as to say that 'it is not just that the play is not about the conventional marriage plot, but [it] is about not being about the marriage plot.'[28] There is much to recommend this view, and there is certainly a sense in which *The Roaring Girl* is not simply a machine to produce marriages but rather a way in which to examine them. Like language and money, marriage is a system that is ultimately undermined by the play. As I see it, Middleton and Dekker work to undermine the epistemological basis of each of these systems. Thus, it is perhaps not so much that the play is about how it is not about the marriage plot as it is that the play is about marriage as one more system by which people organize their lives. In all this, Moll is central. In his study of the economics of *The Roaring Girl*, Jonathan Gil Harris describes her as 'an impossibly complete being ... the one character who cannot answer Mistress Gallipot's question, "what d'ye lack?" because she is represented throughout the play as utterly self-sufficient.'[29] By not lacking anything, Moll is outside the systems that govern the play and can offer an outsider's view of them (or perhaps a bird's-eye view), a function she performs for many of the characters in the play and for us.

However, Moll may not be utterly self-sufficient: near the beginning of the play a tailor comes on stage to say to her, 'I forgot to take measure on you for your new breeches.'[30] I think it is significant that Moll's sole foray into consumerism is connected to her choice to wear masculine clothes and that the tailor comes shortly after Moll declares her determination to remain unmarried: 'I have the head now of myself, and am man enough for a woman' (4.43–5). The episode can be taken as a reminder that what we could call her gender rebellion is made possible by her financial independence, but it can also be taken to suggest that gender – a factor that is of absolute importance to marriages and marriage plots – is more malleable than we might think. In general, I would say that the frequent use of drag in *The Roaring Girl* serves to destabilize gender, to depict gender as a system in the same way that, as I have remarked, language and money are systems. That is, they all are ways of being in the world that can be acquired (and lost) rather than pre-existent entities. That gender is this sort of system is a point that is perhaps made most forcefully by Moll's first appearance in the play: 'Enter Moll, in a frieze jerkin and a black safeguard' (3.180, S.D.). This outfit both is and is not drag: although a jerkin is a garment worn by men, a safeguard is a garment worn by women. We can locate a second ambiguity in the fact that it is difficult, if not here then by the end of the play, to say whether it is the male or the female garment that counts as drag: Moll first appears to us *in utrumque parata / paratus* to signal the extent to which gender, at least for her, is a choice rather than a physiological fact.

Moll's entrance is not the first example of drag in *The Roaring Girl* as it has come down to us. I believe that it appears in the epistle 'To the Comic Play-readers: Venery and Laughter.' Here, Middleton begins by saying, 'The fashion of play-making I can properly compare to nothing so naturally as the alteration in apparel' (1–2), and he goes on to say that the structure of plays resembles – responds to? determines? – the fashion in clothing: for instance, 'as the doublet fell, neater inventions began to set up' (5–6).[31] The play itself, it seems, is 'a kind of light-colour summer stuff, mingled with diverse colours' (10–11). After this characterization of the play, Middleton says that 'Venus, being a woman, passes through the play in doublet and breeches' (14–16). That is, he turns from saying that the play is a kind of garment to saying that garments in the play may be disguises.[32] In this formulation, it is not clear what the status of the play is: is it the covering for something else, perhaps something obscene, or is it the thing itself? If it is the former (and of course it could be both), we could see *The Roaring Girl* as a garment that makes the real Moll more acceptable. This reading is supported by Middleton's statement, a little later, that "tis the excellence of a writer to leave things better than he finds 'em' (23). If the latter, we can understand Middleton to be saying that the play is only a garment, with no real body underneath – that itself it is only a clotheme, a reading that prepares us for what I would describe as *The Roaring Girl* assault on fixity. Like Moll's ambiguous clothing in the third scene, then, we seem to have an outside with an ultimately unknowable inside.

As it happens, the first example of drag in the play itself is provided not by Moll but rather by Mary Fitzallard, who comes on stage at the very beginning of the play 'disguised like a sempster' (1, S.D.). Although the word 'sempster' might seem to indicate that Mary is dressed as a man, Mulholland points out that the term was 'applicable to men or woman at this time' and that 'the use of *needlewoman* at 1.50 below possibly makes the question of sex comically explicit.'[33] When she both enters and begins the play, Mary is in drag as a woman of lower class and, as the passage from Orgel I quoted above reveals, cross-class dressing is another form of drag for which the play's title prepares us. With the exception of Marjorie Garber, who commented that Mary is only 'apparently more conventional' than Moll, critics have tended not to discuss Mary's role in the play in much detail.[34] This is a pity, as Mary is more than the conventional foil to the more adventurous female character that we are familiar with from such relationships as the one between Rosalind and Celia in *As You Like It*. For one thing, in beginning the dramatic action and in introducing the theme of disguise that is so important to *The Roaring Girl*, Mary takes a commanding position in the world of the play. For another, while many of the machinations necessary to move the marriage plot along are conducted by Moll and Sebastian working in tandem, Mary's appearance in disguise at the start of the play should remind us of her agency in the plot. We could even say that the audience's reaction to seeing Moll in disguise in the third scene of the play presents Moll as imitating Mary.

Nor is the first scene the only one in which Mary appears in drag. In the eighth scene, she enters dressed as a page and accompanied by Sebastian and Moll, who is dressed as a man here. That is, Middleton and Dekker present us with a tableau of three men: one real man and two women dressed as men. When Sebastian kisses Mary, Moll says 'How strange this shows, one man to kiss another' (8.45); Sebastian's answer to this is, 'I'd kiss such men to choose, Moll; / Methinks a woman's lip tastes well in a doublet' (8.46–7). Rather like Orsino at the end of *Twelfth Night*, Sebastian appears to find women dressed as men erotically arousing.[35] Moll's line could be cited as evidence of her innate conservatism or her internalization of social rules, but it is also a metatheatrical reminder that we are seeing, in fact, not one man and two women disguised as men, but rather three males. In a way that is useful to the playwrights, Moll points out that both her disguise and Mary's – but especially Mary's, as she is disguised as a boy and the actors who played women's parts were boys rather than men – are not disguises at all but are closer to the clothes they would normally wear. The problematization of gender and of the relation of appearance to reality staged here is typical of the play's dealing with these issues, and Mary's role in this scene and her closeness to the play's clothemes throughout are crucial to Middleton and Dekker's project.

Mary's closeness to Moll is also crucial: in addition to the fact that both appear in drag throughout the play, there is another connection between them. Significantly, this connection occurs at the level of language. I am referring to their names. Although now an independent name, Moll was originally merely a nickname for Mary. Of course, by the time of *The Roaring Girl* the name Moll meant much else besides, a point that is made in a conversation between Sebastian and his father early on. Sir Alexander says to his son, 'Methinks her very name should fright thee from her' (4.157), as there are 'more whores of that name than of any ten other' (4.162). Later in the play, Moll says to Sebastian:

> At your great suit I promised you to come:
> I pitied her for name's sake, that a Moll
> Should be so crossed in love. (8.65–7)

Two important points are made in this passage. One is that Mary and Moll are the same name, a point Moll underlines by using the nickname to refer to Mary, who is not otherwise called Moll in the play. While the one name would seem to guarantee virginity and the other would seem to guarantee whoredom, Middleton and Dekker do not present the two as the opposite poles of feminine reputation (which would be the traditional way), but instead stress the closeness of the two – a point that is also made by the fact that both women are dressed as males in this scene. As so often in the play, we are confronted with the difficulty of interpreting what might initially appear to be unambiguous signs. The system of nomenclature is not, perhaps, as helpful as we would have thought, and the scene as a whole destabilizes both gender, as I have commented above, and, to some extent, language.

The other point that concerns me here is Moll's account of her motives in helping the lovers. She begins by saying that she came because Sebastian entreated her to – 'At your great suit' – but immediately suggests that she came because she and Mary share a name. The implications of this statement are not pursued in the scene; nevertheless, Middleton and Dekker have at least gestured towards female homosociality here – as they do, I believe, in the two songs Moll sings a few lines later. The first song concerns a woman who

> lays out the money;
> She goes unto her sisters;
> She never comes at any. (8.104–6)

The rhyming line for line 106 is 'And comes home with never a penny' (8.109). The second song is about an adulteress who calls Moll a whore. It is not entirely clear what is going on in either song, although the second is one of many things in *The Roaring Girl* that suggest that suspicions that Moll is unchaste are unjustified. The first song appears also to be about a prostitute, but one who does not earn any money. In the reference to 'her sisters' we can see another gesture towards female homosociality. Both songs draw attention to relations between women; these relations occur alongside the women's relations to men and to commerce, but are not, it seems, determined by them.[36]

The possibility of a connection between women that might coexist with (or perhaps even supersede) the marriage plot is only hinted at in the relation between Mary and Moll. We can see another hint in Middleton and Dekker's presentation of the citizens' wives.[37] These women exist at (or function as) the point at which some of *The Roaring Girl* most important systems meet, perhaps most notably the marriage plot and the financial system. For my purposes, one of their most important roles is to provide a commentary on the marriage plot. It is unusual to have a romantic comedy from this period in which there is so much stress on how marriages actually work – that is, in which the playwrights give us not just the young lovers but also a number of married couples. While the lower social class of the citizens might serve to insulate the marriage plot from direct contact with the depiction of married couples, we are nonetheless given the materials for a comparison. The most remarkable aspect of the subplot is the fact that its characters move easily between their participation in marriage and their participation in a homosocial economy, a point that is as true for the women as for the men. What is more, male homosociality is not confined to the subplot, as Jean Howard has pointed out: 'Despite the fact that the plot focuses on getting Sebastian married, the "gentleman" class as a whole seems less interested in marriage that in various modalities of same-sex bonding.'[38] Howard also says that 'homoerotic bonds between men subtend this textual world and are not always easily reconciled with cultural imperatives to marry and reproduce,' but I would argue that the one of the points made by the subplot is that the marriage plot and homosociality can be reconciled.[39] In a way that is crucial for the play as a whole, marriage is presented not as the end (in either sense) of the narrative and not as an exclusive bond that takes primacy over all others but rather as one relation among others. To participate in the marital system, it turns out, is not to remove oneself from other systems of interpersonal relationship.

I shall return to the topic of homosociality when I discuss the play's two final scenes, but now I want to look at a character who does appear to have a certain distance from almost all of the systems in *The Roaring Girl*. This character is Laxton, whose name can be understood as 'lack stone' and therefore both 'without testicles and thus a eunuch or at least impotent' and 'without buildings and land and thus without substance to back up his style.' In his discussion of the play, Harris says that Laxton's 'anatomical lack is emblematic of a more widespread insufficiency shared by virtually all the characters, a lack for which material goods provide the fetishistic stopgap.'[40] Without, it would appear, the money to buy goods or the anatomy to enjoy participation in the traffic in women, Laxton cannot completely enter these systems. Like Harris, I see Laxton's problems as indicating a general inability in the play's characters, an inability either to find satisfaction within these systems or to leave them behind: Laxton's difference from the other characters is thus one of degree rather than of kind. I think it is because of his ambiguous status as both inside and outside the systems of *The Roaring Girl* that Laxton is able, to a greater degree than any of the other characters, to move between the main plot and the subplot. In both of these plots, he attempts to seduce women: Moll in the main plot and Mistress Gallipot in the other. In both cases, the attempt relates, interestingly, to what I see as the main themes of *The Roaring Girl*; I shall concentrate on his attempt on Moll.

In three ways Moll rebuffs Laxton's attempt to have sex with her: she challenges him to fight: 'Draw, or I'll serve an execution on thee / Shall lay thee up till doomsday' (5.69–70); she delivers a long speech (5.72–113) in which, among other things, she criticizes the falseness of gossip:

How many of our sex by such as thou
Have their good thoughts paid with a blasted name
That never deserved loosely or did trip
In path of whoredom beyond cup and lip;   (5.81–4)

and she refers to her financial independence: 'I scorn to prostitute myself to a man, / I that can prostitute a man to me' (5.111–12). For the
audience, much of the point of this scene may lie in the humour of the
idea that Laxton is attempting to seduce a woman, although presumably he could not have sex with her. For me, what is striking is that
Moll's defence challenges the accuracy of some of the play's (and the
world's) key systems: in drawing her sword, Moll transgresses against
gender norms even more sharply than she does by wearing breeches; in
saying that gossip is untrue, she points to the fact that language may
not have any relation to fact; and in mentioning her own financial
power, Moll inverts the traditional relation, in which men provide fi-
nancially for women.[41] As Harris suggests, Laxton's lack leads to the
exposure of a more general lack. Because of him, Middleton and Dekker
are able in this scene to suggest the factitiousness of the systems that
the play has highlighted.[42]

The various themes I have been commenting on come together in the
rather odd conclusion of *The Roaring Girl*, a conclusion that takes place
over the last two scenes of the play. In the first of these scenes we see
Moll dressed as a man and strolling through London with Jack Dapper,
Sir Beauteous Ganymede, Sir Thomas Long, and Lord Noland. Each of
these names is obviously significant: the first name draws attention,
once again, to clothing; the second to the world of male homosociality
of which Moll now appears to be a part; the third to phallic potency; the
fourth is synonymous with one of the meanings of Laxton. Moll's main
activity in this scene is to reveal the truth. Her truth-telling begins when
she informs her companions that Trapdoor is not to be trusted. Once he
appears disguised as a soldier, she is able to see through his clothes and
his attempts to speak Low German. Most obviously, we see Moll as a
truth-teller when she reveals her ability to understand and speak the
cant used by thieves and even to sing a song in it. This may be the most
famous part of the play, and it has attracted a great deal of commentary.
For Stephen Orgel, it confirms his point that Moll 'serves essentially as
an interpreter of [the underworld] to the middle-class world of the
drama';[43] to Jane Baston, 'Moll's role as translator in Act V shows her
capitulation to the dominant practices of class and gender.'[44]

More recently, however, Miles Taylor has 'contest[ed] the prevailing critical view that the recording and dissemination of cant is necessarily and intentionally to the detriment of underclass speakers. An alternative that such readings elide is that translating cant may rather work to subvert the dominant language into which it is transcribed.'[45] Taylor's argument, which also involves an examination of Dekker's pamphlets, is too complex to be quickly summarized here, but the passage I have quoted, which recalls Foucault's point in *The History of Sexuality*, 'Discourses are not once and for all subservient to power or raised up against it ... discourse can be both an instrument and an effect of power, but also a hindrance, a stumbling-block, a point of resistance and a starting point for an opposing strategy,' is suggestive.[46] The play's contemporary audience, faced perhaps for the first time with a language specifically designed to discuss unlawful things, may well have seen cant as offering them new opportunities. While what follows in the scene would seem to indicate that the point of knowing this sort of language is to be able to detect thieves, the existence of a special language just for thieves also makes the point that there is, in fact, a community of thieves and criminals in general, however loosely organized. Within the play, the main point of the use of cant here—and of Moll's activity in the scene as a whole—is that it demonstrates Moll's expertise. Whether or not we regard this expertise as wholly in the service of the dominant interests, by this point in the play Moll has put herself ahead of the other characters both in terms of her knowledge and in terms of her skills in dealing with a wide range of people.

When I referred to what follows the use of cant, I was referring to the questions posed to Moll once the cutpurses have gone:

> Lord Noland. I wonder how thou camest to the knowledge of these nasty villains.
> Sir Thomas. And why do the foul mouths of the world call thee Moll Cutpurse? – A name, methinks, damned and odious. (10.322–6)

The first question is interestingly ambiguous, as it means both 'how is that you know about these things' and 'how do these criminals know you.' Lord Noland's question suggests that knowledge goes both ways: to know about guilt is itself a kind of tacit confession of guilt. This conflation of knowledge and guilt is precisely what Moll combats in her first answer:

> I must confess,
> In younger days, when I was apt to stray,
> I have sat amongst such adders, seen their stings –
> As any here might – and in full playhouses
> Watched their quick-diving hands.   (10.328–32)

Her knowledge of this sort of criminal is merely the result of observa-
tion, she says; what is more, by her instancing the playhouse as a place
where this crime can be seen, the audience itself has access to the knowledge of how pickpockets operate, just as the audience now has access
to the slang used by criminals. In fact, Moll's response to 'any here'
hints that the people watching *The Roaring Girl* themselves may now be
in possession of guilty knowledge. In their study of reproduction and
pedagogy, Pierre Bourdieu and Jean-Claude Passeron point out that 'no
one acquires a language without thereby acquiring a *relation to lan-*
guage.'[47] In her speeches on the thieves' language, Moll is trying to dic-
tate the relation to language that her fellow characters and the audience
will acquire.

Moll's answer does not satisfy Jack Dapper, who asks how she knows
these things. In her response, which is addressed to Lord Noland, Moll
launches into an extended comparison: 'Suppose, my lord, you were in
Venice' (10.346); she goes on to say that if Lord Noland had learnt 'All
the close tricks of courtesans' (10.348) in Venice, he would then feel
obliged to

> proclaim
> Your knowledge in those villainies, to save
> Your friend from their quick danger: must you have
> A black ill name because ill things you know?   (10.351–4)

Moll's statement that Lord Noland would have learnt these tricks from
'some Italian pander' (10.347) rather than from personal experience is
not (or not merely) the deferential tact due from a commoner to a
nobleman, but is also tied to her general point that knowledge of a
thing cannot be taken as indicating either approval or participation.
Furthermore, by choosing fornication rather than, for example, thiev-
ery or counterfeiting, as the hypothetical crime, Moll in effect separates
knowledge in its narrowest sense from knowledge as a synonym for
sexual activity. In general, then, Moll's speech serves to point out that
knowledge means less than we thought it did.

Significantly, Moll ends her defence by responding directly to Sir Thomas's question about her name: she goes from the 'black ill name' that Lord Noland might unjustly gain from his second-hand awareness of prostitutes' wiles to saying, 'I am made Moll Cutpurse so' (10.355), and asking, 'How many chaste whose names fill slander's books?' (10.357), and she concludes by saying ,'let not my name condemn me to you or to the world' (10.365–6). Just as a person's knowledge of an illegal activity cannot be used as proof that he or she performs that activity, so names are not a reliable guide to character: by this point in the play the criminal implications of both parts of Moll's name have been explained away. The point about naming seems unexceptionable, and Moll's defence of herself is in general both spirited and sympathetic, but I think that in the context of *The Roaring Girl* as a whole we should take her speeches at the end of this scene as further indications that the linguistic system on which we all rely has a relationship to truth that is hard to understand and even that language may not indicate truth at all. From the dramatic point of view, Moll's comments could be seen as especially disturbing, as *The Roaring Girl*, like most comedies in this period and after, depends on the absolute equivalence of name and character: we expect to get important information from the fact that a character is called Laxton or Sir Beauteous Ganymede.[48] In other words, Moll's speeches here, in conjunction with the play's general tendency to separate language and fact, might serve to undermine the audience's trust in the playwrights.

Of course, the next scene – the play's last – could be said to restore the public's confidence, as the marriage plot is successfully completed. Even here, however, there is much that is unusual. For example, Middleton and Dekker call our attention to drag once again. Moll enters the scene twice, first as a man and then as a woman; in both cases the emphasis is on her unsuitability for marriage. Moll finishes the play in women's clothing, but this should not be taken as a sign that she has finally returned to her real identity. Her appearance in the last scene is the first time in the play that she has dressed entirely as a woman – which is to say, in the terms of the period, as she should morally and legally dress. Thus, Moll's attire cannot be said to be a return to her true or original femininity, as we have never seen that state. In fact, having become used to seeing Moll in breeches, we are more likely to see her appearance in women's clothing at the end of the play as drag, as a form of disguise. Her clothing now provides a way for the playwrights to foreground the relation of dramatic presentation to reality. Is the real

Moll the woman on whom the play is based or the man she has appeared to be for most of the play or the male actor to whom reference is tacitly made in the first scene of the fourth act? The answer is all three, I believe, and in getting us to think about the body underneath the clothes Middleton and Dekker remind us of the existence of the world outside the playhouse world in a way that will be important to *The Roaring Girl* epilogue. I shall return to this point, but now I want to look at the way in which the play ends.

After Moll's second entrance, the marriage plot can finally conclude: 'Enter the Lord Noland and Sir Beauteous Ganymede, with Mary Fitzallard between them, the Citizens and their Wives with them' (11.168, S.D.). Mary's appearance produces the desired effect and all obstacles to her marriage to Sebastian are removed. However, a number of things qualify the triumph of the marriage plot. Jean Howard has remarked that 'the idealizations of the heterosexual romance plot clash with the competing investments of male homoeroticism and the negative, satirical conventions by which middle-class marriage was frequently represented in misogynist literature and city comedy.'[49] Howard's comment is true of *The Roaring Girl* as a whole, and perhaps never more apt than in the tableau described by the stage direction I have quoted. We see the young woman on the verge of being married to the man she loves, but she is accompanied by one man whose name suggests that he does not have the property to support his aristocratic status and another man whose name suggests that he is the male object of male desire. In production, a director could make Sir Beauteous Ganymede look like Mary as she appeared in page's dress in the eighth scene and could use the fact that both Mary and Moll are dressed as women to stress their resemblances. Furthermore, Middleton and Dekker show us Mary with the citizens and their wives in order to remind us that these are the only examples of married life we have been shown in the play. Considering the deceit and strife that characterize marital relations between the citizens and their wives, the uncertain relation of class to financial assets, and the apparent tendency of aristocratic men to prefer the company of other men, we cannot conclude that the outlook for this particular marriage is especially brilliant.

What is more, Sir Alexander's acceptance – at long last – of Mary Fitzallard as his daughter-in-law does not end *The Roaring Girl*. As Valerie Forman points out, 'the play continues for sixty lines after the marriage plot is concluded to focus on Sir Alexander's attempt to reintegrate Moll.'[50] In this section, Moll pointedly expresses her desire not

to marry (11.216–24), and although Sir Alexander asks for her forgive-
ness, it is still clear that she has no real place in the conclusion, as we see
when Sir Alexander addresses his final speech (the play's last) to his

> worthy friends, my honourable lord,
> Sir Beauteous Ganymede, and noble Fitzallard,
> And you, kind gentlewomen, whose sparkling presence
> Are glories set in marriage .   (11.257–60)

Where is Moll in all this? As the gentlewomen clearly are presented as
wives, she cannot be one of them. She could be included among the
'worthy friends,' but this would be unusual from a man to a woman. I
think the point is that the inevitable wrapping-up typical of comedies
cannot include her, that the marriage plot is ultimately unable to
accommodate a figure like Moll–not, I think, because Middleton and
Dekker want to make a point about transgression, but because they
wish to show the inadequacy of the marriage plot.

   This inadequacy is demonstrated even more forcefully in the play's
epilogue, which returns to the relationship of *The Roaring Girl* to the
world outside the theatre. The epilogue begins with an extended analogy between the play and a painting of a woman and raises the
issue of representation, and specifically of verisimilitude and decorum. In his recent book on Renaissance theatre as a spatial art, Henry
S. Turner draws on Charles Sanders Peirce's distinction between the
icon, a signifier with 'an analogical, motivated, and referential relationship to its signified' and 'arbitrary, unmotivated, and more highly mediated forms of signification such as the symbol or language.'[51]
As Turner points out, theatre depends on the icon in order for the
audience to be able to understand, for example, that an actor represents a character within the play or that stage properties represent
real furniture or weapons. He goes on to say that 'this iconicity, fun-
damental to stage performance, is precisely what enables the theatre
to become a practical epistemology,: a way of coming to knowledge
through representation, or, more precisely, through a mode of representation that is nothing less than a process of doing and making.'[52]
To some extent, the final scene of *The Roaring Girl* has worked in exactly this way: the play has taught us both a particular kind of slang and,
in the final tableau, that marriage and social harmony may be created
out of what seemed, during the play's action, to be very unlikely
sources. But Moll's insistence that to know how criminals talk is not

necessarily to be criminal and her appearance in a wedding dress should be taken to suggest that representation is not always identical with knowledge: we hear her talking cant and we see her in a wedding dress, but it turns out that the status of these representations as icons is not what we might have assumed.

In other words, it may be the case not simply that the marriage plot is inadequate but also that dramatic representation itself – the evidence of our eyes and ears in the theatre – is inadequate, and our sense that this may be true is strengthened when Middleton and Dekker end *The Roaring Girl* with an epilogue that says that if their play has not really worked, 'The Roaring Girl herself, some few days hence, / Shall on this stage give larger recompense' (35–6). As Madhavi Menon points out in her discussion of the play, the epilogue 'creates a residue of desire in the promise of the real Moll's appearance at a future date. The future date will always exist in futurity; instead of sexual and metaphoric completion, the epilogue leaves behind an audience full of lackstones.'[53] At the end of *The Roaring Girl*, it turns out that the marriage plot can neither contain Moll nor satisfy the expectation it has aroused. The reference to the real Moll Cutpurse gestures towards a reality outside the world of the theatre, but by this point, the audience should be aware that her appearance will not provide this reality. For one thing, it is Moll Cutpurse the dramatic character rather than Moll Cutpurse the real woman who will have primacy for the audience that has just sat through *The Roaring Girl*. For another, her appearance 'on this stage' could be said to submit external reality to the artifice of the theatrical environment: wearing male or female clothes that might be her own or might be theatrical costumes, speaking words that might be her own or might be written by Middleton and Dekker, moving freely about the stage or following directorial blocking, Moll Cutpurse's reality can be compromised only by her appearance in the playhouse world. Rather than make a clear epistemological distinction between the theatre and the real world, then, Middleton and Dekker's epilogue might be taken to imply that we only ever have representations and that reality itself is only an effect of signifying systems.

III

In my discussion of *The Two Noble Kinsmen* I shall be almost exclusively concerned with two topics: the association of creativity with same-sex relationships and the way in which the playwrights deal with the marriage plot. To some extent, dealing with the first of these topics will involve the issue of the collaboration, but I have no interest in guessing which lines were written by Fletcher and which by Shakespeare: to me, the collaboration between Fletcher and Shakespeare is merely one of several same-sex collaborations in the play.[54] Indeed, same-sex collaboration (both male and female) is one of the major themes of the play. We can see this theme not just in the fact of Fletcher and Shakespeare's joint authorship but also in the eponymous characters. What is more, the story the playwrights use itself raises the question of collaboration, as the source is Chaucer's *Knight's Tale* and before that Boccaccio's *Filostrato*. And although the story of Palamon and Arcite begins with Boccaccio, the particular backdrop for the story goes back to Statius's *Thebaid*. This work – considered in the Middle Ages and Renaissance to be one of the greatest of all classical poems – focuses on male couples: not just the two sons of Oedipus, whose conflict provides the *Thebaid*'s main plot, but many others as well, including, finally, the male couple formed by Statius and Virgil, the poet Statius names as his poetic predecessor.[55]

Thus, not only is *The Two Noble Kinsmen* the story of a male couple written by a male couple, but it is also part of a literary tradition characterized by what we could call diachronic literary collaborations by men, and it has its ultimate origin in a poem focused on male couples. The reproductive metaphor cannot accurately be applied to this tradition, as sex between men fortunately cannot result in children, but it is not asexual like, for instance, the apicultural metaphor in the *Georgics*. Instead, what we have is an eroticized version of poetic production. Of course, the association of artistic creativity with same-sex eroticism is something that has to be carefully managed, and this is what the play's prologue seeks to do by simultaneously turning the play into an object of sexual desire and employing the reproductive metaphor.[56] But as the playwrights stress that Chaucer is the original author of the narrative, the audience is reminded that if texts and textual productions are eroticized, then homoeroticism rather than heteroeroticism would in most cases be the logical choice. Fletcher and Shakespeare begin by saying, 'New plays and maidenheads are near akin: / Much followed both, for both much money gi'en.'[57] In this metaphor the author appears not so much as the father of the text but rather as its pimp. Presenting the play as a sexually available female has the effect of turning the intense homosociality of the text's narrative and its history into the more acceptable traffic in women.

Still, the attempt to present the text as female breaks down quickly, as the next line adds the qualification that new plays and maidenheads are valuable only 'if they stand sound and well' (3). The reference is primarily to the absence of venereal diseases, but the verb 'stand' suggests tumescence. Nor is this the only change in the gender of the text in the course of the prologue: Susan Green, one of the very few critics to comment on this aspect of the prologue, remarks that 'disorienting gender shifts throughout the prologue ... throw doubt on both the purity of innocence ... and the artistic cum sexual processes that may bring it into the world.'[58] In fact, the text-as-bride quickly becomes the text-as-groom:

> a good play,
> Whose modest scenes blush on his marriage day
> And shake to lose his honour, is like her
> That after holy tie and first night's stir
> Yet still is Modesty and still retains
> More of the maid, to sight, than husband's pains.   (3–8)

The attempt to present the origin of the text as heterosexual has resulted only in the feminization of the masculine subject, something that is underlined when the authors go on to compare the blushing bridegroom to a married woman and specifically to a woman who is no longer a virgin but who still appears virginal despite her 'husband's pains.'

The last phrase creates a further problem: while 'pains' can mean simply efforts, in the context of a description of the first night of a marriage the word would seem most apposite to the female virgin's first experience of sex, and thus even the hypothetical husband of these lines is feminized. In his interesting discussion of the play, Barry Weller has argued that the prologue's presentation of the first night is concerned with 'defloration rather than consummation.'[59] This is not, as it might seem to be, a distinction without a difference, as, while the two are in some respects the same, consummation is a mutual activity, while defloration is something done by one person to another. The stress on defloration clearly foreshadows the insistence on the subjugation of women in the marriage plot that will turn out to be such an important part of The Two Noble Kinsmen, but in the context of the prologue it increases our sense of the fragility of the hermaphroditic text and focuses attention on the husband who does the deflowering. But who, exactly, is this husband? It could conceivably be the spectator, in which case the sexuality would be transferred from textual production to textual consumption, but as Jeffrey Masten remarks, it does not seem to be the authors: 'the more consistent answer to the question of the husband is the theatrical company represented by the prologue-speaker's collaborative "we."'[60] Just as the gender of the text is unfixed, so is the nature – and number – of the text's hypothetical husband(s). In their attempt to present a version of textual production that can be mapped onto the marriage plot, Fletcher and Shakespeare have only managed to raise the possibilities of same-sex marriage, polyandry, and a gender that is ultimately unfixed.

After this image, however, and for the rest of the prologue, the focus turns to Chaucer, who is identified as the play's 'breeder' (10); the play is explicitly called a child in line 16. The speaker entreats the audience to applaud the play for Chaucer's sake, if not for Fletcher's and Shakespeare's: in fact, the speaker admits that *The Two Noble Kinsmen* is 'below his art' (28). The shift towards the reproductive metaphor occurs only when the speaker of the prologue can no longer claim paternity on behalf of the collaborating authors. This may be because the idea of a text's having two fathers would seem odd or because the educated members of the audience would recognize that the play was based on *The Knight's Tale* or for both reasons. But the fact that Chaucer is called the play's 'breeder' rather than its father seems to suggest a difference between the man who is the actual father of a child and the man, or any man, who names and supports the child – precisely the distinction that was so important to Hobbes, as I showed in the introduction. Using contemporary terms, we could say that the prologue establishes Chaucer as the play's biological father and Fletcher and Shakespeare as the gay couple who adopt it and raise it as their own. The passage effectively submits Chaucer to Fletcher and Shakespeare, and heterosexual men are reduced to 'breeders,' whose sole function is to serve homosexuals: reproduction is in the service of homosociality.

Sadly, however, the prologue as a whole shows that after Fletcher and Shakespeare have taken Chaucer's offspring and made it, as they say, dramatic, it re-enters the world of heterosexuality in the drearily familiar role of the sexualized female commodity intended for the straight market. While the prologue appears to want to situate the reproductive metaphor in a thoroughly homosocial context, the attempt breaks down before the prologue is over. In his discussion of this point, Charles H. Frey points out that the prologue draws attention to 'the imprecision of analogies between artistic collaborations and procreative couplings' – one example of this imprecision is the phrase 'husband's pains,' a phrase that suggests that the husband is in labour with the text – and concludes his treatment by observing that 'a play is not literally a child, that any spermatic analogies between artworks and children are extremely questionable, and that possible collaboration on a play may indeed challenge our assumption about the nature of father-hood, breeding, and authorship seem to be issues that the Prologue taken together with the action of the play invites us to consider.'[61] Frey is one of only a few critics to discuss the importance of collaboration to the play as a whole, as the invitation of which he speaks has, as a rule, been declined. I believe we should consider the prologue and the play itself as two phases of one examination of the applicability of repro-duction to textual production and that this examination raises other metaphorical possibilities.

Given the prologue's unsuccessful attempt to use the reproductive metaphor, it is not surprising that the idea of same-sex collaboration remains important, both in the action and language of the play and in the issue of the relation of *The Two Noble Kinsmen* to *A Midsummer Night's Dream*.[62] My concern in what follows is with a particular kind of collaboration in the play: the continued association of same-sex couples with creativity. As Donald Hedrick noted almost twenty years ago, 'The images of friendship are consistently those of artists work-ing together.'[63] I want to begin my examination of this subject not with a male character but with Emilia.[64] The first point to make about Emilia is that she is much more important in *The Two Noble Kinsmen* than in *The Knight's Tale*; in fact, one of the ways in which Shakespeare and Fletcher differ most obviously from Chaucer is in the prominence they give to her. As well, their Emilia is not merely reluctant to marry but actively interested in women. In the first scene, when the three wid-owed queens interrupt the marriage of Theseus and Hippolyta to make their request, the result is an elaborate and carefully plotted masque in which each queen speaks to one of the three main charac-ters. The queen who kneels in front of Emilia makes the longest speech of the three and invokes 'the love of him whom Jove hath marked / The honour of your bed' (I.i.29–30). Emilia's response is 'What woman I may stead that is distressed / Does bind me to her' (I.i.35–7). Ignoring the question of her eventual marriage, which will turn out to be the main issue in *The Two Noble Kinsmen*, Emilia invokes instead the prin-ciple of female solidarity, both as something that would motivate her to help and as something that will result in a bond between her and the woman she has helped.

Emilia's declaration of female solidarity (which is only the first of many in the play) is sufficient to identify her as what used to be called a 'woman-identified woman,' if not perhaps a lesbian.[65] The most significant of these declarations comes in the play's third scene, which I want to look at in some detail. In this scene, Emilia and Hippolyta bid farewell to Pirithous, who is off to help Theseus in the war against the Thebans. As he goes, Emilia exclaims, 'How his longing / Follows his friend!' (I.iii.26–7). The discussion that ensues begins with both women commenting on the close friendship between Theseus and Pirithous. This friendship was one of the most famous examples of masculine friendship in the classical period and was frequently cited in Renaissance literature. Here, however, the topic is raised mainly to introduce a discussion of female friendship, a much less common topic.[66] After each woman has spoken of the friend-ship between the two men, Emilia makes a rather perfunctory and no-ticeably non-committal acknowledgment of Theseus's new status as a married man and the primacy of his relationship to Hippolyta,

> Doubtless
> There is a best and reason has no manners
> To say it is not you,   (I.iii.47–9)

and she begins to talk about Flavina:

> I was acquainted
> Once with a time when I enjoyed a play-fellow.
> You were at wars when she the grave enriched,
> Who made too proud the bed.   (I.iii.49–52)

The bed is at once the metaphorical bed of the grave and a literal bed in which the enjoyment Emilia mentions took place. That is, Emilia's char-acterization of her friendship is strongly sexual, a point that is empha-sized just after these lines when she speaks of the love between Theseus and Pirithous in obviously sexual terms:

> their needs
> The one of th'other may be said to water
> Their intertangled roots of love.   (I.iii.57–9)[67]

The important difference between Emilia's relationship with Flavina and Theseus's with Pirithous thus is not the difference between chastity and sexuality, but rather the difference between adolescents and adults (and, to a lesser extent, the difference between females and males). When Emilia says 'she I sigh and spoke of were things innocent' (I. iii.60), she means not that their relationship was not sexual but that they were unaware of any rational basis for their love – precisely the point made by Montaigne in his description of his love for la Boétie in the course of his essay on friendship, an essay that Shakespeare clearly had in mind when he was writing this scene.[68] Emilia begins her description of her love by Flavina by stressing its seriousness. While it may be tempting to see the love of the two girls as permitted because it is expressed in elegiac mode, Emilia's speeches in this scene insist instead on its maturity, and Emilia's speeches and actions in the rest of the play demonstrate her ongoing commitment to female-female relationships rather than mixed-sex ones.[69]

I shall return to this topic when I discuss the marriage plot, but now I want to look at the extent to which Emilia's account of her love for Flavina provides a model of artistic production that is unconnected to the reproductive metaphor. In this account, Emilia stresses the sameness of their tastes: 'What she liked / Was then of me approved; what not, condemned' (I.iii.64–5). She gives three examples, beginning with the notably erotic image of a flower that, Emilia says, '[Flavina] put between my breasts (then but beginning / To swell about the blossom)' (I.iii.67–9), and then proceeding to fashions in clothing and finally to music. We can summarize this progression as a movement from decorating (and eroticizing) the body with something natural to decorating the body with something artificial and then to art itself: in other words, this is a movement from nature to art that is motivated by same-sex eroticism. In Emilia's account of the music the girls shared, the tune is either one that she has 'Stol'n from some new air' (I.iii.75) or one that comes 'From musical coinage' (I.iii.76). In this case, the movement is from art as something we imitate to art as something that we create ourselves; once again, the motivation here is the relationship between the girls. Once Emilia has 'at adventure hummed' (I.iii.75) the tune, Flavina learns it. Emilia presents homosociality as important not just to artistic production but also to the circulation of the work of art. Furthermore, as Will Fisher points out, in the Renaissance 'unnatural sexualities and unnatural economics were coded through each other.'[70] The 'coinage' in which the girls participate may also suggest the sexual pleasures they shared.

At this point, we should remember that the story of the play as a whole is simultaneously something 'Stol'n' by Fletcher and Shakespeare (from Chaucer, who stole it from Boccaccio, who stole it from Statius) and, insofar as they turned it into a play and added characters and incidents, something Fletcher and Shakespeare coined, to use Emilia's term. What is more, Emilia's speech about Flavina is obviously modelled on Helena's aggrieved speech to Hermia in *A Midsummer Night's Dream* (III.ii.195–219). Like Emilia, Helena speaks of her intimate friendship with another girl using erotic imagery – 'So we grew together, / Like to a double cherry' (III.ii.208–9) – and stressing the friendship as artistically productive:

> We, Hermia, like two artificial gods,
> Have with our needles created both one flower,
> Both on one sampler, sitting on one cushion,
> Both warbling of one song, both in one key.   (III.ii.198–201)

Both *The Two Noble Kinsmen* and *A Midsummer Night's Dream* depend, to a greater extent than has usually been acknowledged, on the opposition between same-sex relationships that are artistically productive and erotic and mixed-sex relationships engineered by fraud and force. Or, to put it another way, art is shown to be produced by same-sex relationships, while marriage, within the limits of the play's plot, does not produce anything but rather is produced by means that are at best undignified and at worse tragic.

In the form of an opposition between elective and familial bonds, the opposition between production and reproduction also characterizes the relationship between Palamon and Arcite. At the very beginning of their first scene in the play, Arcite says, 'Dear Palamon, dearer in love than blood / And our prime cousin' (I.ii.1–2). While acknowledging the close relationship, Arcite is careful to emphasize that their connection is due to love rather than to the fact that their mothers were sisters.[71] Arcite's opening speech is an invitation to his friend:

> let us leave the city
> Thebes and the temptings in't, before we further
> Sully our gloss of youth.   (I.ii.3–5)

His concern is echoed by Palamon. While their concern for their honour might seem almost maidenly (it recalls the presentation of the 'bridegroom' in the prologue), it should be remembered that Thebes was generally a bad place in Greek literature, and in the reign of Creon in which

The Two Noble Kinsmen is set Thebes was at an especially low point. Indeed, it turns out that their uncle Creon is the problem:

> A most unbounded tyrant, whose successes
> Makes heaven unfeared and villainy assured
> Beyond its power there's nothing.   (I.ii.63–5)

The two friends resolve to leave Thebes in order that they 'may nothing share / Of his loud infamy' (I.ii.75–6).

Up to this point, then, the first scene between the eponymous characters shows a clear movement away from familial relationships – specifically, as they are related to each other and through Creon through their mothers, from relationships through women – to elective bonds between men. Palamon and Arcite seek to establish or find a private homosocial world removed from dynastic considerations. In this, they resemble Emilia and, like her, they are doomed to be disappointed. While Emilia's homosocial desires are most obviously frustrated by the death of Flavina long before the play begins and then, of course, by the relentless motion of the marriage plot, Palamon's and Arcite's desires are ended by the arrival of a summons from Creon just after they have decided to leave their city. The decision to attack Thebes taken by Theseus in the first scene of the play has been acted upon and the two kinsmen are called to the defence of the city. Although Arcite declares that he will not be able to fight with any particular zeal, Palamon says, 'Leave that unreasoned. / Our services stand now for Thebes, not Creon' (I. i.98–9). The distinction he makes here is of no consequence, of course, once he and Arcite are captured by the Greeks, and, as tyrant of the city, Creon is effectively identical to Thebes in any case, but for the two friends the decision to fight the Athenians represents the victory of familial over elective bonds. In this sense, the second scene of the play demonstrates the basic action of *The Two Noble Kinsmen* as a whole: the desires of the characters for a different way of living are unavailing against the ability of the familial system to turn everything and everyone to account.

The victory of the family might seem assured when we next see the two friends. In this scene, Palamon and Arcite lament all they have lost and will lose through their captivity. First Palamon says,

> Oh cousin Arcite,
> Where is Thebes now? Where is our noble country?
> Where are our friends and kindreds?   (II.ii.6–8)

In naming his blood relationship to his friend and in mourning the loss of the city and the people they were formerly so eager to leave, Palamon seems to see things through the lens of the family, and this impression would appear to be confirmed when he proceeds to speak of the war and war games in which he and Arcite contended (II.ii.9–25). The speech as a whole presents Palamon as someone who sees himself as part of a family and whose idea of homosociality is no longer the exclusive bond that once motivated him to plan to flee his home with his friend but rather the combative relationship in the service both of organized heteroeroticism – Palamon points out that they shall never again see 'The hardy youths strive for the games of honour, / Hung with the painted favours of their ladies' (II.ii.10–11) – and of the state that was, and to some extent still is, the primary socially sanctioned form of male bonding.

Arcite's response further supports our sense that the vision the two men shared in their first appearance is irrecoverable. He says that his particular regret is that the two shall remain

> unmarried.
> The sweet embraces of a loving wife,
> Loaden with kisses, armed with thousand Cupids,
> Shall never clasp our necks; no issue know us;
> No figures of ourselves shall we e'er see.   (II.ii.29–33)

While the shift from the singular wife to the plural cupids and figures may be significant, the overall point is clear. Arcite instances the joys of family life, of marriage and reproduction, as the greatest losses they will suffer. That Arcite imagines what they would have said to their children – 'Remember what your fathers were, and conquer' (II.ii.36) – suggests that he still conceives of himself and Palamon as a couple, but their association is now in the service of the state, and specifically of training up new soldiers. When he says, 'This is all our world. / We shall know nothing here but one another' (II.ii.40–1), he seems explicitly to refute the idea of male bonding as self-sufficiency, as the image of the two men together and separated from everything else that was once their ideal can now appear only as a misfortune.

Nevertheless, the two friends do not completely surrender to the imperatives of the plot. Arcite says that he sees two good things arising from their imprisonment:

> to hold here a brave patience
> And the enjoying of our griefs together.
> While Palamon is with me, let me perish
> If I think this our prison.   (II.ii.59–62)

While the first of these invokes the conventional stoicism of classical literature, the second resuscitates the idea of the two men as a complete unit in themselves. As well, it could be argued that the difference is not great between Arcite's vision of their lives in prison and his vision of what their lives would be like if they were free and could get married. While he speaks wistfully of the 'sweet embraces of a loving wife,' the contrast between the singular wife and his statement that these embraces will 'clasp *our* necks' (my emphasis) suggests that even marriage will not replace the primacy of their homosocial bond. As well, the hypothetical children will be 'figures of ourselves' and will be exhorted to resemble their father and 'conquer': in other words, their children will be copies of themselves. Arcite thus gestures towards the idea of reproduction without alterity that was one of the Renaissance's goals. In this speech, as in the prologue's reference to Chaucer as the play's breeder, heterosexuality is in the service of bonds between men.

When Arcite elaborates on the second advantage of their incarceration (the fact that they will always be together), he begins by returning to the idea of escaping the 'corruption of worse men' (II.ii.72). As was the case in his first speech in the play, Arcite shows a concern for male purity that, as I have suggested, recalls the gender confusions of the prologue. Here, he sees their youth as especially subject to temptation:

> We are young and yet desire the ways of honours,
> That liberty and common conversation,
> The poison of pure spirits, might, like women,
> Woo us to wander from.   (II.ii.73–6)

It is not clear whether the reference to women means that women themselves are a danger in that they tempt men to immoral conduct or rather that women are particularly prone to being tempted, but in either case the meaning is obviously that safety lies in the right sort of same-sex attachment.[72] In conjunction with the comment later in the speech, 'A wife might part us lawfully' (II.ii.89) – although even here there appears to be only one wife for the two men – the implication is that Arcite, at least, correctly identifies the marriage plot as their principal danger.

Arcite's enumeration of the blessings of their imprisonment is the most famous part of this scene, and one of the most famous parts of *The Two Noble Kinsmen*:

> What worthy blessing
> Can be but our imaginations
> May make it ours? And being here thus together,
> We are an endless mine to one another;
> We are one another's wife, ever begetting
> New births of love; we are father, friends, acquaintance,
> We are, in one another, families;
> I am your heir and you are mine. This place
> Is our inheritance.   (II.ii.76–83)

This is a vision of absolute self-sufficiency; significantly, it is one in which all the existing channels of relationship in Renaissance England are supplied within the male couple. According to Arcite, the two men will have no need of the families that give the individual a place in the society in which he lives or of the wives who supply new people to inhabit those places. When he says that the prison will be their inheritance, he severs all ties with the world into which he and Palamon were born and in which they were raised. Of course, the dramatic irony here is that the prison is indeed their inheritance, as they have been sentenced to life imprisonment precisely because they are Thebans (all their property – their real inheritance – would have been confiscated by the Athenians). Still, Arcite is able to envision a same-sex connection that will render the marriage plot unnecessary.

When Arcite says 'We are one another's wife,' the corollary is clearly that the two men are also one another's husband. Thus, the aim is not so much to avoid marriage altogether but rather to avoid the mixed-sex marriage on which the marriage plot, both in life and in literature, depends. Perhaps the crucial image in this connection comes in the line before the reference to wives, when Arcite says that the two men will be 'an endless mine to one another.' The endless mine, with its suggestion of anal imagery, indicates that the prison will be a place of inexhaustible sodomy and that this sodomy will be inexhaustibly productive. In this passage, then, Arcite uses the reproductive metaphor in a way that renders it homoerotic. The physical connection of the two men will produce everything that marriage – whether literal marriage or the metaphorical marriage subtending the reproductive metaphor – is intended to provide. I see this passage as central, not only to the depiction of Palamon and Arcite's relationship, but to the play's association of homosociality and textual production. As Hedrick has suggested, *The Two Noble Kinsmen* as a whole 'desires to be another "new birth of love" of a collaborative homosocial labor.'[73] But just as the prologue's attempt to depict male collaboration ran into trouble, here too the vision of male love as productive breaks down almost instantly when Emilia and her woman appear and the two friends both fall in love with her. From this point on, the marriage plot, like a juggernaut destroying everything in its path, is unstoppable.

What has never, I think, been remarked about the intrusion of heteroeroticism at this point in the scene–an intrusion that will provide *The Two Noble Kinsmen* with its plot–is that Palamon and Arcite do not only see a beautiful woman, they see two women engaged in a conversation that is at once sexual and creative.[74] As Shannon remarks, the imagery of 'flowers and dress, blossoms and pattern' is common both to the conversation of Emilia and her woman and to Emilia's earlier speech about Flavina: 'the feminine space inhabited by the women is a creative economy.'[75] Thus, while the rupture of Palamon and Arcite's friendship because they both fall in love with Emilia is the main plot action in this scene, what the audience actually gets at the moment of viewing the play is a tableau composed of two examples of same-sex love, each of which is associated with artistic production. In other words, what is at stake here is not only the individual fortunes of the characters but also the viability in the world of the play of non-reproductive sexuality and artistic production. After this decisive scene, the woman vanishes, although she may appear as a mute in other scenes, and the men are now enemies, competing for the unwilling prize that is Emilia. However, their collaboration does not entirely vanish from the play. In III.vi, the scene in which Palamon and Arcite arm each other for their duel, we see the two working together to achieve a common purpose in a manner that has erotic undertones.[76] Furthermore, when Theseus speaks to Emilia near the end of the play, he incongruously compares the two combatants to 'Two emulous Philomels' (V.iii.124). Hedrick says of this image, 'The play returns to the circumstances of its production through the striking analogy of a singing contest.'[77] Arcite and Palamon's contest for the love of Emilia does not remove the possibility of homosociality from the play, then, but it turns their bond into the competitive, violent, and ultimately fatal version of passionate attachments between men that is so often, as it is in *The Two Noble Kinsmen*, in the service of the marriage plot.

I want to conclude my discussion of the play with a consideration of the marriage plot and the havoc it wreaks. The action of *The Two Noble Kinsmen* begins at the moment when one marriage plot has been concluded and the next is about to begin. The former is the marriage between Theseus and Hippolyta, a marriage in which the two are not only, and perhaps not primarily, dramatic characters but also representatives of two opposed ways of life: the masculine, Athenian world and the feminine, Amazon world.[78] To some extent this dynamic is evident both in *A Midsummer Night's Dream* and in *The Knight's Tale* – after all, in the preamble to his poem Chaucer tells us that Theseus 'conquered al the regne of Femenye' – but Shakespeare and Fletcher have arguably made it the most important force behind the plot of their play.[79] The defeat of the Amazons brings women under male control in a general sense; what happens to Emilia and to the Jailer's Daughter in the course of the play demonstrates the subjugation of particular women. Emilia's singleness is presented as a problem from the first scene, in that I think we are intended to read the noticeably elaborate (both visually and verbally) tableau with which the play opens as one that celebrates the union of a particular man and a woman and emphasizes the isolation from this union of a second woman. Among other things, the character of the Jailer's Daughter, simultaneously marginal and central, shows the extension of the marriage plot through different levels of society. But before I look at the Jailer's Daughter I want to consider briefly the character of Pirithous.

In the first scene it is in some ways Pirithous, rather than Emilia, who matters.[80] As Frey has pointed out, in 'a standard romance, the bride's sister, Emilia, would fall in love with and marry the groom's best friend, Pirithous.'[81] Instead, Emilia and Pirithous are conspicuously not coupled with each other and no longer coupled with their same-sex partners – Hippolyta and Theseus, respectively. While Theseus and Pirithous are a standard part of the catalogues of pairs of male friends that are so familiar a part of much Renaissance literature, in *The Two Noble Kinsmen* Pirithous's connection to Theseus becomes chiefly background knowledge. He occasions the comparison of male and female friendship between Hippolyta and Emilia that I have already discussed, he has Arcite released from prison, and he tells Emilia of Arcite's fatal accident; these are all significant aspects of the play and they all serve to connect Pirithous to the main characters and to do so in a way that stresses his association with homosociality. Still, Pirithous never quite becomes, as might have been expected by readers with a knowledge of the classical tradition, a character in his own right. Like Emilia in his isolation from the happy couple at the beginning of the play, Pirithous, in this and in his reported rather than acted-out connections to more important male characters in the play, registers the defeat of same-sex bonds as primary in the world of *The Two Noble Kinsmen*. His utility to the main characters and the main plot serves as a demonstration of the peripheral and secondary nature of same-sex bonds.

Just as Pirithous fails to become a possible husband for Emilia, so the Jailer's Daughter, who is Fletcher and Shakespeare's addition to the story, fails to solve the problem of the competition of two men for one women.[82] As Peter T. Hadorn points out, 'we should not forget that creating a second woman character is the solution Shakespeare chose for *The Two Gentlemen of Verona* ... and *A Midsummer Night's Dream* ... Shakespeare and Fletcher surely created the character of the Jailer's Daughter in part to suggest this very option: one of the cousins could find someone else to love.'[83] That Palamon refuses to fall in love with her despite considerable encouragement could be said to make the valuable point that the marriage plot does not work according to a simple binary difference between heterosexual and homosexual bonds; just as the latter are acceptable when they serve the former, so the wrong kind of heterosexual bond – here, a cross-class love – is useless except insofar as it leads the Jailer's Daughter to free Palamon and thus to make possible the violent conclusion that is necessary for the plot's resolution. But if the Jailer's Daughter does not succeed in entering the marriage plot, she does a great deal of other work in *The Two Noble Kinsmen*.[84] As Sandra Clark has shown, the play's 'focus on female desire is unusually prominent, and the number and length of the self-reflective speeches and soliloquies allotted to Emilia and to the Jailer's Daughter renders them as important to the play's design as are the kinsmen.'[85] While Palamon and Arcite are a same-sex couple that is broken apart by the marriage plot, the Jailer's Daughter and Emilia are a same-sex couple that never has the chance to form. In adding this character, Shakespeare and Fletcher are able to double the number of female victims.

It is tempting to see the Jailer's Daughter as in some sense the unconscious of *The Two Noble Kinsmen*, particularly in her madness.[86] For instance, Masten suggests that 'the Jailer's Daughter may signify an escape from the very idea of constraining authorial attribution, for her discussion is a patchwork of songs and ballads – some associated with recognizable poets like Philip Sidney, others that echo and rewrite the borrowed voicings of other staged madwomen.'[87] The Jailer's Daughter's conflation of texts could thus be seen as offering a different model of authorship, one in which there is no single author and not even a pair of authors but only a compilation of various kinds of literature all freed from the constraints of the marriage plot and of any plot whatsoever. This compilation may at times be a kind of parody: Douglas Bruster has remarked of some of her mad speeches that 'in counting things that the main plot does not require she count ... the Jailer's Daughter comes close to parodying the play's need.'[88] In focusing on counting, the Jailer's Daughter makes explicit the reductive and ultimately deadly romantic mathematics of the plot of *The Two Noble Kinsmen*. What is more, the extraordinary copiousness of her discourse connects her to the female textual production previously associated with Emilia and Flavina. When the Doctor exclaims after one of her outbursts, 'How her brain coins!' (IV.iii.40), for example, he recalls Emilia's reference to 'musical coinage' in her description of her love for Flavina.

While the Jailer's Daughter is interesting and significant not just for her role in the plot but also for her own textual production, it is important to remark that she is not only counting but counted. When the Schoolmaster is organizing the performance for Theseus, he counts his players and observes, 'Here's a woman wanting' (III.v.39). Shortly after, the Jailer's Daughter arrives and is pressed into service by the troop, after which she is returned to her family. The line of the first Countryman, 'A madwoman? We are made, boys' (III.v.77) – Green's choice for her article's title – aptly illustrates the play's dependence not only on a single woman but specifically on a woman who has lost the ability to assert her autonomy. Lief and Radel have suggested that the Schoolmaster can be seen as a parody of Theseus;[89] I would add that he is also a parody of Fletcher and Shakespeare: like him, they have 'a woman wanting' and are able, in the name of the marriage plot, to turn everything to account, even–or perhaps especially–the misery of this unfortunate woman. When we last see the Jailer's Daughter, she is being tricked into marrying the man her father has chosen for her. Carol Thomas Neely argues that 'the mad Jailer's Daughter cure becomes the vehicle for both the tying up of the plot and for whatever satisfaction ensues from it.'[90] The fate of the Jailer's Daughter precedes and prefigures the fate of Emilia, who is also forced to marry. The latter's position at the top of the social hierarchy does not protect her. In both plots, Shakespeare and Fletcher demonstrate that a single woman associated with artistic creation is in need of a husband. We can see Theseus's allusion to Philomel in the fifth act as providing a context for the connection of these female characters with musicality and enforced sexuality. In both stories and in *The Two Noble Kinsmen* what matters is the shift from production to reproduction.

One way to observe this shift in the play is to note the increasing use of unpleasant images of reproduction towards the end of *The Two Noble Kinsmen*. Writing of what she calls the play's 'unwholesome obstetrics,' Paula S. Berggren argues that 'one of the most disturbing elements of the final movement of the play is a sequence of childbirth images that reverse the hopeful sense of organic continuity.'[91] As she remarks, in context these images are associated with impending death; taken as a whole, they work to undermine any feeling that the marriages at the end of the play will be happy. For me, the crucial image of 'organic continuity' in the play is not reproductive but rather the 'New births of love' that Arcite envisions in prison at the beginning of the second act, an image, as I have pointed out, of inexhaustible productivity arising from the love between men. In comparison, the literal obstetrics towards which the forced marriages of the play tend can only be unwholesome. It need not have ended this way. As Mallette points out in his analysis of the play's final scene, 'The marriage tetrad the ending of the play fails to construct is between Arcite-Palamon and Emilia-Flavina.'[92] Or, rather, it does not fail to construct it but instead refuses to construct it. These same-sex marriages, elective, loving, and associated with artistic production, must be eliminated in favour of reproductive futurism. Much more thoroughly and much more grimly than the other plays I have discussed in this chapter, *The Two Noble Kinsmen* demonstrates that the marriage plot leads to a reduction of possibilities. In fact, the play suggests that textual production – a play, for instance – must be supported not by the reproductive metaphor but by actual reproduction, no matter what the cost. It is in detailing this cost and in forcing us to take account of what is foreclosed by the marriage plot that *The Two Noble Kinsmen* directs our attention, however unprofitably, to alternative modes of textual production.

2 Seductions

In this chapter I discuss three works from the 1590s: Daniel's *Delia*, Marlowe's *Hero and Leander*, and Marston's *The Metamorphosis of Pigmalions Image*. These works represent two of the most popular genres of the period: the sonnet sequence and the epyllion (in fact, in England these genres flourished only in that period). The 1590s have long been distinguished as a decade in which much of the greatest English literature was written and in which many writers who are now central to our sense of what Renaissance literature is began or ended their careers. But it was not merely a good, or even an exceptionally good, decade for literary production in England. Georgia Brown has argued that the 1590s were also a decade in which the concept of literature itself changed. While her thesis has been controversial, I find it convincing. Brown suggests that in this period 'literature started to be conceived as a valuable activity in its own right'; along with this went what Brown calls 'the wholesale sexualization of literary culture.'[1] All the works I discuss in this chapter are situated at the junction of these ideas; their writers are concerned with the extent to which literature is or should be directed towards an external aim, and they see literature as connected to sex – perhaps even as a form of sexual activity. Daniel, Marlowe, and Marston deal with these ideas very differently, however, and by way of setting up the discussion that follows, I want to look briefly at the genres of the works in greater detail.

Looking back at the sonnet sequence, today we are chiefly concerned with those written by Shakespeare, Sidney, and Spenser (and, increasingly, with those by Barnfield and Wroth). Except for a couple of sonnets that can be found in most anthologies, Daniel's sequence has now receded into the very crowded background against which we place the sequences we consider major. My intention here is not to argue that the sonnets of these now more famous writers are not good, but I want to stress that *Delia*, which was first published as a complete sequence in 1591, is one of the first sequences in English. While Daniel obviously drew on *Astrophil and Stella*, which I shall discuss in the next chapter, and on numerous sonnets by French poets, he was also in some ways an innovator.[2] What he inherited from Sidney, from the French poets, and, of course, from Petrarch, was the sonnet sequence as a narrative characterized by romantic disappointment and by generally futile aspirations. Recent criticism has taught us to see that many of these aspirations were, in fact, social as well as or even rather than romantic.[3] Daniel's social ambitions are indeed a factor in *Delia*, but I shall be more concerned with his literary ambitions insofar as the latter can be distinguished from the former. To what I see as a greater extent than the other sonneteers of the period, Daniel is explicitly concerned with the status of sonnets as printed poems. In *Delia*, the teleology initially is not moral or social advancement but romantic success. Daniel hopes that his poems will move Delia to love him or, at least, that they will move the public to pity him. When he finally gives up all hope of a poetic career, we are left with what we could call the real teleology of the sequence: the printed book. One of the things Daniel interrogates in his sonnet sequence is the effect of this still relatively new technology on the status of poetry in late sixteenth-century England.

This teleological focus links Daniel's poems to Marlowe's and Marston's, as does his consideration of the power of poetry more generally, although their texts are both more cheerful (most of the time) and more clearly connected to sex. Indeed, the eroticism of their poems seems to us now to be one of the indispensable features of the genre as opposed to the sonnet sequence in which the unattainability of sex is one of the chief topics. I shall call the genre of *Hero and Leander* and *The Metamorphosis of Pigmalions Image* the epyllion throughout, as although it was not the term used then, the fact that the word is a diminutive of epic makes it useful as a reminder of the way in which to write an epyllion is simultaneously to engage with and to decline to engage with the task of writing an epic, a task that seemed to be the inevitable ambition, or fate, of a poet given the model of Virgil's career and the influential adoption of that model by Spenser. As Brown suggests, 'The epyllion is a reduction, truncation, and trivialization of epic.'[4] In addition to the content of the poems, then, the mere fact of writing an epyllion instead of a more serious poem can be read in the context of the

1590s as a questioning both of the genre of epic and of the teleology that is seen as one of its inevitable concomitants. One very popular way of putting this is to say that while the epic is Virgilian, the epyllion is Ovidian. In this understanding of the texts of these two great Latin poets, Virgil stands for teleology and fixity, while Ovid stands for endless play. This understanding is simultaneously true and false, and I want now to look at these classical poets and at how their teleology and lack of teleology were useful to Renaissance writers.

The *Aeneid* is obviously a work that deals with the foundations of the Roman empire; in this sense, Virgil's poem is clearly teleological. Nevertheless, the poem does not end with the establishment of Aeneas's kingdom but with the death of Turnus. As Turnus is Aeneas's chief enemy, his death removes the primary obstacle from the way of the Trojan refugees, but in context it is merely one death among many in the last half of the *Aeneid*, a poem that focuses on loss and death rather than on triumph. We could say that in Virgil's poem teleology is an unattainable telos. In contrast, although the *Metamorphoses* is not unified around a single hero and the connection between the poem and the empire seems tenuous at best, the poem is nevertheless strongly teleological, as it is composed of a multitude of narratives, each of which ends decisively – much more decisively than the *Aeneid*. Furthermore, while the omnipresence of metamorphosis seems to depict a world characterized by fluidity, many of the metamorphoses arguably do not represent change at all. In the example of Iphis and Ianthe that I mentioned in the previous chapter, for instance, when Iphis is turned into a boy, the magical change only makes physical what had been true in all other ways, as Iphis was brought up as a boy. And in the story of the Propoetidae that introduces the story of Pygmalion the transformation of these shameless women is, as Ovid admits, slight: he says to turn them into stone was only the result of a 'paruo ... discrimine' (small difference; X.241–2).[5]

These are only two examples out of the hundreds of metamorphoses in the poem, of course, but many, and perhaps most, of the metamorphoses work to restore order or to punish crimes or to make the metaphorical literal or all of the above. Thus, the *Metamorphoses* is not particularly open-ended, nor does it depict a world in which anything goes: it does not represent the polymorphous perversity that so many critics have yearned to find. The poem is most decisively teleological, appropriately enough, at the end. While the *Aeneid*, which is admittedly an unfinished poem, ends with a death, the *Metamorphoses* ends with Ovid's praise of himself. In contrast to Virgil's rather tentative estimation of his poem's future – for example, when he says that he will preserve the memory of Nisus and Euryalus, he is careful to say 'si quid mea carmina possunt' (if my songs can do it; XI.446) – at the end of his book Ovid passes from praise of Augustus to declaring, 'opus exegi, quod nec Iouis ira nec ignis / nec poterit ferrum nec edax abolere uetustas' (I have made a work that neither the wrath of Jove nor fire nor the sword nor gnawing age will be able to obliterate; XV.871–2); and, when he is dead, 'parte tamen meliore mei super alta perennis / astra ferar, nomenque indelebile nostrum' (yet with my better part I shall be carried immortal above the stars and my name will be indelible; XV.875–6). Among the bewildering changes that the poem relates, Ovid remains immutable, which is as important to Renaissance poets as the fact that he offered models for writing about sex: he showed that a poet could be the real subject of his poem and that the telos towards which poems, and especially narrative poems, were supposed to tend could be the poet's personal happy ending.

Hero and Leander and *The Metamorphosis of Pigmalions Image* are Ovidian both in the sense that they are concerned with sex and in the sense that poetry becomes not the means to an end but the end itself, although the speaker in the former poem is clearly happier about this than the speaker in the latter poem, as there is an important contrast between Pygmalion's successful union of art and love and the speaker's frustration. In Marston's poem sexual desire is essentially private, while in Marlowe's the private love between the eponymous protagonists is always seen against a social background that eventually becomes the foreground. In recent years, queer theory has often been criticized for being too focused on texts and not enough on the social. For instance, the sociologist Adam Isaiah Green has said that 'queer theory tends to lapse into a discursively burdened, textual idealism that glosses over the institutional character of sexual identity and the shared social roles that sexual actors occupy.'[6] Interestingly, of the two poems I am discussing here it is Marston's heteroerotic text that is solipsistic and narrowly focused while Marlowe's distinctly homoerotic treatment of his two young lovers most insistently returns again and again to 'the institutional character of sexual identity.' Still, Green is certainly right about the criticism of *Hero and Leander*, which has tended to concentrate on the polymorphous perversity towards which the poem also returns and to evaluate Hero and Leander as individuals rather than as people who occupy social roles.[7] In my analysis, I want to focus on the poem as a critique of the sexual regime.

What unites all the poems I discuss in this chapter is their focus on rhetoric, on the ability or inability of people to do things with words. In all three texts men attempt to use highly elaborate rhetoric to persuade women to have sex with them: Leander succeeds, while Marston's and Daniel's narrators do not. Nevertheless, I believe that the difference between success and failure in this one point is not particularly important – for one thing, it is clear that Hero's willingness has nothing to do with rhetoric: as William Keach has pointed out, Leander's arguments 'have little effect on Hero compared to [his] sheer physical energy and attractiveness.'[8] In all three poems, I would argue, rhetoric is important not so much for its ostensible aim or for whether that aim is achieved, but rather because it provides an especially clear example of the disciplining of language itself. A rhetorical poem, as opposed to a purely descriptive one, can always be evaluated for its usefulness. Furthermore, the teleological nature of rhetoric disciplines poets as well as the language they use. As Joel Fineman points out, 'the Renaissance sonnet ... is acutely aware of its own rhetoricity' and, by focusing on praise, the sonnet 'establishes, by virtue of its self-foregrounding epideixis, a kind of grammar of poetic presence that controls the way the poet can articulate himself.'[9] In the narratives of Marlowe and Marston as well, our attention is drawn to the limits of possible expression.

In his study of classical rhetoric, Jeffrey Walker notes that it was divided into two kinds, *epideiktikon* and *pragmatikon*, and that the difference between the two was 'the nature of the audience and forum to which the discourse speaks, and the function of the discourse for the audience in that forum' (the latter, often called forensic rhetoric, was used before judges); as Walker admits, however, the distinction has often been blurred and the former term 'came to include everything that modernity has tended to describe as rhetoric.'[10] In this later distinction between *epideiktikon*, as a kind of rhetoric associated with literature, and *pragmatikon*, as a kind of rhetoric associated with the law, there is potentially a space for a non-teleological poetics. James Longenbach has recently said that 'if the assumption of poetry's relevance can be oppressive to poets, the assumption of its irrelevance can be liberating.'[11] If freed of the requirement to be relevant – with 'relevant' given the narrow sense of contributing to a socially approved purpose – poetry might be able to focus either on pleasure or on examining why certain kinds of behaviour are approved and others are not. And, of course, a non-teleological poetics could do both, as I think it does in *Hero and Leander*, if not, or at least not to the same extent, in the two other poems I look at in this chapter.

As Walker points out, however, by the time of the Renaissance there was 'a poetics ... that makes poetry a medium of epideictic rhetoric whose end is moral suasion.'[12] Indeed, by the end of the sixteenth century many writers were only too willing to concede that a poetry focused on pleasure and on resisting official ideas about morality (especially sexual morality) was immoral. However, these writers did not make this point in order to enable a different kind of poetry, but in order to stamp out most kinds of poetry altogether. In response to these attacks, sixteenth-century English writers tended to argue for the clear moral purpose of the poetry they and others wrote. In the passage I have just quoted Walker is writing specifically about Sidney, but the idea is generally applicable throughout the Renaissance, as not only Sidney but many other writers stressed poetry's ability to provide moral suasion or, to return to the terms of rhetoric, to turn *epideiktikon* into *pragmatikon* in ways that were socially approved.[13] For these writers, poetry's undeniable affective power, its ability to inspire pleasure of various sorts, made it especially suitable for moral purposes. Daniel, Marlowe, and Marston all were writing poetry against this sort of discourse, and all their poems raise, in very different ways, the problems for poets of defining poetry through its teleologies.

I

Delia was published in 1592 as part of Daniel's first book of original poetry. One of the distinctive features of this book and of the rest of the books Daniel published throughout his career is his concern with publication itself. He appears to have seen publication as dangerous in that control over the text passes from the poet to the reader, and I think that his sense of publication as a decidedly mixed blessing is related to his doubts about poetry. Daniel began his poetic career by worrying in print about what poetry could and could not do and to what extent its powers of persuasion might legitimately be used. In the dedication to the Countess of Pembroke, which begins the 1592 volume – *Delia Contayning certayne Sonnets: with the complaint of Rosamond* – he explains why he decided to publish: 'I was betraide by the indiscretion of a greedie Printer, and had some of my secrets bewraide to the world, vncorrected: doubting the like of the rest, I am forced to publish that which I neuer ment.'[14] Daniel is telling the truth, as some of his sonnets

had been printed without his permission the year before. But his anxieties about publication do not only concern the process of submitting a
manuscript to a printer who will then release it to booksellers. While
the preface discusses what led to his decision to publish, the poems
themselves are concerned with publication both in the sense of having
a book printed and in the more general sense of making something
public. For Daniel, the problem was that, once a book is published, the
poet can no longer control it, and readers are free to make whatever use
of the book they choose and to interpret the poems – and their author
– in any way they wish.

When Daniel says, 'I am forced to publish that which I neuer ment,'
he means two things. The more obvious is that he is declaring that the
had not intended to make these poems public, but I think that he is also
trying to disassociate himself from the speaker of the poems: that is, he
is saying that he did not mean the sentiments expressed in the poems.
Of course, as the speaker in a sonnet sequence typically appears at a
disadvantage, it is entirely plausible that a poet would be reluctant to
be identified with the speaker of the poems. Daniel expresses this reluctance at various points in *Delia*, but his clearest statement of unease at
the prospect that the sentiments and situations expressed in his poems
will be taken to be his own personal experience appears in his address
'To the Reader,' which was first published in 1607:

> I know no work from man yet euer came
> But had his marke, and by some error shewd
> That it was his, and yet what in the same
> Was rare, and worthy, euermore allowd
> Safe co[n]uoy for the rest. (43–7)

Daniel's formulation is pessimistic in that a poem's faults enable readers
to identify its author, and while its virtues can excuse the faults, it appears that they are not considered to be as typical of the poet. Daniel feels
that the reading public is only too apt to make a straightforward equivalence between a poet and his works: to read a man is to know him.

Daniel's published reluctance to publish is, of course, a conventional
gesture: by the beginning of the 1590s many poets prefaced their books
with similar disclaimers. In an important article on the role of poets in
sixteenth-century England, J.W. Saunders points out that, while publication is now thought to bestow a certain approval on poetry, the situation was different then, at least for those who had to earn their living by

their poetry: 'whereas for the amateur poets of the Court an avoidance of print was *socially* desirable, for the professional poets outside or only on the edge of Court circles the achievement of print became an *economic* necessity.'[15] Poetry is an achievement in two senses: it is an accomplishment, and it can also function as a bourgeois equivalent to the heraldic achievement, which is one of the proofs of gentle status. But Daniel makes this achievement seem problematic. What if to publish a poem is to publish your faults to the world? What if poetry's power to persuade is misused? Or, to return to the words of the dedication, what if you publish something you never meant? Daniel's stated unwillingness to publish cannot merely be read as convention, although admittedly much of what he writes throughout his first book is conventional in the sense that other poets were making similar statements at the time. In the case of the 1592 volume, Daniel's ambivalence about publication is not confined to the dedication but emerges as one of the central themes of the collection as a whole.

In his influential book on the relations between manuscript circulation and publication, Arthur F. Marotti says of Daniel's dedication that 'despite his protestations of humility and dependence, Daniel was asserting authorial authority and defining poetic texts in ways proper to print culture' and that by reprinting these poems he 'brought back texts that had passed out of his possession back under authorial control, and, erasing their original social coordinates, re-presented them ... as self consciously literary works.'[16] He goes on to say that 'Daniel expressed his antagonism to the general public ... [by] omitting any epistles to readers and presenting the book as a gift to one person, who, in effect, becomes the owner of the text.'[17] Marotti makes many excellent points, but I think that his characterization of the status of the poems needs to be qualified. Rather than hand over ownership of the his poems to the countess, Daniel enlists her support in the fight against the misrepresentation to which any text is subject, and by increasing the number of readers of a publication he also increases the number of (possible) misrepresentations. As well, since some of the sonnets in *Delia* had originally appeared in the first edition of *Astrophil and Stella*, in dedicating the book to Sidney's sister Daniel is not 'erasing their social coordinates.' Indeed, I would say that he is insisting on them.

Furthermore, the dependence Daniel expresses in his dedication is not entirely a fiction: as the tutor of the countess's children he was literally dependent on her and continued to be so for several years, after which he found other patrons, including, eventually, Queen Anne herself.[18] Such was the life of a professional poet without private means. In making public his connection to the countess at the beginning of his first book of original poetry, Daniel foregrounds the social context of his poems as a way of stating his credentials. As Marotti suggests, Daniel is 'asserting authorial authority' in his dedication, but I think that his plan is also to stress the social context of his poetry in order to use the authority of the countess, a famous and powerful figure in the literary world of late sixteenth-century England. Rather than hand over the ownership of his poems to the countess, Daniel invokes her as a figure who has the power to support Daniel's claim to own his poems. As Christopher Warley comments, Daniel 'deploys [her] nobility in the service of his own work and in his own interests. The dedication to the Countess assists his work in its efforts to "purchase grace."'[19] Daniel's metaphorical use of the word 'purchase' reminds us of the material basis both of publishing and of the countess's status. After all, she was not only famous and powerful but also rich.

The humility Marotti mentions is a more complex subject. Although Daniel tends to speak quite humbly throughout the book, this could be considered a pose prompted by the customary haplessness of the speaker in a sonnet, although if by humility is meant humble status, it may well be an accurate term. As very little is known about Daniel's background, it is not clear what his claims to gentility were.[20] His father was a musician, which might or might not imply gentle status. Daniel attended Oxford, and it is true that a university degree legally conferred gentle status, but sometimes this status was only legal. It is not even entirely clear that Daniel ever obtained a degree. After leaving Oxford, he published a translation of Paulus Jovius in 1585 and worked for the first in a series of aristocratic patrons. He appears to have entered the countess's employ in 1592, although, as Rees points out, ' Precise information is lacking about Daniel's activities from 1586–1592.'[21] What we do know is that when Daniel published *Delia*, he was a man in his late twenties who had achieved neither literary renown nor financial security. Both were to come (the former with the publication of this book), although obviously he could not have known that. Part of Daniel's aim in the dedication is to connect himself with the countess as his patron. Thus, the conventional narrative situation of the sonnet sequence – that the man is at a disadvantage with regard to the woman he loves – can be said to reflect his actual situation. The 1592 volume can be read as Daniel's attempt to establish an autonomous realm where, as a celebrated poet, he will to some extent be free from his low social standing.

He appears to be deeply ambivalent about both the feasibility and the propriety of such a step, however, and in this volume publication often seems to be equivalent to presumption.

The most obvious way for Daniel to establish an autonomous realm for himself is to stress the power of poetry. Although *Delia* as a whole is ultimately pessimistic about the success of this strategy, Daniel's references to the power of poetry feature prominently throughout his book, beginning with his praise of the countess as a patron of the arts: 'Whereby you doe not onely possesse the honour of the present, but also do bind posterity to an euer gratefull memorie of your vertues, wherein you must suruiue your self' (9). The immortality Daniel promises the countess is a forerunner of the immortality he promises Delia, and in 1592 this was a novel feature of the sonnet sequence. As Thomas P. Roche Jr points out, 'Daniel is the first of the English sonneteers to promise immortality to his beloved.'[22] But the poetic survival Daniel promises to both women is ultimately more a compliment to him than to them. Although Daniel presents the renown he aspires to confer as merited, the renown will nevertheless have the effect of reversing the power dynamic between the poet and each of these powerful women. Daniel ends the dedication by telling the countess, '[I am] vowed to your honour in all obseruancy for euer,' but he also comments that this will only come about as a result of his publication: 'if my lines ... shall purchase grace in the world, they must remaine the monuments of your honourable fauour' (9). His poetry will preserve the memory of their relationship, and in that sense the poetry is not and never can be entirely independent of the countess's patronage, but in becoming a monument to her it assumes the dominant position: a monument is one of the proofs that someone is dead.

It may not seem surprising to us that sonnets themselves begin with a consideration of the role of poetry, but like the promise to bestow immortality on the beloved, this is one of Daniel's innovations. Michael R.G. Spiller points out, 'the first sonnet ... takes the unusual course (in the long history of the sonnet) of treating writing as writing.'[23] In fact, the beginning of the sequence as a whole is unusual. Lars-Hakan Svensson comments that the first four sonnets 'form a kind of extended *proemio* to which there are no counterparts in the sequences usually connected with Daniel's.'[24] For my purposes, the most important of these sonnets are the first two, in which Daniel presents various themes and images that are crucial to his project: the collection as a book, the question of immortality, the image of the ocean, and the story of the birth of Minerva. Daniel begins the sequence by dedicating it to Delia: 'Vnto the boundles Ocean of thy beautie / Runs this poore riuer' (1.1–2). The dominant image in this sonnet is of the book itself, which need not be a printed book like the 1592 volume: Daniel could be referring to a manuscript.[25] The second option is perhaps the more likely at this point, since the emphasis here is on the speaker's declaring his love to Delia rather than to the reading public, but the sequence itself goes on to focus our attention on the poem's transition from completely private objects to objects with a readership of one to public documents that anyone may read.

In the first sonnet, the speaker still thinks of Delia as the only reader of his book. However, the verb he uses is not 'to open,' but rather 'to unclasp.' This verb also suggests the end of an embrace (and perhaps of a relationship as a whole), but as it becomes clear early on that Daniel has never had any success with Delia, I think we should take the unclasping as Daniel's ultimate revelation of himself to the reading public:

> Heere I vnclaspe the booke of my charg'd soule,
> Where I haue cast th'accounts of all my care:
> Heere haue I summ'd my sighes, heere I enroule
> Howe they were spent for thee.   (1.5–8)

In an analysis of the poem in her book on gender and Elizabethan poetry, Wendy Wall points out that 'the speaker's active assertion ... and his identification of the text with his interiority ... constitutes a secondary and belated claim subordinate to and originating from the mistress's more crucial power.'[26] I would expand this comment to say that the mistress's power itself is 'secondary and belated' in relation to the countess's power, which is the subject of much of the dedication. In both the dedication and the beginning of the sequence, then, Daniel presents himself as subservient. So far, at any rate, publication has not enabled him to achieve independence.

In the rest of the first sonnet Daniel develops the image of the book as an account book or ledger. With a gesture that recalls the traditional obeisance of the lover, the poet submits the book to Delia: 'Looke on the deere expences of my youth' (9). He goes on to ask Delia to evaluate the poems as the return on an investment made with the capital of her beauty: 'see how just I reckon with thyne eyes: / Examine well thy beautie with my trueth' (10–11). In his use of 'reckon,' Daniel draws on two meanings of the word: to narrate and to make calculations. He makes a similar play on words when he says, 'crosse my cares ere greater summes arise' (12). As a verb, 'cross' may mean to preclude or hinder and to cancel a debt. The poet simultaneously pleads to be reimbursed for his outlay and begs for kind treatment. The images tie love to economic considerations, but they also bolster the status of the book itself. From the beginning, this record of unhappy love is presented as a financial document with legal status. By working out the implications of his images, Daniel stresses that writing, particularly published writing, has legal weight. Nevertheless, the greater status of the book does not confer greater wealth or status on the poet. In using the metaphor of the account book presented to a powerful woman Daniel in effect represents himself as steward for a noblewoman such as the countess herself. Rather than elevate the poet, then, the image maintains him in the position of reasonably genteel servitude that he held as the tutor for her children.

In the second sonnet Daniel moves to a different metaphor. As Spiller notes, the first two sonnets 'offer contrasting views of [Daniel's] own writing.'[27] In the second, the emphasis is on speaking rather than writing and, while in the first sonnet the poems are presented as a book, here Daniel resorts to the reproductive metaphor – in fact, to the most conventional example of all the uses of the reproductive metaphor I examine in this book. He addresses the poems directly – 'Goe wailing verse, the infants of my loue' (2.1) – and adds that they are '*Minerua*-like, brought foorth without a Mother' (2.2). In the context of a collection of romantic poetry addressed by a man to a woman, the reproductive metaphor is especially marked, as the poet's evident failure means that the children he might have had with the woman can be only metaphorical. The statement that the poems were produced 'without a Mother' simultaneously emphasizes the speaker's lack of romantic and sexual success and implies that he does not need women to reproduce: both readings are plausible. In the second sonnet, the poet would be like Jupiter, who was able to appropriate and tame female power that had threatened to endanger him. Daniel's use of the allusion is a parable in which women are the raw materials for the artist's work but they are indispensable for only the first step in the poetic process. If we return to the themes of the dedication, we could say that Daniel has figured out how to bypass feminine power. And although the poems are characterized as 'wailing verse,' the book is no longer a ledger that must be submitted to a superior, but something with an independent existence, however depressing that existence may be.

Daniel develops the idea that his poems may have an independent existence in the second half of the sonnet. They will be, he says, a 'Monument that whosoeuer reedes, / May iustly praise, and blame my loueles Faire' (2.7–8). The lines recall his use of 'monument' in the dedication; in both cases it is important to remember that a monument is designed to replace a person. In this sense the poems are not so much independent as interdependent with Delia, but they will have the power to shape the ways in which she is remembered. Jane Hedley points out that the second 'sonnet is prospective in a double sense: it refers to the already-written sonnets we have not read yet, and it looks beyond the end of the sequence, hoping that as a completed "monument" it may have more power to move Delia than any of the individual poems had.'[28] And the monument will move more people than Delia: a monument is a public artwork that is expressly designed to inspire an appropriate reaction in anyone who sees it – 'whosoeuer reedes.' Although the dedication demonstrates Daniel's trepidation about the consequences of publishing his poetry, by the second sonnet he appears to have found a way to see publication as advantageous. In these first sonnets Daniel draws our attention to the poems as public artefacts and as things with a life of their own. He may not obviate his fear that the book may not redound to his credit, but he does increase our sense of the power of publication.

Daniel begins the third sonnet by returning to the image of his poems as children and then proceeds to speak of his readers:

If so it hap this of-spring of my care,
These fatall Antheames, sad and mornefull Songes:
Come to their view, who like afflicted are;
Let them yet sigh their owne, and mone my wrongs.   (3.1–4)

This imagining of his readership represents a significant enlargement of the world of the poems, which up to this point has focused on the speaker and Delia. The next lines reveal that the speaker still has not entirely grasped the meaning of publication or, at least, that he is unwilling to accept all of its implications: 'But vntouch'd harts, with vnaffected eye, / Approch not to behold so great distresse' (3.5–6). He goes on to make explicit the restriction of his potential readership to those who resemble him: 'you, and none but you my sorrowes read' (3.11). In fact, in the next sonnet he disavows any strictly poetic ambitions: 'No Bayes I seeke' (4.9). All he now wishes is to give himself some relief: 'These lines I vse, t'nburthen mine owne hart; / My loue affects no fame, nor steemes of art' (4.13–14). In these first four sonnets, Daniel situates his sequence in the middle of the contemporary discourse on publication and on the uses of poetry and ends this initial group of sonnets by retreating to a private realm, having apparently concluded that poetry has only a personal use. This is not a teleological view of poetry, but it is one that provides only limited pleasure.

After these first four sonnets, the bulk of the sequence is concerned with expressing his misery. Although this misery is often beautifully expressed, the overall impression is of stasis. We may now consider this stasis to be an essential feature of the sonnet sequence, but if we do so, it is largely because of Daniel's example here. While the sequences of Sidney, Spenser, and Shakespeare do not feature particularly brisk narratives, and while the same is true of Petrarch's *Rime Sparse*, I would argue that Daniel increases the narrative deadlock. Events occasionally occur to trouble most other sequences, but *Delia* is written almost entirely in a retrospective mode. Whatever happened – or, rather, whatever did not happen – happened or did not happen before the first sonnet. Still, despite this stasis an important change occurs in sonnet 26 and it is clearly significant this is the beginning of the sequence's second half.[29] The speaker attempts to look retrospectively at his love for Delia, not because he has ceased to love her but because he plans to die: all the final couplets of sonnets 26, 27, and 28 end with references to his death. Of course, he does not die, nor does he continue his retrospection. Many of the sonnets in the second half would work just as well in the first half, although I think there is a perceptible shift as Daniel begins to concentrate on the theme of the immortality that poetry can bestow, although not in ways that are helpful to the speaker of the poems.

The shift in the sequence is not the result of Delia's relenting or even of her further cruelty but rather concern the poet's attitude to his work. In sonnet 39, for example, he presents himself as a book:

Read in my face, a volume of despayres,
The wayling Iliades of my tragicke wo;
Drawne with my bloud, and printed with my cares,
Wrought by her hand, that I haue honoured so.   (39.1–4)

In producing a book, the poet has merely succeeded in turning himself into one, by producing himself as a text. We could see the shift from active to passive as mirroring the difference between the poet who

controls his manuscripts, and thus the dissemination of his texts, and
the poet who is read by anyone who can command the price of his
book. Furthermore, if the poet as book is 'Wrought by her hand,' then it
is Delia who has become the active force, the writer (or, at least, limner)
of the poet. Undone by his own work, the poet passes from being a
speaking subject to being a poetic subject. And as the poem made from
his sorrows is compared to the *Iliad* , we are reminded of the scope of
the poet's failure, since writing an epic (as opposed to figuring in one)
was seen as the best conclusion of a literary career.

Perhaps as a consequence of this vision of the sequence as self-
destructive, the poet tries to re-imagine himself, beginning with his
statement that Delia would prefer to read 'Lines of delight, whereon
her youth might smyle' (43.2). The poet then moves from an image of
Delia as his magnetic north to a celebration of England as a northern
country: 'Florish faire *Albion*, glory of the North, / *Neptunes* darling
helde between his armes' (44.9–10). But the attempt to become a patri-
otic poet is instantly abandoned, and this sonnet is followed by two
that demonstrate a retreat into the personal mode. In the first ('Care-
charmer sleepe'), poetry appears to have been abandoned altogether, as
the speaker says that he wants to sleep for ever, 'imbracing clowdes in
vaine: / And neuer wake to feel the dayes disdayne' (45.13–14). In the
second ('Let other sing of Knights and Palladines'), the speaker rules
out the heroic poetry that Spenser has just made famous by saying, 'But
I must sing of thee and those faire eyes' (46.5). This is the speaker's
admission that he can imagine no other subject for his verse, a point he
develops in the next sonnet:

> Like as the Lute that ioyes or els dislikes,
> As is his arte that playes vpon the same;
> So sounds my Muse according as she strikes,
> On my hart strings high tun'd vnto her fame.   (47.1–4)

Sonnet 39's picture of Delia as the one who wrought the poet has become a picture of the poet as a mere instrument. Publishing poems that
celebrate England or that tell heroic tales has an important public purpose, but these sonnets have no purpose at all: they refuse to be teleological in any way except one that is personally humiliating to the poet.

The last three sonnets of the sequence can be understood as Daniel's
attempt to resign himself to what is now a public failure. He begins by
stating that he is not seeking the usual rewards of the poetic life. First

he denies any wish for fame – 'None other fame myne vnambitious Muse, / Affected euer but t'eternize thee' (48.1–2) – and then for money: 'For God forbid I should my papers blot, / With mercynary lines, with seruile pen' (48.5–7). Money is usually considered a bad telos, but fame is typically considered a worthy motive for a poet – as it is, for example, for Ovid at the end of the *Metamorphoses* and for Virgil in the third book of the *Georgics*. Indeed, as I showed in the introduction, Virgil ends the *Georgics* by contrasting his private poetry unfavourably with Caesar's public career. But while I argued that Virgil could see possibilities for textual production in the very privacy and abjection of his posture (both his metaphorical posture and his posture as presented in the poem's sphragis), it appears that Daniel could see his abjection only as gradually closing off all avenues for the writing of poetry. I think that his attitude has something to do with the changing status of poetry in an age of mechanical reproduction and, therefore, of unprecedented disseminative capacity. I think that Daniel wants to suggest that the shift from the circulation of poems in a relatively small number of manuscripts to the circulation of easily printed books to the market as a whole puts increased pressure on poems – and on the people who write them – to be teleological, to make some sort of contribution that is not merely private.

Interestingly, Daniel presents the narrowing of his poetic focus chiefly in geographical terms:

No no my verse respects not Thames nor Theaters,
Nor seekes it to be known vnto the Great:
But *Auon* rich in fame, though poore in waters,
Shall haue my song, where *Delia* hath her seate
Auon shall be my Thames, and Song;
Ile sound her name the Ryuer all along.   (48.9–14)

We can see this as an attempt to reverse the usual flow of poetic talent and of poems from the province to the metropolis, the place where the presses are. Daniel is also invoking the original meaning of publication, one that does not depend on the economic realities of the printing press. I would also say that the passage recalls the famous beginning of Virgil's first eclogue, in which Meliboeus says to Tityrus: 'formosam resonare doces Amaryllida siluas' (you teach the woods to echo lovely Amaryllis; 1.5). Daniel implicitly suggests that he can be identified with the shepherd Tityrus, singing love songs in seclusion and enjoying his land, which, although of poor quality, is sufficient for his needs. The allusion is also, I think, a coded reference to Virgil's move from pastoral to epic as a precedent for poets like Edmund Spenser. The move to the country and to pastoral poetry in sonnet 48 inverts the standard model for poetic careers in Daniel's time.

In any case, Daniel quickly abandons this plan and he begins the next sonnet by bewailing his 'Vnhappy pen and ill accepted papers' (49.1). At the beginning of the sequence, his poems were 'the booke of my charg'd soule' (1.5) and were presented in language that suggested a printed book or, at least, a collection of bound papers, rather than individual sheets. Publication is supposed to fix a manuscript in a form in which it can be transmitted from the private world of the poet to the public world of the literary marketplace in a relatively durable container. In *Delia*, it appears that the reverse has happened and that the poems have reverted to their original form. The poems' inability to maintain the tangible form of the book can be seen in the progression in this sonnet's first quatrain. After referring to his poems as papers that 'intimate in vaine [his] chaste desier' (49.2), he describes the desires themselves as 'euer burning tapers' (49.3). Thus, the poems metaphorically embody that which will destroy them, a point stressed by the papers / tapers rhyme. As well, the idea of a thing containing its own destruction recalls the story of Jupiter and Minerva. But while that story depicts the male ability to appropriate female power and to resist a female challenge, in sonnet 49 it seems that Daniel is not only powerless but even in danger, chiefly from himself. Like his poems, his desires can affect only himself and only for the worse.

We can see another version of this myth at the end of this sonnet when Daniel resolves to 'content me that her frownes should be / To my infant stile the cradle and the graue' (49.11–12). In the second sonnet, Daniel is the Jupiter who brought forth offspring without a woman, as he has told us that his poems are '*Minerua*-like, brought foorth without a Mother.' Part of the achievement here, both for Daniel and for Jupiter, is the male usurpation of women's ability to bear children, but there is always the possibility (for Daniel, at least) that the bringing forth may appear not as a man's victory over women but rather as a man's becoming like a woman. By this point in the sequence, the latter appears to be the case. Delia is not the mother of his poems but rather the one who tends them, the one who calls them forth (insofar as her frowns are their cradle), and the one who has absolute power over them (insofar as her frowns are their grave). Daniel's entire poetic production is dependent upon Delia. He continues to present himself as a woman when he ends the sonnet by saying 'What though my selfe no honor get thereby, / Each byrd sings t'herselfe, and so will I' (49.13–14). It is not unusual for poetry to be compared to birdsong, but it is significant that the bird in question is female. As well, this couplet expresses Daniel's renunciation of a poetic career and his declaration that from now on his poetry will once again be a solitary and private thing rather than a public commodity.

As part of this renunciation, Daniel tries to sum up the sequence in his last sonnet: 'Loe heere the impost of a faith vnfaining, / That loue hath paide, and her disdaine extorted' (50.1–2). The use of 'impost' returns to the financial imagery of the first sonnet and also recalls the description of the sonnets as 'the Posts of my desire' (4.1). The assumption that the publication of private papers gave them legal power was, at least implicitly, one of the most important ideas behind the presentation of the poems at the beginning of the sequence. By contrast, the last sonnet emphasizes the futility of publication. The sonnets have failed to gain Delia's love, and in publishing his poetry, Daniel has merely succeeded in spreading the news of his failure. His return to the themes and metaphors of his *proemio* underlines that he has failed to progress. In fact, the most significant change has been the narrowing of his poetic scope and of his audience. In the final couplet of the final sonnet he gives up poetry altogether: 'This is my state, and *Delias* hart is such; / I say no more, I feare I said too much' (50.13–14). This statement does not only imply a farewell to poetry; it also suggests that the sequence as a whole is excessive and that his plans for a poetic career were mistaken. It is crucial that this statement is made in a published book, as he no longer has the power to suppress his excessive speech. His failure is now part of the historical record.

Daniel's determination to cease to speak turns out to be merely the latest in a series of attempts to end the sequence. He is still unable to stop writing poetry about Delia, and his next solution is to give up sonnets rather than poetry as a whole. Carol Thomas Neely points out that this is not an uncommon conclusion for a sonnet sequence: 'detachment from conflicts is achieved by a shift to forms of poetry other than sonnets.'[30] Still, I see Daniel's abandonment of the sonnet form as part of what we could call his poetics of renunciation. He ends the sequence with an ode set in the landscape in which the sonnets end, the pastoral world that was intended to provide a refuge but that turns out to be a world in which he has no place. This landscape is described in terms of love and generation from which he is excluded:

Whilst the greatest torch of heauen,
With bright rayes warmes *Floras* lappe,
Making nights and dayes both euen,
Cheering plants with fresher sapper;
My field of flowers quite be-reauen,
Wants refresh of better happe.   (7–12)

The poet's isolation is underlined by the contrast between the solitary birdsong in sonnet 49 ('Each byrd sings t'herselfe , and so will I' and the amorous birdsong of the ode ('One byrd reports vnto another' [3]). The poet's exclusion from the regeneration celebrated in the ode leads to his death: 'And well he'ends for loue who dies' (24). This is the logical conclusion of the narrowing of focus that has dominated the second half of the sequence.

Of course, Daniel did not die after putting down his pen at the end of the ode; the 1592 volume continues with *The Complaint of Rosamond*, in which he deals with many of the same issues as in the sequence.[31] The next year, he published his first play and in 1595 he published the first version of his historical epic, *The Civil Wars*. Daniel established himself as a successful writer in a variety of styles and genres. The demand for his work allowed him to put out new editions of his work, and these were often extensively revised and expanded. *The Civil Wars* grew from four books in 1595 to eight books in 1609; *The Complaint of Rosamond* eventually gained twenty-three stanzas; and *Delia* itself was expanded from fifty to fifty-eight sonnets in the 1594 edition before ending up at sixty sonnets in the 1601 edition (Daniel also changed the order of several of the sonnets). His success in publishing his works meant that he was able to resist what I described at the beginning of this chapter as the teleology of the printed book. The finished product that is the printed book is the property of anyone who has the money to buy it, but the people who bought the 1592 volume would soon have discovered that they did not have what we would call the definitive edition. Daniel's revision to the sonnet sequence and to his other poems can be seen as attempts to keep the work under the control of the author and to resist the teleological power of the publishing industry. As I have pointed out, however, he continued to be dependent on female patrons, and in this respect the reproductive metaphor, with its insistence that textual production depends on a man and a woman, was still suitable for his poetry.

II

Christopher Marlowe's *Hero and Leander* is one of the most popular of all Renaissance poems and has been the subject of numerous critical discussions, but there is still no consensus as to whether the poem is finished or unfinished or what its genre is or even whether it is comic or tragic.[32] To some extent, this confusion is the result of the frames through which readers approach the poem. As the story of Hero and Leander is familiar from the classical versions by Musaeus and Ovid as well as Renaissance versions, such as the one by the Spanish poet Juan Boscán, these other versions have functioned as a control against which Marlowe's poem are evaluated. Most obviously, of course, while the other versions end in the deaths of the lovers, Marlowe's poem ends, if it does end, with the lovers still alive. I think the first point to make here is that Marlowe's poem is not in any strict sense a translation of Musaeus, and while in some ways it is more like Ovid's treatment of the story (and more like Ovid in general), it is not really a translation of the *Heroides* either.[33] The possibility that Marlowe used Boscán's *Leandro* is more interesting, as this version contains a lengthy (448 of the poem's 2,792 lines) digression that, in essence, translates most of the second half of the fourth book of the *Georgics*, telling the story of Aristaeus and ending with the head of Orpheus.[34] If Warren Boutcher is correct in saying that for Boscán and, as I suggested in the introduction, for poets generally, the story of Aristaeus functions 'as a threshold leading to the heroic poetry of the *Aeneid*,' then it could be argued that Marlowe's decision not to include this story is part of a larger refusal of the idea of posterity.[35] As Helga Duncan has recently observed, *Hero and Leander* 'pays attention [neither] to the perpetuation of family and kinship structures, nor to a world of work, accumulation, and lineage.'[36]

I think Duncan is entirely correct, but I should acknowledge that this is the minority view and that the attempts to connect the poem to 'the perpetuation of family and kinship structures' go back as far as Marlowe's publisher, Edward Blunt. When Blunt published the first edition of *Hero and Leander* shortly after Marlowe's murder, he prefaced it with a dedication to Sir Thomas Walsingham in which he wrote, 'wee thinke not our selves discharged of the dutie wee owe to our friend, when wee have brought the breathlesse bodie to the earth.'[37] Although the body has been buried and we can no longer look at it, 'the impression of the man, that hath beene deare unto us, liv[es] an after-life in our memory.' Blunt's dedication is touching, and the idea of a beloved dead man surviving in his friend's memory suggests that posterity may be personal and homosocial. But the impression of which Blunt writes is not merely a metaphor for the way in which people affect us power-fully even after they die but also a reference to the impression on which publishing depends and thus to the book Walsingham held in his hands. At this point, Blunt's language switches from the personal to the legal. Thinking about the dead man leads him to consider what 'farther obse-quies' are owing, and appointing himself '(as by an intellectuall will) ... executor to the unhappily deceased author of this Poem,' Blunt decides to publish. The legal language initiates a switch to the reproductive metaphor, and referring to Marlowe's unpublished works as 'issue of his brain,' Blunt suggests that Walsingham is the proper legal guardian: his support 'would proove more agreeable and thriving to his right children, than any other foster countenance whatsoever.' As is often the case in writing about textual production, the idea of the writing body quickly turns into the discourse of reproduction within the legal frame-work of the family.

When Blunt characterizes *Hero and Leander* near the end of his dedica-tion as 'this unfinished Tragedy' the adjective seems to emerge from the legal talk of settling the unfinished business of the dead man's estate and can serve as a useful reminder of the way in which discussions about whether the poem is finished (and about texts more generally) are connected to larger questions of the distribution of wealth and property. From this point of view we can see George Chapman's div-ision of the poem into two parts and his composition of four more parts – including, crucially, an account of the deaths of the lovers – as an attempt to make the poem more socially and literarily legible. This at-tempt can be seen in Chapman's dedication to Lady Walsingham, in which he says, 'This poore Dedication (in figure of the other unitie be-twixt *Sir Thomas* and your selfe) hath rejoyned you with him' (456). Poetry is enrolled in the service of the marriage bond. But the fact that Chapman's additions are both antithetical and inferior to Marlowe's poem does not alter the fact that his meddling was able to change the way in which the poem is perceived. As Marion Campbell pointed out in 1984, 'Even those who are most contemptuous of Chapman's poem – even readers who don't attempt to read it – cannot escape its influence on their conception of Marlowe's *Hero and Leander*.'[38] Partly as a result of Campbell's superb article – which inaugurated an interesting debate on the poem's status – it is now easier to find editions of *Hero and Leander* that do not include Chapman's poem or his division into 'sestiads.'

Nevertheless, I agree with Campbell that Chapman's influence is now to a great extent an inescapable part of the poem and for that reason I have decided to use an edition that divides the poem into two.

Another advantage of keeping the question of the poem's incompleteness in sight rather than settling it in one way or the other is that to do so is to maintain the focus on one of the most interesting aspects of *Hero and Leander*, which is that it leads us to consider the extent to which we expect or even require a narrative to have an ending. In her article, Campbell usefully commented that the poem resists narration in a number of ways, perhaps especially in Marlowe's 'elevation of the role of the narrator at the expense of narration.'[39] More recently, Judith Haber has remarked that in telling a tale whose ending is, in effect, a foregone conclusion, Marlowe 'makes us recognize the contingency not only of narrative but of all that it implies.'[40] For my purposes, this is one of the most important features of *Hero and Leander* – its problematization of narrative both in the sense of the narrative of the two young lovers as we know it from Musaeus or Ovid or any of the other writers who have told the story and in the sense of the narratives by which we organize and understand our lives. Foremost among these narratives for Marlowe is the narrative of sexuality, a larger narrative to which he constantly relates the smaller narrative of the two lovers. Furthermore, as Haber suggests, in *Hero and Leander*, the 'disruption of end-directed narrative is paralleled by, and equivalent to, the disruption of end-directed sexuality.'[41] It is this equivalence that concerns me most here.

That sexuality is the dominant subject of *Hero and Leander* is hardly news, but the extent to which sexuality in the poem is always associated with larger social constructions is only beginning to be realized, as discussions of the poem have hitherto tended to focus on the eponymous characters. One of the first critics to deal thoroughly with this association was Gregory Bredbeck, who said in 1991 that the poem demonstrates 'the discursive base of supposedly natural heteroerotic desire.'[42] To some extent, this focus on the discursive derives from Marlowe's reading of Ovid; as Jim Ellis points out, 'for Marlowe ... [Ovidian narratives] are principally about rhetoric.'[43] Marlowe is interested in what words can and cannot do and in the ends of language; he is also interested in seeing mixed-sex relations as only one form of available sexuality. The epyllion is an especially suitable genre in which to pursue these interests, since, as Georgia Brown has remarked, 'through its indulgence in peripheral sexualities and its exploitation of eroticism, the epyllion promotes what is marginal and even what is transgressive.'[44]

I would add that *Hero and Leander* goes beyond most epyllia in its focus on marginal and transgressive sexuality and on how the personal is political – that is, on the connection, to adapt Haber's words, between an end-directed narrative about two young people in love and a socially mandated system of end-directed sexuality – and, crucially, on expressing these issues through rhetorical and narrative form rather than rhetorical and narrative content

In some ways, both the entire narrative of the poem and the distinctive nature of Marlowe's treatment of the story are contained in the opening four lines:

> On *Hellespont* guiltie of True-loves blood,
> In view and opposit two citties stood,
> Seaborderers, disjoin'd by *Neptunes* might:
> The one *Abydos*, the other *Sestos* hight.   (I.1–4)

The phrases 'guiltie of True-loves blood' and '*Neptunes* might' remind us of the end of the story; in beginning with the ending, Marlowe signals his lack of interest in narrative as such. Also significant is the image of the two cities 'In view and opposit.' Here, Marlowe gives us a picture of the two lovers and foreshadows the vital importance of seeing to his poem. It is through sight that we fall in love, and we are supposed to fall in love with that which is opposite to us. Of course, it makes no sense to speak of men and women as opposite sexes, but this prevalent fiction is crucial to Marlowe's focus on binaries in *Hero and Leander*. The sense that 'In view and opposit' simultaneously suggests sameness and difference is heightened by the next line, in which the cities are simultaneously 'Seaborderers' and 'disjoin'd,' together and apart. As Ellis remarks, in this description the Hellespont is 'both a passage and a bar to desire.'[45] In the rest of the poem it is what we could call the sexual system that has this function. In the world of *Hero and Leander*, the elaborate system of rules governing sexual relations between the sexes is both a template for lovers and something that interferes with actually having sex – that is, the sexual system frustrates any sex that is not properly teleological.

In the context of the opening lines the reference to Neptune appears to be a fairly common metonymy for the sea, but the rest of the poem shows that Neptune is not mentioned here solely as the god of the sea. For one thing, he turns out to be a character in one of the poem's most famous episodes. For another, one of the most important themes in the poem is the difference between humans and gods, a difference that is presented chiefly, although not exclusively, in sexual terms. The clearest example is the description of Venus's temple. The floor of the temple contains depictions of many of the best-known stories of divine lust: 'There might you see the gods in sundrie shapes, / Committing headdie ryots, incest, rapes' (I.143–4). In his description Marlowe mentions Jupiter as lover of Danae, of Juno, of Ganymede, of Europa; Venus caught with Mars by her husband; and Sylvanus's love for Cyparissus: in other words, infidelity, homoeroticism, incest, and, uniting almost all the stories, the ability of the gods to change both their own shapes and the shapes of the humans they desire. The only human story depicted here is the reference to the destruction of Troy, and the implication is that while the gods may pursue a variety of sexual activities with only relatively minor consequences for them, humans are endangered by sexual transgression. Jupiter can turn himself into a golden shower in order to have sex with the imprisoned Danae, and the human lovers of the gods may be changed into other forms (and, like Ganymede, may evenbecome immortal); Venus's adultery with Mars leads only to embarrassment, but Helen's adultery with Paris leads to the utter destruction of a great empire.

The contrast between divine sexual freedom and the constrained sexuality of humans is most forcibly expressed in the fact that Hero's virginity is the result of her oath as priestess of Venus. Leander finds this inexplicable and tells her, 'thou in vowing chastitie, hast sworne / To rob her name and honour' (I.304–5). Never much of a thinker, Leander does not realize that human society is to some extent premised on human regulation of sexuality. The scenes depicted in the temple represent forms of sexuality that are denied to humans rather than a preview of coming attractions. One way to approach this point is to recalls Foucault's narration in *The Order of Things* of his response to the fantastical classifications of animals in a story by Jorge Luis Borges. At first Foucault's response is laughter, but then 'arose in its wake the suspicion that there is a worse kind of disorder than that of the *incongruous*, the linking together of things that are inappropriate; I mean the disorder in which fragments of large number of possible orders glitter separately in the dimension, without law or geometry, of the *heteroclite*.'[46] The subtitle of Foucault's book is *An Archaeology of the Human Sciences*, and my point is that the law and geometry to which he refers in this passage are human sciences (in the sense of ways of knowing) rather than divine ones. The 'headdie ryots, incest, rapes' and the full panoply of divine sexual freedoms that glitter in the 'Christall shining faire' (I.141) of the temple floor and that occur throughout *Hero and*

Leander represent other orders of sexuality and of experience in general. But while Foucault sees the other orders of the heteroclite as possible, within the poem they are possible only at the level of art – that is, they may be represented in the temple and in the epyllion, but the lovers themselves have no access to these sexual options the pictures depict.

That many things are impossible for humans is one of the main themes in the poem, which as Claude J. Summers has pointed out, focuses on 'the limits of human power.'[47] These limits are most explicitly treated in both of the narratives in *Hero and Leander* in which gods are characters. These narratives are usually called digressions or inset narratives. The latter term is better than the former, but both suggest a separation, whereas I think both are connected to the story of the young lovers in important ways: Jane Adamson notes that 'each inset tale of sexual action becomes a gloss on the others. Hero's and Leander's strivings are assimilated to, not distinguished from, those Marlowe sees in every aspect of nature.'[48] It is important for Marlowe to present the contrast between human and divine sexuality in action. What is more, I would argue that rather than make a hierarchical division of the poem into the story of Hero and Leander (the main narrative) and the stories of Mercury and Neptune (the inset narratives or subplots), we should consider the stories as connected thematically rather than narratively. We should see Marlowe as having consciously refused either to unify the poem around the story of Hero and Leander or to relegate the other stories to minor status, and we can connect this to the fact that the poem does not reach the expected ending. In their anomalous narrative status, the two stories of divine sexuality in *Hero and Leander* offer concrete examples of Marlowe's conflation of end-directed narrative and end-directed sexuality.

Both mythological stories are about attempts by the gods to seduce humans. The focus on seduction obviously connects these stories with the story of Hero and Leander, but there is an important difference. While Leander attempts to seduce Hero with words, the preferred method of the gods is ultimately to seduce through gifts. In the first story, for example, Mercury lusts after a country maiden. When she runs from him, he stops her by his narrative gifts: he

>   us'd such cunning,
> As she to heare his tale, left off her running.
> Maids are not woon by brutish force and might,
> But speeches full of pleasure and delight.   (I.417–20)

It might seem that Marlowe wishes to highlight the power of discourse, but we learn that what is decisive is Mercury's granting of her request for 'A draught of flowing *Nectar* ... / Wherewith the king of Gods and men is feasted' (I.431–2). Mercury's speech is only the ostensible cause of his success; the story is really the record of a material transaction. The story of Neptune is similar in that he tries to seduce Leander through words but finally decides to give him treasure, at which point the narrator sagely comments that ''Tis wisedome to give much, a gift prevailes, / When deepe perswading Oratorie failes' (II.225–6). In both stories, then, elaborate discourse, which is to say precisely the sort of discourse in which poets specialize, is shown to be ineffective if it is not backed up by material assets.

This undermining of poetic speech is amplified in the conclusion of the tale of Mercury. The god is able to grant her request by enlisting the support of the Fates, whom Cupid compels into love with Mercury. He asks a favour of his own: the banishment of Jove and restoration of Saturn:

> They granted what he crav'd, and once againe,
> *Saturne* and *Ops* began their golden raigne.
> Murder, rape, warre, lust and trecherie,
> Were with *Jove* clos'd in *Stigian* Emperie. (I.455–8)

But 'long this blessed time continued not' (I.459), as Mercury begins to neglect the Fates, who return Jove to power and punish Mercury, who is the god of scholars, by ordaining that scholars will always be poor. One effect of this punishment is 'That *Midas* brood shall sit in Honors chaire, / To which the *Muses* sonnes are only heire' (I.475–6). The story of Mercury and the country maiden can thus be seen as an etiological tale that explains why it is that poetry does not produce results and gifts do. Marlowe presents the powerlessness of poetry as a sign of injustice on a cosmic scale – and, what is more, an injustice in which the gods themselves are complicit.

The inability of rhetoric to persuade is something that affects both gods and humans, but what is decisive for the narratives of these stories are the strictly human limits that become important. When the country maiden asks for a draught of nectar, after all, she is asking for the substance that preserves the eternal youth and life of the gods: she wishes to do away with the basic human limit imposed by mortality. This nectar was originally served to the gods by Hebe, the daughter of

Jupiter and Juno, and it is she who is mentioned by Marlowe in this tale: Mercury steals the nectar 'from *Hebe* (*Hebe, Joves* cup fil'd)' (I.434), but Jupiter replaced her by his lover Ganymede. As Ganymede had originally been human, his becoming not only immortal but also the means by which the gods maintain their immortality is the exception that proves the rule. Marlowe emphasizes Ganymede's status as an exception in the tale of Neptune, who initially takes Leander to be Ganymede – 'The lustie god imbrast him, cald him love, / And swore he never should return to *Jove*' (II.167–8) – but then realizes his mistake: 'he knew it was not *Ganimed*, / For under water he was almost dead' (II.169–70). Except in his beauty and appeal to men, Ganymede cannot serve as a precedent for Leander. In fact, that Ganymede was originally a Trojan prince and that Jupiter's neglect of Juno for him is cited by Virgil as one of the causes for her enmity to the Trojans (and we should recall that Marlowe puts a depiction of the destruction of Troy into the temple of Venus) should point out the strength of the limits placed on humans in Marlowe's poem.[49]

What is most significant about the tale as a whole is that it is Leander's mortality that is presented as the problem rather than Neptune's homo-erotic lust.[50] When Neptune accidentally wounds himself, Leander feels sorry for him and the narrator explicitly recommends a similar attitude on our part:

>   In gentle brests,
> Relenting thoughts, remorse and pittie rests.
> And who have hard hearts, and obdurat minds,
> But vicious, harebraind, and illit'rat hinds?   (II.215–18)

I am sorry to say that the answer to this seemingly rhetorical question is 'many of the critics who have written on *Hero and Leander*.' When Leander reveals his ignorance of homoeroticism, Neptune smiles and tells a story about a shepherd in love with

>   a boy so faire and so kind,
> As for his love, both earth and heaven pyn'd;
> That of the cooling river durst not drinke,
> Least water-nymphs should pull him from the brinke.   (II.195–8)

Leander, significantly presented here as a fan of narrative simplicity, interrupts 'ere halfe this tale was done' (II.201) and swims off to Hero.

More important than Leander's impatience, however, is that the tale
tells a story of human homoeroticism set in the realm of pastoral possibilities that I have called homoerotic space; as a result, same-sex sexuality is not restricted to gods after all. Bredbeck identifies the boy as
Narcissus, but it seems to me that this is wrong.[51] While an exact identification of the boy is obviously impossible, he is closer to Hylas, the
lover of Hercules, whom water-nymphs abducted because of his beauty.
In any case, the sudden opening of the poem into homoerotic space
signals to the reader that the limits placed on human sexuality – limits
carefully depicted by Marlowe throughout the poem – are not abso-
lutes. We, if not Leander, can see how different this story, and stories in
general, might be. 'Perhaps,' as M. Morgan Holmes has suggested, 'in
Marlowe's retelling and our own responses, the tale does not have to
end tragically; perhaps, the fantasy of homoerotic engagement is there
to rescue Leander from death and the story, and its readers, from history.'[52] As I see it, Holmes is suggesting that in *Hero and Leander* it is
heteroeroticism, in the service of a reproductive futurism that seeks to
ensure that history is really just repetition, that brings about the tragedy. Freed from this tyrannic repetition, both texts and readers might
live in spaces of potentiality and change.

In *Hero and Leander*, this potential is only hypothetical and is instantly
foreclosed by Leander's natatory and narrative drive. He return us to
the world of binary oppositions set up at the beginning of the poem, the
most obvious of which is female and male. The human sexual system
under which Marlowe lived and under which to a considerable extent
we live today, depends on reducing all the possible sexual differences
among people to the one difference between men and women and on
insisting that only that difference should be eroticized. Other differences, such as class or race, to name only two, are not supposed to signify,
and sameness, itself reduced to the supposed sameness of one woman
with another woman or of one man with another man, can signify only
at the price of not being eroticized. We can see this in the way that the
poem's initial difference (the difference between Sestos and Abydos or,
in larger terms, between Europe and Asia, a highly significant opposition then as now) is collapsed into the difference between Hero and
Leander and turns out not to make any real difference at all: it is the
shared sea rather than the separate cities that turns out to be decisive in
the poem. Many love stories stress the similarity of the lovers (except,
of course, for the requisite difference of their genders), but after establishing the setting of his poem, Marlowe has two long descriptions of

Hero and Leander that stress their differences. These descriptions depend on a further opposition – the one between nature and art that was so frequently discussed in the Renaissance – but as we shall see, Marlowe complicates this opposition as well.

The ostensible point of the descriptions is to establish how beautiful the two lovers are, but the methods employed are very different. With Hero, Marlowe concentrates on the semiotic goldmine that is her clothing. She wears a long dress, covered in transparent fabric, which features the memorable combination of purple, gold, blue, green, and red. She also wears a wreath, a veil that goes to the ground, necklaces, and buskins of coral, pearl, and gold. I want to begin my examination of Hero's outfit by making the point that the description is not a description of Hero at all but rather a description of clothes and jewellery. It should be obvious that any humanoid figure wearing that outfit would look like Hero and would presumably be equally attractive. Marlowe begins by saying that Hero's beauty led Apollo to offer 'his burning throne, / Where she should sit for men to gaze upon' (I.7–8), but from the description itself it would appear that they would be gazing not at a woman but at a dizzying sartorial spectacle. Feminine beauty is thus initially presented not as an essence but as something that is created and assembled. It recalls Miller's discussion of homosexuality, mentioned in the preface, as something not only that is recognizable through signs but that may even consist solely of signs. At this point in the poem, Hero resembles the 'cloathed image' that is Pandora at the beginning of *The Woman in the Moone*, and like that image, Hero will turn out to be situated somewhere between nature and art.

From my summary of the description it would appear that Hero is associated only with art, with products made by humans, but the description is actually more complex. As Haber notes, in this passage 'reality is conflated with rhetoric, the natural is confounded with the artificial, and the image seems to displace the thing itself.'[53] In other words, rather than placing Hero on one side or another of a clear line between nature and art, Marlowe suggests that this binary – and, to some extent, binaries in general – cannot be maintained. In the description of her veil, for instance, art is clearly paramount: 'Her vaile was artificiall flowers and leaves, / Whose workmanship both man and beast deceaves' (I.19–20). Here, art imitates and surpasses nature. What is more, as Fred Tromly points out, this is 'a slyly self-referential passage [which] sets forth the power of art to attract and misdirect desire.'[54] I would rephrase this statement to say that art here creates desire and that art itself is premised on deception. Our sense of this deception is increased by Marlowe's focus on the veil. As Cindy L. Carlson has remarked, not only does the costume as a whole conceal the body of the person wearing it, it could also lead us to be unsure of what kind of body is behind it: 'Hero's body, heavily attired in kirtle, sleeves, buskins, and veil is, itself, in transvestic disguise. Only the veil reads as unambiguously feminine attire.'[55] There are thus two possible levels of deception: 'both man and beast' may take the veil's depictions as real flowers and leaves, and while people might assume anyone wearing a veil to be female, the veil may hide a male body.

The deception is increased by what follows the description of the veil:

> Many would praise the sweet smell as she past,
> When t'was the odour which her breath foorth cast.
> And there for honie, bees have sought in vaine,
> And beat from thence, have lighted there againe.   (I.21–4)

Here, it is not the clothing that is deceptive but rather the product of her own body. Hero is, it turns out, naturally artificial. The other thing that is naturally artificial in the passage is of course honey, a natural product. In taking her breath for honey, then, the bees are merely confusing one artificially produced substance for another. This understanding of the reference to honey is underscored by the description of Hero's buskins, which are 'of shels all silvered' (I.31) and 'brancht with blushing corall' (I.32); on the buskins 'sparrowes pearcht, of hollow pearle and gold' (I.33). Like honey, shells, coral, and pearls are all natural products. What is more, as we have just learnt that bees swarm around Hero, it does not seem surprising that sparrows would as well but Marlowe instantly undeceives us by telling us that the sparrows are themselves artificial. The picture of Hero teaches us two crucial lessons: one on the difficulty of distinguishing between the natural and the artificial and one on how easily desire may mistake its object.

While Hero is elaborately dressed, Leander is gloriously naked. Marlowe's move from clothing to nakedness might seem to indicate the desired progress of seduction, but in that case it is notable that the two descriptions could be read together as confirming our suspicion that the female veil might hide a male body. As well, Leander's nakedness might seem to obviate any hermeneutic difficulties, but even here desire is complicated, and not in the way one might expect. By way of showing us how desirable Leander is, Marlowe lists those who desire him: Cynthia, 'wilde *Hippolitus*' (I.77), 'the rudest paisant' (I.79), and 'The barbarous *Thratian* soldier moov'd with nought' (I.81). Leaving aside Cynthia, whose lust, in any case, is transgressive because of her chastity, we might think that what makes the other examples of lust here transgressive is their homoeroticism, but Marlowe's point is actually that these are people who are supposed to be immune to lust. In fact, their desire for Leander has a softening effect on them: Hyppolitus becomes 'Enamoured' (I.78), the peasant 'melt[s]' (I.79), and the soldier 'Was moov'd with him, and for his favour sought' (I.82). Male sexual desire for other men is presented as a civilizing force, and this is emphasized by the fact that Marlowe has already said that Leander's 'bodie was as straight as *Circes* wand' (I.61). This wand turned men into beasts, but homoeroticism here makes men less like beasts. As we shall see, male desire for sex with women is not so favourably presented.

Even in this passage, however, Marlowe reminds us of the limits on humans. When he writes that '*Jove* might have sipt out *Nectar* from his hand' (I.62), he implicitly compares Leander to Ganymede, but what follows makes it clear that Ganymede is, once again, the only exception to the limits placed on humanity:

> Even as delicious meat is to the tast,
> So was his necke in touching, and surpast
> The white of *Pelops* shoulder.   (I.63–5)

The synaesthesia is erotic, but the idea of Leander as something to be literally rather than figuratively eaten up or consumed reminds us of the powerlessness of humans against the gods, especially given the move from drinking in line 62 to eating in line 63. The idea of eating is underlined by the reference to Pelops, whose shoulder was so white because it was made of ivory.[56] This prosthesis replaced the original shoulder, which was eaten by the gods when Tantalus, Pelops's own father, served him as food. The story as a whole is a story of hubris and could be said to serve as a warning. Furthermore, the ivory's status as both natural and artificial (in that it is a prosthesis), reminds us of the confusion of nature and art in the description of Hero.

The crucial point about human homoeroticism in this passage comes when Marlowe says about Leander that 'Some thought he was a maid in mans attire, / For in his lookes were all that men desire' (I.83–4). This statement has often been misinterpreted as meaning that Leander looked like a woman; the error has spawned a discourse of its own.[57] The couplet actually means that, because men find Leander desirable, they can see him only as a woman (and, in any case, Leander is not attired). Bredbeck makes the point well when he says that Leander 'is ... a man in maid's attire: a masculine body anatomized and substantiated through the typically feminine rhetoric of the Renaissance blazon.'[58] In other words, the femininity here is not in Leander's appearance but rather in the conventional understanding of male desire: like the veil, the ability to inspire lust in men is read as indicating femininity even when there is a male body behind it. The critics are not the only ones to find this concept baffling: Leander's response to Neptune's seduction is to say 'You are deceav'd, I am no woman I' (II.192). Our sense of Leander's spectacular dimness in assuming that the god who has swum all around his naked body is unaware of his sex is heightened by the fact that, apart from Cynthia and, of course, Hero, only men find Leander desirable. That he should be unable to understand this simple point – should, in fact, be seemingly unaware of the very existence of homoeroticism – is one of the best jokes in *Hero and Leander*.

Leander's stupidity is also comic in the first scene with Hero. Throughout this scene, Marlowe stresses both the inexperience of the lovers and the extent to which the sexual system under which they live is actually an obstacle to sex. We see Hero, for instance, forced by the rules of feminine propriety to appear demure and coy, as when she leaves him and 'would have turn'd againe, but was afrayd, / In offering parlie, to be counted light' (II.8–9). Instead, she drops her fan in the hope that this will lead Leander to follow her, but 'He being a novice, knew not what she meant, / But stayd, and after her a letter sent' (II.13– 14). Leander's ignorance of this transparent stratagem is humorous, but there are two serious points to be made here. For one, while the effect of this passage and of much else in *Hero and Leander* is to demonstrate that Leander is simply simple, Hero emerges as a more sympathetic character, and Marlowe, in a way that may seem surprising to those who feel that he has little sympathy for or interest in women, shows that the rules of the sexual system restrict women more than men. Hero is prevented from achieving her desires not by anything on her part resembling Leander's mental incapacity, but by ideas about how maidens should behave. The second serious point made in this passage is that in the substitution of a text for a desired human contact we can see the larger point that language is not necessarily teleological and, in fact, as it does here, may interfere with the desired teleology.

In Leander's long and elaborate seduction speeches, we see a different sort of interference with the goal of having sex. Marlowe gives us a dizzying succession of arguments – many obviously specious, as when he urges her to compare virginity and marriage in order to make an informed decision (I.262–4) – and images, many obviously poorly thought out, as when he says 'Who builds a pallace and rams up the gate, / Shall see it ruinous and desolate' (I.239–40). Leander has learnt the form of rhetorical argument so prized in the Renaissance, but he is unable to supply a cogent content. Of course, it does not matter anyway and, as Marlowe's summary makes clear, the irrelevance of Leander's complicated rhetoric is precisely the point: 'These arguments he us'de, and many more, / Wherewith she yeelded, that was woon before' (I.329–30). This couplet suggests that elaborate rhetoric may not lead anywhere. Hero is already in love with Leander, already eager to have sex with him, so all the verbal strategies that were intended to be productive have been a waste of time from the point of view of the characters themselves. From our point of view, however, these speeches have not been a waste of time at all, as the experience of reading them has given us pleasure: the generally solitary and unproductive pleasure of the text. Marlowe's separation of the pleasure language can give from the result it is intended to produce registers a protest against the calculation of use value that is part of the reproductive metaphor.

Leander refers to reproduction in his seduction speech, although his aim is presumably not to seduce Hero by suggesting that sex with him might lead to pregnancy:

> treasure is abus'de,
> When misers keepe it; being put to lone,
> In time it will returne us two for one.   (I.234–6)

As so often, Leander's ineptitude is comic, but his equation of Hero's hymen with treasure and his belief that money should be invested and bring a return conflates sexuality and economics in a way that is only too familiar. The equation has already been made in the poem's most famous passage, in which Marlowe tells us, 'It lies not in our power to love, or hate, / For will in us is over-rul'd by fate' (I.167–8). These ten lines, ending with the rhetorical question 'Who ever lov'd, that lov'd not at first sight?' (I.176), have often been cited out of context either as an example of Marlowe's fatalism or as a romantic statement or as both, but I see them as a grim examination of how sexuality is reduced to being merely a financial activity and, like other financial activities, subject to control. Arguing that the poem is more like Marlowe's plays than has usually been thought, Robert A. Logan says that 'Marlowe's pervasive interest in the effects of power unifies individual passages as well as the whole of *Hero and Leander*,' and I would add that power in the poem is presented primarily as power over sexual expression.[59]

As the opening couplet of this passage suggests, fate is stronger than will, but Marlowe goes on to define what he means by fate in a way that reveals he is not talking about the supernatural:

> When two are stript, long ere the course begin,
> We wish that one should loose, the other win.
> And one especiallie doe we affect,
> Of two gold Ingots, like in each respect.   (I.169–72)

The lines draw attention to our status as voyeurs: readers are judges, not lovers. The romantic couple is first presented as two naked athletes, an image that has an erotic charge, although the charge is homoerotic, as the athletes can only be two men. The eroticism is vitiated, if not by the idea that love is a spectator sport (as readers would hardly have made it this far into the poem without liking to watch), then by the idea that love is a competition in which there is a winner and a loser. Worse follows: the two runners become bars of gold. While two naked people are different – are, in fact, more different to the sight than two clothed people – bars of gold really are identical. What is more, our picking one of the athletes could be explained by a preference for a particular body type or colouring (for example), but in preferring one ingot to another, our judgment is revealed to be entirely arbitrary. Marlowe presents us with the most basic of narratives: we pick one of two objects and judge it to be a winner. This ultimately pointless narrative is revealed to be our basic narrative paradigm, even in love.

The crucial movement in this passage is not the narrative movement from the contest to the outcome that we expect but rather the collapse of the human into the monetary. What is important about people and about the things they do is what their use is and, ultimately, what financial return they bring. Leander reveals, or betrays, his awareness of this fact at various points in his seduction speeches, which are a verbal investment intended to bring about a sexual profit. In the example of the athletes, both participants were male, but in the poem itself it is the woman who is made to pay (in both senses). As Summers argues, one of the major themes of *Hero and Leander* is 'the inequities of a gender system that commodifies women.'[60] And it is this commodification that Marlowe focuses on at the end of the poem when Hero stands naked in front of Leander: 'Whence his admiring eyes more pleasure tooke, / Than *Dis*, on heapes of gold fixing his looke' (II.325–6). In having sex with Leander, Hero has attained neither the happy ending of one kind of love narrative nor the tragic ending of another kind (and of the standard version of the narrative of Hero and Leander) but has succeeded only in becoming the asset that is indispensable to the financial narrative that underwrites all other narratives. This, Marlowe says, is the point to which insistence on use and production and reproduction leads.

One sign of the poem's decisive turn from romance to finance is Marlowe's pairing of the reference to Dis, king of the underworld, with an explicit mention of the underworld itself. He tells us that the advancing day

> mockt ougly night,
> Till she o'recome with anguish, shame, and rage,
> Dang'd downe to hell her loathsome carriage.   (I.332–4)

This completes the process begun when Leander first touched Hero and

> The aire with sparkes of living fire was spangled,
> And night deep drencht in mystie *Acheron*,
> Heav'd up her head, and halfe the world upon,
> Breath'd darknesse forth (darke night is *Cupids* day).   (I.188–91)

Cupid's metaphorical day, so beautifully described, has given way to the literal day in which assets can be seen and counted and the wiseness of sexual investments can be assessed. As W.L. Godshalk remarks, 'Something more important than night has died here.'[61] With the return of night to hell, Marlowe's poem ends. While the lovers are still alive, it seems clear that the real tragedy has already occurred.

However, it could all have been different. In the sex scenes, Hero discovers another way of being sexual, one which offers an alternative to the financial mode, although it is unfortunately too late. Up to this point, Marlowe has depicted Hero as held back by maidenly decorum. In the sex scene itself, however, just as Marlowe depicts a bolder and more active Hero, he also shows that the rules preventing women from acting on their sexual desires are perhaps prudent, as love here is presented not as a race or a financial transaction but as a fight to the death:

> the truce was broke, and she alas,
> (Poore sillie maiden) at his mercie was.
> Love is not full of pittie (as men say)
> But deaffe and cruel where he meanes to pray.   (II.285–8)

In this scene, the war between the sexes appears to be literal rather than metaphorical. When Marlowe says 'Treason was in her thought, / And cunningly to yeeld her selfe she sought' (I.293–4), the idea of treason should carry its full weight, although Hero is betraying only herself. The yielding Marlowe mentions has both the meaning of acceding to a sexual advance and of declaring a surrender. In these lines, and in the poem's conclusion more generally, we see Hero as the defenceless victim of male sexual aggression and, when Leander looks at her the next morning, he does so with the gaze of a conqueror.

I want to conclude by looking at two passages in the sex scene: the simile of the bird and the description of Hero's striving. Here is the description of Hero:

> She trembling strove, this strife of her (like that
> Which made the world) another world begat,
> Of unknowne joy.   (II.291–3)

And here is the bird simile:

> Even as a bird, which in our hands we wring
> Foorth plungeth, and oft flutters with her wing.   (II.289–90)

Any discussion of these lines is complicated by questions about their order. In the original order, after 'gentle parlie did the truce obtaine' (II.278), we are told of Hero's striving; the passage as a whole ends with the bird simile. In this case, the word 'truce' remains metaphorical and both the literalization of the war between the sexes – the reference to breaking the truce, for instance – and the simile of the bird present a sad ending to Hero's brief moment of bliss. In the revised order in which the poem was first printed (and this order is still standard today), the

literalization of the metaphor of the truce and the simile of the bird pre-
cede the description of Hero's pleasure and thus the moment of a radical
revision of sexuality and, especially, of women's place within it, is over
before it starts. It has been argued that the revised order makes better
sense, but Haber has intriguingly suggested that 'the original order could
more effectively be defended as making nonsense.'[62] I take this to mean
that the original order gives us, not the 'Poore sillie maiden' who is such
a familiar figure, but a woman who is, however temporarily, independent and powerful and thus socially and literarily incomprehensible.

For my purposes, Marlowe's description of Hero's movements during sex is the most important passage in the poem. When Marlowe
describes Hero's creation using the verb 'begat,' he invokes the reproductive metaphor, but it is clear from the context that this is creation
without procreation and that the result is pleasure rather than use. The
joy that cannot be known is a joy that cannot be quantified or commodi-
fied; to use Barthes's terms, this is the text of bliss. The fact that this joy,
like the other periods of happiness in *Hero and Leander*, is of short
duration should not qualify our sense of Hero's achievement. And if we
are to agree with David Lee Miller that the bird image is a reference to
the story of Philomel, then this too, however depressing, is a story of
woman as artist.[63] I am claiming not that Hero is victorious, but rather
that Marlowe uses her to gesture towards other sexual and literary possibilities. That they are so decisively foreclosed by the conclusion of
Hero and Leander is part of his point. Marlowe emphasizes this point by
his use of chiasmus. The opening descriptions appear to separate Hero
and Leander on opposite sides of the difference between art and nature.
Indeed, Leander, naked and forthright about his desires, seems the very
picture of nature, while Hero, weighed down by her bizarre costume
and by the rules governing female behaviour, can appear only as linked
to culture, if not to art in the strict sense. At the end, however, it is
Leander who is associated with the culture imperative to reproduce, to
turn any situation into a narrative leading to profit (and thus to loss for
someone else). It is Hero who moves, if only for a short time, into the
realm of pure pleasure.

III

The kind of fetishistic looking that ends *Hero and Leander* dominates
Marston's *The Metamorphosis of Pigmalions Image* throughout. This poem
first appeared in 1598 in a volume that included a series of satires called

'The Scourge of Villanie,' and as a rule critical discussions of the poem have focused on the poem's situation somewhere between the genre of the epyllion and the genre of the satire.[64] Recent critics have tended to assume that the poem is of mixed genre and have concentrated on discerning what the targets of its satire are. For Jim Ellis, Marston 'is satirizing those who do not admit that sexual desire is part of the pleasure of reading.'[65] In her analysis, Lynn Enterline suggests that 'what draws the satirist's fire is not merely that the Petrarchan poet loves his own images more than he loves his mistress, but that he loves what he sees *of himself* in those images.'[66] The situation is complicated by the fact that Marston prefaces and follows the poem with references to it that function as ways of interpreting it. I shall deal with these paratexts later, but I would like to say at the outset that my concern is not to decide Marston's authorial intentions.[67] Instead, I follow most of the poem's recent critics in considering *The Metamorphosis of Pigmalions Image* as a text about textuality and about the representation of sexual desire.

This focus on the connections between sexuality and textuality is inherent in the story of Pygmalion, which Marston derived from Ovid. As Keach remarks, 'the interrelationship of artistic and erotic imagination ... stands at the centre of Ovid's story.'[68] And by focusing on description to a much greater extent than Ovid did, Marston makes his version of the story a fully fledged ecphrasis, a kind of poetry, as Gordon Braden reminds us, that is often connected to sexuality.[69] Enterline says that 'Marston, like both Ovid and Petrarch before him, is drawn to the rhetorical dimensions of the story and turns it into a provocatively eroticized commentary on his own scene of writing';[70] I would qualify her comment only by saying that it is not so much that the commentary becomes erotic but rather that in *The Metamorphosis of Pigmalions Image* writing itself is ultimately indistinguishable from eroticism. I would connect Marston's insistence on a sexual textuality with his insistence on the power of rhetoric: the poem takes place in a world characterized by linguistic determinism, something that raises the questions of the purpose and teleology of literature with which I have been concerned throughout this chapter. Marston's position on these matters is clear from the poem's dedication to 'The worlds mightie monarch, Good Opinion.'[71] As he goes on to say, Good Opinion not only forms the basis for judgments but also is the force 'by whom all things are that that they are' (49).

In the poem that follows the prose dedication, Marston depicts Good Opinion as the supreme rhetorician: 'Thou moouing Orator, whose

powrefull breath / Swaies all mens iudgements' (4–5). But if Good
Opinion's power depends on the power of rhetoric, then Marston can
challenge it with his own rhetoric. Although he vows to 'sing an Hymne
in honor of thy name' (11) if his poems are successful, if they are not,
he threatens

> that all the World shall ken
> How partiall thou art in Honours giuing:
> Crowning the shade, the substance praise depriuing.   (16–18)

This is precisely the distinction Marston makes in the first stanza of the
poem itself when he says that Pygmalion shunned women until 'Loue
at length forc'd him to know his fate, / And loue the shade, whose
substance he did hate' (1.5–6). In both passages, Marston makes distinctions (between appearance and reality in the dedicatory poem, between artistic representation and the thing represented or, in linguistic
terms, between signifier and signified) that are familiar to us, but the
general tendency of the poem is to blur these distinctions: that is, Good
Opinion's error is not only Pygmalion's error as well, but also our own.
The Metamorphosis of Pigmalions Image takes place in a world where
there is only phenomenology and no epistemology, and as a result teleology cannot operate: there is nothing to which the words of the poem
can lead.

Of course, my last sentence is an exaggeration. In the poem to his
mistress (and pointedly not to his muse, whom he describes as 'dulled'
[4]) that immediately precedes *The Metamorphosis of Pigmalions Image*
Marston praises her power:

> Thy fauours like *Promethean* sacred fire,
> In dead, and dull conceit can life inspire.
> Or like that rare and rich Elixar stone,
> Can turne to gold, leaden inuention.   (7–10)

In the first couplet, Marston is not the artificer but instead the raw
material or, in the terms of the Pygmalion story itself, the work of art
awaiting the breath of life, while his mistress is the 'sacred fire' of
poetic inspiration. In the second couplet, while Marston remains inert,
the mistress becomes a stone like the statue itself, but one that is productive, and, furthermore, is productive in a financial sense.[72] His
mistress here is the power that acquires Good Opinion and turns the

thoughts that fill a poet's mind into marketable commodities. In this formulation, textual production is not like reproduction but like alchemy, and Marston eliminates the middle term in the equation: texts = children = assets. He presents money rather than offspring as the transcendental signifier in the world of his book, as that which shows that the expense of effort was worthwhile after all. In this, we could say that Marston resembles Leander.

As it turns out, however, the idea that thoughts – conceits – can take material form is the dominant one in the poem, and money does not play a role in *The Metamorphosis of Pigmalions Image* itself. This is to say not that Marston abandons all teleology but, as he goes on to say in the poem to his mistress, that he adopts a strictly personal one:

> And as thou read'st, (Faire) take compassion,
> Force me not enuie my *Pigmalion*.
> Then when thy kindnes grants me such sweet blisse,
> I'le gladly write thy metamorphosis.   (13–16)

The aim of the poem, then, is the familiar one of seducing the woman the poet desires, and one meaning of the word metamorphosis in this passage is the orgasm that the poet will write with his penis / pen. What is most important, however, is that in this passage the word *metamorphosis* also means the process by which a human being becomes a work of art – in other words, Marston uses the word to mean exactly the opposite of what it means in the Ovidian original. In writing about how an artistic creation turned into a woman, Marston will turn a woman into an artistic creation. Although this passage indicates that the poem's *telos* is sexual activity, it also gestures towards other possibilities. Perhaps the work of art is not the means by which an aim is achieved but rather the aim itself: both the beginning and ending of an entirely circular process.

The themes I have been discussing in the preliminary paratexts also appear in the poem that follows *The Metamorphosis of Pigmalions Image* and that is unsurprisingly called 'The Authour in prayse of his *precedent Poem*.' This is the poem in which Marston attacks his epyllion and pronounces that the joke is on us if we took it seriously as a work of literature. Critics have tended to take this poem (and the similar disclaimers in the sixth satire of 'The Scourge of Villanie') at face value, which seems an odd reaction to the words of a satirist. In any case, in the poem that follows the epyllion Marston, employing a martial metaphor, speaks of the poem's stanzas as 'like odd bands / Of voluntaries and mercenarians' (17–18): although they are 'rich bedight' (20), 'Glittering' (21), and dressed in 'pleasing sutes' (22),

> Yet puffie as Dutch hose they are within,
> Faint, and white liuer'd, as our gallants bin:
> Patch'd like a beggars cloake.   (23–5)

Although the stanzas look promising, they will not stand and fight: here, as so often, Marston draws attention to the difference between shade and substance. On the other hand, the difference between the fancy new clothes of the soldiers and the 'beggars cloake' could be at once the difference between appearance and reality and the beginning and ending of the narrative, familiar from so many Renaissance texts, of the soldier returned from the wars and cast adrift in an uncaring society.

A similar ambiguity related to narrative occurs just after this point in 'The Authour in prayse of his *precedent Poem*' when Marston summarizes the epyllion by saying 'And in the end, (the end of loue I wot) / *Pigmalion* hath a iolly boy begot' (27–8). This couplet does accurately summarize Marston's poem, which ends with a reference to Pygmalion and Galatea's daughter Paphos, but in the *Metamorphoses* itself she is not the end of anything but instead serves merely as the transition to her son, of whom Ovid says 'si sine prole fuisset, / inter felices Cinyras potuit haberi' (if he had been without offspring, Cinyras could have been held to be among the blessed; X.298–9).[73] Cinyras, of course, was the lover of his daughter Myrrha and thus the father and grandfather of Adonis. In other words, the child that results from Pygmalion's love for his statue is best known as the beginning of two more stories – and, in fact, two of the most famous stories of the *Metamorphoses*, both of which, in very different ways, focus on reproduction – and Marston's presentation of this child as the end of the narrative is an obvious falsehood. Thus, Marston emphasizes the extent to which his poem can be seen as teleological not only by referring to Pygmalion's child, but also by punning on the meanings of the word 'end,' particularly in the phrase 'the end of loue,' which could mean either the conclusion of love (and, for that matter, of his poem) or the purpose of love. In following his epyllion with a poem that raises the questions of teleology, interpretation, and the distinction between shade and substance, Marston undermines the possibility that the epyllion really ends at all.

As I have pointed out, Marston ends the first stanza of the poem by making one of the poem's crucial distinctions when he tells us that Love forced Pygmalion to 'loue the shade, whose substance he did hate.' The substance is 'woman-kinde' (1.3), as he knows 'their want, and mens perfection' (1.4), but what is most important about Marston's formulation here is that he does not say that Pygmalion eventually learnt to love the substance as well; instead, he refuses the theory that the beauty one sees leads one to appreciate that person's inner qualities. Both the poem and its protagonist will stay on the surface. When Marston tells us in the second stanza that Pygmalion made

> So faire an Image of a Womans feature,
> That neuer yet proudest mortalitie
> Could show so rare and beautious a creature,   (2.2–4)

and in the third that Pygmalion 'thought that Nature nere produc'd such fairenes' (3.3), it seems clear that he is correct. Although the statue he creates changes from being a work of art to being a human being, I would argue that even when Pygmalion is united at the end of the poem with the woman he has created his focus is still on the work of art.

One implication of this statement is that since Pygmalion is, of course, the maker of the work of art, his focus is on himself rather than being directed outwards. Marston draws our attention to this by the implicit comparison he sets up between himself and Pygmalion early in the poem. After the passage I quoted above, which says that the statue's beauty surpasses any that 'mortalitie' could produce, Marston makes an important exception: 'Vnlesse my Mistres all-excelling face, / Which giues to beautie, beauties onely grace' (2.5–6). In these lines (which are parenthetical in the original), Marston reiterates the teleology he mentioned in the dedicatory poem to his mistress and thus distinguishes himself from the subject of his poem, who turns to art as part of his retreat from humans. Marston then goes on to tell us that Pygmalion 'was amazed at the wondrous rarenesse / Of his owne workmanships perfection' (3.1–2) and that he 'was enamored / On that fayre Image himselfe portraied' (3.5–6). As Brown notes, the word 'himselfe' has an 'uncertain function' here: it could mean either that he himself made the image or that in making the image he portrayed himself; what is more, the preposition 'On' has an 'arresting physicality.'[74] That is, Pygmalion is enamoured on the image both in the sense of being in love with it and in the sense of being on top of it. Brown says that the poem 'is, among other things, a poem about masturbation,' and in this respect as well Pygmalion is removed from teleology.[75] At least at this point in the poem, his sexuality is really directed only towards himself and not to any socially recuperable end.

The extent to which Pygmalion's love for the statue is really self-love is the subject of much of Marston's humour. For instance, when Pygmalion is gazing at the beauty of his sculpture early in the poem, he begins to think that it is alive: 'He thought he saw the blood run through the vaine / And leape, and swell' (5.1–2). Marston is able to emphasize that Pygmalion is in error by the visual pun of 'vaine' (at once 'vein' and 'vain'), but what is most noticeable about this passage is that it suggests that when Pygmalion looks at his statue he is really looking at his penis, since the lines offer an unmistakable description of tumescence. Later in the poem, Marston compares Pygmalion's love for his statue to idolatry:

Looke how the peeuish Papists crouch, and kneele
To some dum Idoll with their offering,
As if a senceles carued stone could feele,   (14.1–3)

Significantly, we are told that the stone of which the idol is made is not only 'senceles' but also 'carued': Marston draws attention to the complicity of idolaters in their own error. This point is most often made in *The Metamorphosis of Pigmalions Image* by the frequent use of the word 'conceit': for instance, when Marston says that to Pygmalion 'no lips did seeme so faire / In his conceit' (7.1–2), he means both 'in his mind' and 'in the image that he created.' The story of Pygmalion seems to tell of how art can become nature, but in Marston's hands it is chiefly the story of how art replaces nature: art is something that traps the artist in his own 'conceit.'

Of course, the narrator himself is guilty of precisely this error. While he mocks Pygmalion for thinking that by kissing and fondling his statue 'he might procure the loue / Of his dull Image, which no plaints coulde moue' (13.5–6), since the statue is immune to rhetoric, to the elaborate language of seduction in which some poets specialize, Pygmalion does at least manage to have sex with his statue. And while the narrator generally tries to present himself as a somewhat cynical and detached figure, not unlike the narrator of *Hero and Leander*, there is an unmistakable wistfulness to his asides, as, for instance, when he says, after his description of Pygmalion staring at the statue's crotch,

'O that my Mistres were an Image too, / That I might blameles her per-
fections view' (11.5–6). By the end of the poem it is clear that Pygmalion
is a more successful lover than the narrator, and a more successful artist
as well. I think that it is to stress the latter point that Marston goes out
of his way to criticize his poem, not only in 'The Authour in prayse of
his *precedent Poem*,' as I have shown, but also in the sixth satire in 'The
Scourge of Villanie,' in which he describes *The Metamorphosis of Pigmalions
Image* as 'nastie stuffe' (7) and 'maggot-tainted lewd corruption' (8). I
would say, however, that the poem does not fail on moral grounds –
nor, indeed, on aesthetic ones – but rather on rhetorical grounds: for the
narrator, *The Metamorphosis of Pigmalions Image* fails to become teleological in a way that helps him.

The crucial point at which the relative positions of Pygmalion and
the narrator as artist become clear occurs when Pygmalion undresses:
'straight he strips him naked quite, / That in the bedde he might haue
more delight' (25.5–6). These lines seem to be the prelude to masturbation, which itself (at least in the poem) could be said to be a question of
conceit or the shadow rather than the substance of sexuality. As well, in
being naked, Pygmalion presents himself to our gaze just as the statue
has been presented to his gaze. But as Pygmalion's apostrophe makes
clear, the statue is no longer naked: 'Sweet sheetes, he sayes, which
nowe doe couer, / The Idol of my soule' (26.1–2). As Enterline notes,
these 'sheetes' are simultaneously the bedclothes and the paper on
which the poem is written and published.[76] Another way to paraphrase
this ambiguity is to say that the sheets simultaneously reveal and conceal: the bedclothes hide the naked bodies, but the poem narrates their
embraces. This, at any rate, is what Marston has seemed to promise us,
but from this point on in *The Metamorphosis of Pigmalions Image* the
sheets that are real in the fictional world become more important – more
powerful – than the sheets that are real in the real world. Conceit, that
is, becomes reality, and shadow becomes substance; or, to put it another
way, the work of art becomes real both in the story of Pygmalion and in
Marston's poem about Pygmalion.

The narrator's acknowledgement of this change comes directly after
he tells us that Pygmalion and his statue 'dally, kisse, embrace together'
(27.5) or, in other words, that the statue has become a woman:

Yet all's conceit. But shadow of that blisse
Which now my Muse striues sweetly to display
In this my wondrous metamorphosis.   (28.1–3)

At first, Marston appears to be saying that the embraces themselves are 'conceit' in the sense, now familiar to us from the poem, of being only in Pygmalion's head. It immediately becomes clear, however, that conceit in this case refers to the poem itself. The 'blisse' of the lovers is real, and it is Marston's poem that is only a shadow. Furthermore, I think we should see the phrase 'wondrous metamorphosis' as ambiguous. On the most obvious level, the metamorphosis is the transformation of a statue into a woman, but to me the possessive pronoun suggests that we can also see it as the transformation of Ovid's poem into Marston's and as the narrator's own tumescence, a tumescence that is pointless, unlike Pygmalion's.[77] The characterization of the muse as sweetly striving – words that recall Marlowe's 'She trembling strove' – call attention to the vast difference between erotic and literary effort in this case, in which only the former will produce issue.

A few stanzas later, the narrator makes the last of his references to his own desires and returns to his idle erection:

Had I my Loue in such a wished state
As was afforded to *Pigmalion*,
Though flinty hard, of her you soone should see
As strange a transformation wrought by me.   (32.3–6)

Using the well-established Petrarchan metaphor according to which the mistress is hard, the narrator hopes that the poem will soften her, but in context the transformation from hard to soft seems more accurately to foreshadow his lack of erotic success. Significantly, the narrator describes Pygmalion as at first apprehensive that the transformation of his statue is only a dream before realizing that she touches him and kisses him: 'He's well assur'd no faire imagery / Could yeeld such pleasing, loues felicity' (31.5–6). The statue is no longer imagery but rather it has become a woman; on the other hand, the poem's own 'faire imagery' remains exactly that and does not yield any felicity.[78] To return to Karmen MacKendrick's concept of the counterpleasure, the poem's happy ending is now shown to be something 'so absurdly difficult in attainment that we must sometimes suspect that the pleasure comes in the intensity of the challenge itself.'[79] In the case of *The Metamorphosis of Pigmalions Image*, however, the pleasure is all ours and the difficulty all Marston's.

Drawing on Freud's theory of forepleasure, which was also the origin of MacKendrick's theory, Enterline comments on the way in which the poem does not achieve consummation: 'Integral to the poem's temporality of forepleasure – its coy allusion to and evasion of the act of intercourse – the mute, "senceless" statue never comes alive.'[80] That is, Marston never narrates the transformation itself. Neither does he narrate the sexual act, and his refusal to do so is, in fact, the subject of several of the poem's last stanzas. Speaking scornfully of 'the wanton itching eare' (33.1) of the person hearing the poem (an image that becomes the 'gaping eares that swallow vp my lines' [38.2] – voracious orifices indeed), he refers to sex as 'that, which is not fit reporting' (35.6). He then performs the depressing, and depressingly familiar, bait and switch, in which we hoped to read about sex but instead find ourselves reading about reproduction. Before I also turn to reproduction, I want to comment on Marston's refusal to write explicitly about sex (he says of the reader, 'Let him conceit but what himselfe would doe' [34.1], so that sex is relegated to the imagination, just as Pygmalion's imagination becomes reality). To some extent, Marston's decision might have been motivated by prudence (although if this is the case, his caution was unsuccessful, as *The Metamorphosis of Pigmalions Image* was banned and burned with *Hero and Leander* in the year in which it was published), but his refusal to narrate sex is also, I think, a way to compel readers to consider the extent to which the sexual act is not the telos of narratives but only a way to produce reproduction. In disappointing the prurience he has so skilfully aroused, Marston might be leading us to ask ourselves how happy we are with the expectation that narratives should lead to reproduction. Perhaps, after all, masturbation is better.

Fittingly, Marston's turn towards reproduction is accomplished in a notably odd way. He begins with an extended metaphor that describes Pygmalion's joy:

> Doe but conceiue a Mothers passing gladnes,
> (After that death her onely sonne hath seazed
> And ouerwhelm'd her soule with endlesse sadnes)
> When that she sees him gin for to be raised
> From out his deadly swoune to life againe.   (30.1–5)

Unlike most metaphors, which explain something by producing an example that is easier to understand (comparing a fictional character's situation to something that the reader will have experienced, for instance), Marston remains in the realm of miracle: neither the vehicle (the shadow) nor the tenor (the substance) is the real thing here. The joy

of someone who sees a dead person come to life again is really no closer
to us than the joy of a man who finds that he can have sex with the
statue he carved. We literally cannot conceive it; and the choice of 'con-
ceiue,' with its double meaning of artistic inspiration and human reproduction is obviously crucial here. The reproductive metaphor can be
only a metaphor in this context. That the poem narrates a story in which
artistic conception is literally rather than figuratively reproductive
gestures towards the possibility of an artistic realm in which everything
is possible.

The gesture is no sooner made than revoked, however, and in the
final stanza Marston turns firmly to literal reproduction:

> that same happy night
> So gracious were the Gods of marriage
> Mid'st all there pleasing and long wish'd delight
> . *Paphus* was got: of whom in after age
> *Cyprus* was *Paphos* call'd, and euermore
> Those Ilandars do *Venus* name adore.   (39.1–6)

Whereas Ovid says only that Pygmalion and Galatea had a child,
Marston makes the conception of the child happen as soon as the two
have sex – 'Long this blessed time continued not,' as Marlowe would
say – and thus strengthens our sense that it is important that sex be reproductive. But even here all is not lost. When Marston says that the
Cypriots worship Venus because of the miracle she performed, he actually says that they worship '*Venus* name.' He raises the possibility
that there is a gap between the goddess herself and the name by which
she is known – and, of course, the Greeks often called Venus, or rather
Aphrodite, 'Kypris' because she was born on the island, so her name
is variable in any case – and the question of shade versus substance
remains unsettled.

Furthermore, Paphos is the mother of Cinyras, who is, as I have said,
the father of Myrrha and thus the grandfather and father of Adonis,
with whom the line ends. The union of Pygmalion and his statue thus
leads to Myrrha, who reproduces with the wrong person, and Adonis,
who refuses to reproduce at all (or, in fact, even to have sex with the
very goddess whose name the Cypriots adore). She becomes a tree, he
becomes a flower: what begins as art ends as nature. One way to understand the story of this family is to see it as suggesting that both art and
non-human nature (the tree or the flower) have a permanence denied to

merely human products. Although Ovid says of Myrrha's transformation that 'tanti noua non fuit arbor' (a new tree was not worth so much; X.310), Marston, I think, disagrees, or at least hints that disagreement is possible. While Daniel ultimately presents the power of poetry as something that is probably harmful, and while Marlowe suggests that a world in which pleasure, rather than profit, is the desired end can be only temporary, Marston demonstrates that even the turn towards reproduction is not irrevocable: the story of Pygmalion and his descendants shows the limits of teleology. Not only does the family line end, so that the transformation of a work of art into a human being is not the end of anything but only a phase, but while Myrrha becomes a tree whose product itself is useful and highly valuable, Adonis becomes only a flower. The 'wondrous metamorphosis' is a circle rather than the infinitely extended line of genealogy, as the statue's ultimate descendant becomes something that has no use to us and that we value only for its beauty.

3 Beginnings

To a greater or lesser extent, all the texts I have discussed to this point in the book employ the reproductive metaphor. For the poems I discuss in this chapter, however, any metaphor that attempts to describe the process and purpose of literary composition is especially important. Sidney's *Astrophil and Stella*, Milton's *Paradise Lost*, and Bunyan's 'The Author's Apology for his Book' all focus on beginnings and introductions. Bunyan's poem does so because it functions as a preface to *The Pilgrim's Progress*, of course, but the situation is rather more complex in Sidney's and Milton's texts. We are accustomed to see sonnet sequences as narratives in which nothing happens, but in *Astrophil and Stella* many things happen (and have happened): it is just that they do not happen in an order that is helpful for the lover. Nor is Astrophil clear about what exactly his poems are for: what can – and what should – they do for him or for Stella or for anyone? In a way that was to prove influential for Daniel when he came to write *Delia*, Sidney makes his uncertainties about his poetic project central to the sequence as a whole. Throughout *Astrophil and Stella*, Sidney raises questions about inspiration and composition, and also about the issue I discussed in the previous chapter: that is, the extent to which a poem's value depends on its successful teleology. Furthermore, for Sidney the question of poetic teleology includes not only the question of whether the poems will serve to seduce the beloved woman but also, much more explicitly than was the case with Marlowe and Marston and even more explicitly than was the case with Daniel, the question of whether he even wants a poetic career.

In *Paradise Lost*, beginning has a very different status, since Milton is concerned both with how to begin (and begin again, and again) his poem, but also with the beginning of our world, of the human race, and even, we could say, of time itself. Time is always at issue in *Paradise Lost*, as in telling his story Milton has to be conscious of his own present day, of the distant biblical past, and of all the time in between. Among other things, this means that while *Astrophil and Stella* is a narrative from which we know we cannot expect much, *Paradise Lost* is a narrative from which we know exactly what we can expect. This aspect of the poem simplifies teleology in one respect, but it also increases the magnitude of Milton's task, as his teleology is not personal (as is the case with Daniel and Sidney) but collective. Much depends on *Paradise Lost*. Specifically, much depends on the invocation to *Paradise Lost*, and Milton's work here is further complicated by the fact that the poem has more than one invocation, since he begins again when the poem turns from Hell to Heaven at the beginning of Book III, for instance. What is more, the poem as a whole can be described as an invocation, as a text that can be completed only outside its bounds: in the Bible (and especially in the New Testament), in human history, in the life of the individual Christian, and, above all, in the inscrutable workings of God. In focusing on the very beginning of the book of Genesis, Milton proclaims his belief that beginnings are crucial; in *Paradise Lost* itself one of the ways in which he demonstrates this belief is by his focus on invocations and on questions of poetic inspiration and composition.

I shall end this chapter and the book with a short discussion of Bunyan's poetic preface to *The Pilgrim's Progress*. Although *The Pilgrim's Progress* is strongly influenced by the Bible and although it is also in some ways a response and a reaction to seventeenth-century English religious issues, Bunyan's focus is on the life of the individual Christian. He undertakes to teach his readers how to live, but he famously does so primarily through allegory. What interests me here is 'The Author's Apology for his Book,' the poem that precedes the prose narrative, in which we see Bunyan writing to some extent *in propria persona*, giving an account of the text's composition, his hopes for it, and an extended defence of his allegorical method. In fact, this poem is one of the most detailed accounts of textual production from the English Renaissance, and for this reason alone it deserves more scrutiny than it has typically received. However, there are other reasons as well. As the writer of a work of advice for Christians, Bunyan is naturally concerned with moral instruction, and much of the prefatory poem suggests ways in which people can derive spiritual profit from his book. In this regard the teleology of *The Pilgrim's Progress* is sufficiently clear, but what I think is unusual about the poem is that Bunyan could be said to be as interested in producing the right kind of reader as in producing the right kind of text. In other words, Bunyan proposes not only a theory of how to live but also a theory of how to read. For him, at least in 'The Author's Apology for his Book,' textual production is inseparable from textual consumption.

I

Near the beginning of *The Defence of Poesie*, Sidney explains that the word *poet* comes from the Greek: 'ποιητην, which name, hath as the most excellent, gone through other languages, it commeth of this word ποιεῖν which is to make: wherin I know not whether by luck or wisedome, we Englishmen have met with the Greekes in calling him a Maker.'[1] Sidney's point in this passage is not to show off his classical learning (or not only that), but rather to set up his discussion of what poetry can do. After commenting rather scornfully on the ways in which historians, lawyers, arithmeticians, and other learned men are limited in their work by what actually exists in nature, Sidney launches into the boldest of his claims:

> Onely the Poet disdeining to be tied to any such subjectio[n], lifted up with the vigor of his own invention, doth grow in effect into an other nature: in making things either better then nature bringeth foorth, or quite a new, formes such as never were in nature: as the *Heroes, Demigods, Cyclops, Chymeras, Furies*, and such like; so as he goeth hand in hand with nature, not enclosed within the narrow warrant of her gifts, but freely raunging within the Zodiack of his owne wit. Nature never set foorth the earthe in so rich Tapistry as diverse Poets have done, neither with so pleasaunt rivers, fruitfull trees, sweete smelling flowers, nor whatsoever els may make the too much loved earth more lovely: her world is brasen, the Poets only deliver a golden. (8)

I have quoted this famous passage at length partly because of its ranking of poetry above nature and partly because of its beauty and verve; perhaps especially pleasing is the breathtaking condescension of 'the narrow warrant of her gifts.' Considerable classical and Renaissance artistic theory presents nature as a guide to art; Sidney follows this topos only to invert it.

In much of what follows this passage Sidney is careful to demonstrate that what he values most about poetry is its ability to instruct, to tell people what to do and what not to do, what sort of person to be and what sort of person not to be; throughout *The Defence of Poesie* he is clear that poetry is intended to have a moral result in the real world, although at a number of points he also draws attention to poetry's strictly emotive powers. But despite Sidney's stress on the didactic nature of poetry, the point that poets surpass nature and that they are makers, not solely in the sense of makers of texts but even in the sense of makers of worlds, remains an essential part of Sidney's case in *The Defence of Poesie*. In a way that should influence our sense of his presentation of poetic composition in *Astrophil and Stella*, Sidney, in effect, pre-empts the reproductive metaphor. For him, a poet is not like a person giving birth to a child, but rather like a god creating all of humanity – in fact, we could almost say that the poet creates humanity twice: once because the poet creates a new world and a second time because the poet can make human beings better. Furthermore, poetry is not a reproduction or imitation: not only does the comparison between the poet's world and the natural world show nature at a disadvantage, but in his depiction of the poet's world as made of gold and nature's world as made of brass, Sidney effectively presents nature as a cheaper and less satisfying version of art.

This, at least, is the case in *The Defence of Poesie*. As we shall see, in his great sonnet sequence, *Astrophil and Stella*, Sidney has more trouble with the question of what poetry can and cannot do. Although he begins the sequence by imagining that his poems will lead to real world results, the possibility emerges that all he can create through his poetry is the poetry itself. In this sense, then, the world of *Astrophil and Stella* is a closed world, one in which poetry cannot be turned to account – either in being literally profitable or in persuading Stella to have sex with the poet. I would argue that it is precisely to emphasize this point that Sidney's sequence focuses on poetic issues and specifically on questions of vocabulary and of the methods and motives of textual production. These issues will be my focus, too, in this highly selective look at *Astrophil and Stella*. In this respect, my approach is very different from the standard discussion of these poems, a discussion that is almost invariably historicizing and that looks at the biographical basis for the poetry, often to the exclusion of the poetry itself. To some extent, this is a result of Marotti's extraordinarily influential argument that 'Love is not love' – in other words, that what seem to us to be poems about love are instead chiefly poems about social anxieties.[2] As a man with a particularly fraught (and famous) set of social anxieties, Sidney has seemed a natural candidate for this sort of analysis.

My point is not that historicist criticism is bad: a great deal of interesting and perceptive work has been done on the relation of Sidney's poems to his life and to the society in which he lived.[3] Nevertheless, here, as elsewhere in Renaissance literary studies, historicism has had an unduly restrictive influence on critical discussions, and in what follows I shall concentrate on the ways in which Sidney uses *Astrophil and Stella* to present ideas about textual production, and I shall do so at the expense of a historical approach.[4] My focus will be on the points at which Sidney reflects self-consciously on his own poetic practice and on the motives for poetic composition, which is to say on those aspects of the poem that relate to Sidney's larger interest with what poetry can and cannot do. Aside from, or in addition to, Sidney's real desire to have sex with Penelope Rich, the central importance of seduction to a sonnet sequence gives the question of the power of poetry an immediately personal relevance that adds drama to what might otherwise be considered a merely theoretical concern. We could say that Sidney uses *Astrophil and Stella* to raise two related questions. One of these is the one raised to some extent by all sonnet sequences (and much love poetry of any kind): can poetry obtain sex? The other is the question of how far poetry can be a substitute for sex, whether in providing a form of communication that is like sexual communication or in demonstrating the mastery of the poet and thus compensating for his sexual failure or in providing a similarly intense pleasure.[5] In this context, Sidney's use of the reproductive metaphor is especially pointed, as the absence of any possibility of real children – given Astrophil's failure to win Stella – emphasizes the inaptness of the metaphor.

In what is still one of the best analyses of the sequence, Anne Ferry remarks that *Astrophil and Stella* 'begins with two sonnets clearly designed as an introduction to the sequence. They focus on the speaker's uneasiness about the distinction between loving in verse and love shown in poetry, a subject considered *explicitly* in approximately one-fifth of these 108 sonnets.'[6] Indeed, as Maria Teresa Prendergast has argued, the sequence as a whole is to a considerable extent about literature.[7] Here are the first four lines of the first sonnet:

Loving in truth, and faine in verse my love to show,
That the deare She might take some pleasure of my paine,
Pleasure might cause her reade, reading might make her know,
Knowledge might pitie winne, and pitie grace obtaine.[8]

Sidney's use of gradatio and a colloquial tone initially make these lines seem easy to apprehend, but the easiness soon disappears. For one thing, the theory of reading that Astrophil adumbrates here is both hard to follow and, I think, displeasing. Stella will take pleasure in his pain; this pleasure is somehow simultaneously something that is produced by reading and something that leads to reading; and the ultimate result of this reading pleasure will be her agreeing to have sex with Astrophil because she feels sorry for him: in other words, a sadistic Stella and an abject Astrophil. It could thus be argued that the sequence begins by denigrating the poetic project altogether; in the context of this book, we can understand Sidney as saying, like Virgil and Montaigne, that poetry comes from abjection.

What is more, the vocabulary of these lines turns out to be ambiguous. While 'faine' most obviously means 'desirous' in the first line, the fact that the word follows 'truth' so closely hints at the play on words with 'feign,' the opposite of telling the truth.[9] Prendergast argues that the collocation of 'faine' (understood as feign) and 'in verse' (understood as inverse) 'encode[s] a desire to invert conventional meanings by validating the feigning, sophistical poetics to which both Ovid's Orpheus and Sidney's Astrophil adhere.'[10] The tension between plain speaking and misleading poetic speaking which animates so much of *Astrophil and Stella* thus begins in the first line of the first sonnet. In fact, this tension occurs twice in the first line if we accept Ferry's argument that the line shows a 'distinction between Astrophil's inward experience and his poetic term for it,' between, that is, 'loving' and 'my love.'[11] I would say that these first lines set up a picture of poetry as something that is motivated by real emotion and that strives to bring about a result in the real world, but that poetry itself instantly turns out to be fiction and, as such, suspect. Catherine Bates has remarked that 'the inaugural poem' of the sequence is 'the product of a split between the "I" that loves and the "I" that writes,' and this seems to me to be one of the best descriptions of how *Astrophil and Stella* works.[12] Perhaps the most significant pairing in the first four lines is 'in truth' and 'in verse'; while Sidney presents the relation between the two as cause and effect, we should instead see them as introducing an opposition that the sequence never resolves.

The problem is made even clearer in the next four lines. As Ronald Levao shows, 'The first quatrain proclaims a poetic teleology, the employment of verse as a conduit joining subjective desire and objective fulfillment, yet the outward movement toward "grace" is immediately stalled in the second.'[13] By 'poetic teleology' Levao refers to the result the poems are intended to produce, but one of the things that interests me about *Astrophil and Stella* is the extent to which poetry becomes both the means and the end for Sidney. Here is the second quatrain:

> I sought fit words to paint the blackest face of woe,
> Studying inventions fine, her wits to entertaine:
> Oft turning others leaves, to see if thence would flow
> Some fresh and fruitfull showers upon my sunne-burn'd braine.   (1.5–8)

As Heather Dubrow has pointed out, to paint can mean both to depict (the obvious meaning here) but also to disguise or falsify, and the word is thus the same sort of troubling pun as 'faine.'[14] And, as Levao suggests, the teleology in these lines is not so much the seduction of Stella but rather the composition of poetry: 'The persuasiveness of "the deare She" remains the objective goal, but the entertainments of method – both for the speaker and for us – are never far from center stage.'[15] As we shall see, poetic method is not only the focus of the first sonnet but rather a theme to which Sidney returns throughout *Astrophil and Stella*.

Sidney immediately tells us that this particular method has not worked, that the 'inventions fine' of other poets have not helped him to write:

> But words came halting forth, wanting Invention's stay,
> Invention, Nature's child, fled step-dame Studie's blowes,
> And others' feete still seem'd but strangers in my way.   (1.9–11)

This passage provides still more ambiguity. In this sonnet, invention means at once the works of other poets and his own poetic ability; furthermore, while invention is artificial in that it is apparently a process of arrangement, it is also 'Nature's child.' The last phrase prepares us for the reproductive metaphor and I shall return to that in a moment, but now I want to look at the metaphors of 'leaves' and 'feete.' Both are common metaphors for poetry, but the difference between them is important. The leaves are poetry as a finished product, either written in manuscript of printed in a book. The feet are the basic metrical units of a poem – in this context, the method by which words becomes poetry: without feet, Astrophil's words are 'halting.' What is most significant, I think, is the extent to which the metaphors (which are almost dead metaphors in sixteenth-century poetry) become real. Sidney makes the leaves seem real by using the very vivid image of the leaves of a tree that hold rainwater, and he makes the feet seem real by turning them into the feet of strangers who impede his own progress. The extent to which these metaphors take on a life of their own indicates the extent to which both this sonnet and the sequence as a whole refuse to be merely teleological – or, as I have suggested, the extent to which poetry is the real telos of *Astrophil and Stella*.

The crucial shift here is from poems as either written or as the leaves of a tree to poems as personified; the personification of poems in the phrase 'others' feete' is only one of several personifications in the poem: woe, invention, study. The change from real people (the poet and the woman he loves) to personifications sets up the reproductive metaphor, in which the mental activity of poetic composition is imaged as a physical process:

> Thus great with child to speake, and helplesse in my throwes,
> Biting my trewand pen, beating my selfe for spite,
> 'Foole,' said my Muse to me, 'looke in thy heart and write.'   (1.12–14)

As Leonard Barkan remarks, 'the poet's own body ... act[s] as scene for his progression.'[16] In using the metaphor of himself as pregnant, the poet aligns himself with 'Invention, Nature's child' rather than with 'Studie,' who as a stepmother is not associated with childbirth. But this sense of poetic composition as physical is immediately undermined by the reference to his 'trewand pen' and by the appearance of his muse. Whoever his muse may be, she resembles 'Studie' in being associated with mental activity rather than with physical activity. The muse's injunction to look in his heart continues to present poetry as something that comes from the body, but it also points out the inadequacy of the reproductive metaphor by suggesting that poetry comes from the heart rather than the womb and that it is solitary rather than the result of the sex between a man and a woman that the sequence as a whole is ostensibly designed to produce.

The suggestion that good poetry comes from the heart would seem to separate *Astrophil and Stella* from the poetry that has failed to help Astrophil to write his poems, but here, as well, the situation as ambiguous. Given the Elizabethan tendency not to pronounce initial 'h,' Dubrow suggests that we could read (or hear) the final line as saying 'looke in thy art and write.'[17] Whether or not this is the case, I think it is important to realize that the first sonnet does not oppose art and (human) nature. As David Kalstone notes, 'The complaint is not against art, but against false art. The poet is asked to devise, to find conceits that fully articulate the strength and particularity of his love'; Kalstone goes on to point out that 'with its elaborate rhetorical figures and its attention to Stella's image, [the first sonnet] uses a formal literary manner and sonnet conventions quite ostentatiously.'[18] Or, as Patricia Fumerton says of this sonnet, 'Only through con-vention can he find in-vention.'[19] Art, in the sense of love poetry, is necessary, but it is insufficient to ensure that Astrophil's own poems are accurate and authentic. In a recent book, Daniel Juan Gil perceptively comments that 'Sidney's project ... is, in a sense, to prop up the social values of words by trying to imagine words that are tied to a sort of biological gold standard, the physical bodies of elite ladies and friends.'[20] Thinking of *Astrophil and Stella* as a whole, I would say that both the reproductive metaphor and the metaphor of poems as coming from the heart are designed to provide a 'biological gold standard' of authenticity. One of my themes in the rest of this section is Sidney's attempts to use these metaphors and the difficulties that result from attempting to refer to both an internal and an external standard.

The second sonnet, in which Astrophil tells the story of how he fell in love with Stella, could be seen as his taking his own advice: he has looked into his heart and now he tells us what is in it. But the sonnet ends with three lines that suggest that the price of using an internal standard for poetry is that the resulting poems will remain focused on the internal, on what is private. Sidney resolves to

> employ the remnant of my wit,
> To make my selfe beleeve, that all is well,
> While with a feeling skill I paint my hell.   (2.12–14)

We can get some sense of the narrowing of focus from the first sonnet to the second by comparing Astrophil's description of his poems in the last line of this sonnet with his statement in the fifth line of the previous sonnet: 'I sought fit words to paint the blackest face of woe.' And the narrowing of focus continues in the third sonnet. Astrophil begins this by speaking once again of the kinds of poetry he is not writing; tellingly, he begins by saying 'Let daintie wits crie on the Sisters nine' (3.1). These sisters are the muses, of course, one of whom advised him on writing at the end of the first sonnet. Now he disdains their help and concludes this sonnet by saying 'all my deed / But Copying is, what in her Nature writes' (3.14). We could see this as a move from the artificial to the natural, but it is also a move from the reproductive metaphor to presenting his poetry as literal reproduction. While in the *Defence of Poesie* Sidney praises the poet for outdoing nature, here he reduces the poet to a mere copyist of nature.[21]

In moving from thinking of his poetry as a record of whàt is in his heart to thinking of his poetry as a record of Stella, Astrophil moves from an internal to an external standard, but not in a way that will help him to obtain Stella's love. For the rest of the sequence, he will try to regain control of his poems and to establish his autonomy as a poet. It is for these reasons, I believe, that he has so many poems in which he speaks of his methods and motives. His attempts are unsuccessful, however, and they are so at least partly because of the power of Stella. Prendergast argues that over the course of the poems it becomes clear that Stella 'is ... the author who governs the sequence,' and while I would not go quite that far, it is certainly obvious that Stella's prominence steadily increases throughout the sequence.[22] As Nona Fienberg points out, Sidney's 'sonnet sequence does give space to a Stella who is not simply a projection of the speaker's desires.'[23] Astrophil's description of his composition at the end of the third sonnet as copying what nature wrote in Stella is developed into several references to Stella as a book to be read. While we could choose to think that Astrophil is still the person who wrote this book, Sidney's emphasis is on the book rather than its writer, which should remind us that in speaking of himself as a copyist Astrophil, in effect, is giving up any claim to be the shaper of raw material. Perhaps the most extreme example of his presentation of himself as a secretary, as someone who takes dictation, appears in what may well be the most beautiful line in the whole sequence: 'And love doth hold my hand, and makes me write' (90.14). The 'trewand pen' of the first poem has been brought under control, but not under Astrophil's control.

There are, of course, many moments throughout the poems in which Astrophil writes of himself as a writer, not merely a secretary, but many of these are qualified by his presentation of Stella as the performer of his works and, significantly, as someone whose performance changes the very nature of the poems. Probably the best example of this aspect of Stella comes just after the halfway point in the sequence:

She heard my plaints, and did not only heare,
But them (so sweete is she) most sweetly sing,

With that faire breast making woe's darknesse cleare:
A pretty case! I hoped her to bring
To feele my griefes, and she with face and voice
So sweets my paines, that my paines me rejoyce.   (57.9–14)

Although the poems have had an effect – which is what Astrophil hoped at the beginning of the first sonnet – the effect is only on Astrophil himself. While in the first poem he hoped that Stella 'might take some pleasure of my paine,' now it is he who takes pleasure in his pain. What is more, this pleasure is produced by Stella's sound rather than by his own sense: apparently, the words of the poems no longer matter.

The meaning of Astrophil's self-abnegation has been debated. In a discussion of the fiftieth sonnet (to which I shall return), Jacqueline T. Miller argues that his 'complete humility provides the poet with the very fame he began by pretending to renounce: now his artful transformation allows him to accept it as a gift from his beloved.'[24] One of the things that is at issue here is the extent to which we are supposed to believe Sidney's disclaimers of his poetic ambition whether here – as when Astrophil says 'In truth I sweare, I wish not there should be / Graved in mine Epitaph a Poet's name' (90.7–8) or elsewhere in his works. Readings like Miller's, in which these disclaimers are read as merely conventional or as examples of Renaissance sprezzatura, have been influential. Specifically, Astrophil's statements of dependence and powerlessness are understood as tacitly asserting his independence and power. Bates refers to this sort of reading when she writes of 'the dialectic of mastery – the dialectic that cancels abjection by making the poet master of it' and adds, 'To write about loss is to disavow loss – to substantiate it and to offer words as a fetishistic surrogate.'[25] Bates is not convinced, however, and neither am I. Throughout the sequence, Sidney draws attention to the poems as texts whose fate is not in his hands, as in the lines I quoted above in which Stella's performance inverts the meaning of the poems or in the image of a child pleased with a book because of its physical appearance rather than because it is 'the fruit of writer's mind' (11.8).

I think the question cannot be definitively settled, but in the context of this book what is especially significant to me is Sidney's return to the reproductive metaphor in sonnets 37 and 50. In the first of these, the metaphor is used only briefly to introduce the poem: 'My mouth doth water, and my breast doth swell, / My tongue doth itch, my thoughts in labour be' (37.1–2). The shift from what we might be inclined to see as literal physical symptoms to what is clearly a metaphor is surprising, but what is perhaps more surprising is what follows: 'Listen then Lordings with good eare to me, / For of my life I must a riddle tell' (37.3–4). What Astrophil delivers in the rest of the sonnet is, in context, one of the easiest riddles ever told, not just because in using the word *Rich* five times it obviously puns on the married name of Penelope Devereux. Although Astrophil begins by saying that the riddle is about him – 'of my life' – it is actually about Stella: he is only the container for the story. The deferential (and pseudo-medieval) nature of Astrophil's appeal to his audience further stresses the extent to which we can now consider him not as an original poet or even as a man who is presumably the social equal of Stella, but rather as a paid entertainer who serves both a great lady and a male aristocratic audience. Here, the reproductive metaphor leads to the further abjection of the poet.

Fienberg notes that the reproductive metaphor in 37 and 50 is very different from the reproductive metaphor in the first sonnet: 'Instead of delivering his poetry, he now labors to create his beloved.'[26] In fact, while in 37 the 'riddle' Astrophil delivers occupies most of the sonnet, the situation is different in 50. As in 37, he begins by using the language of making external what is internal (although the reference here is not to childbirth):

> *Stella*, the fulnesse of my thoughts of thee
> Cannot be staid within my panting breast,
> But they do swell and struggle forth of me,
> Till that in words thy figure be exprest.   (50.1–4)

The crucial word here is 'exprest,' which has both its (now more usual) metaphorical meaning of saying or writing that which is within one and its (now less usual) literal meaning of pressing out something (such as a baby, for instance) by force. The first of these meanings indicates that Astrophil is doing what the muse told him to do at the end of the first sonnet (although in this case he says he is doing it at 'my Lord *Love's* behest' (50.6). In 37, Astrophil seemed happy with what was expressed, but in this sonnet he sees the 'weake proportion' (50.7) of what he has done and is dissatisfied.

In the sestet of the sonnet Astrophil presents himself as trapped in a terrible dilemma:

> I cannot chuse but write my mind,
> And cannot chuse but put out what I write.
> While those poore babes their death in birth do find.   (50.9–11)

In this version of the reproductive metaphor the poet's fertility is a curse, as he keeps expressing things that he knows to be bad. We could say that Astrophil resembles Montaigne in his description of himself in 'Of Idlenesse,' helplessly giving birth to monstrosities of all sorts, but where Astrophil is in a better position than Montaigne is in his love for Stella:

> And now my pen these lines had dashed quite,
> But that they stopt his furie from the same,
> Because their forefront bare sweet *Stella's* name.   (50.12–14)

However, this glimmer of hope has a price: if we continue to read these last lines through the reproductive metaphor, we see not only that Astrophil is the woman but also that Stella, insofar as she passes on her name to the children / poems, is the man. Astrophil's return to the reproductive metaphor demonstrates his total subjection both of himself and of his poetry to Stella. It is now no longer a question of the ability of his poems either to seduce or to make her famous; instead, she controls the poems.

Of course, these issues are not settled at this point – not even halfway through – in *Astrophil and Stella*. Throughout the sequence we see Astrophil attempting to begin again, to clarify his poetic ambitions, and to get concessions of various sorts from Stella. But as readers know, despite a number of hopeful moments he does not make any real progress, and I believe that his refashioning of the reproductive metaphor in the fiftieth sonnet should be taken as one sign of Astrophil's inability to write powerful and independent poetry. In her discussion, Dubrow mentions what she sees as the first sonnet's characteristic 'preoccupations with failure and dependency,' and we could see these as central to the sequence as a whole.[27] For instance, one of the most important things the reproductive metaphor does in sonnet 50 is to demonstrate that both Astrophil's poetic activity and even the survival of the poems themselves are dependent on Stella. Obviously, in real life we know that the poems have survived, but if we take their survival (something that might not have been welcome to Sidney) as evidence of Astrophil's bad faith, we fall into the error of being excessively historical, or rather excessively historicizing. Within the sequence, Astrophil becomes and remains abject and, most important for my purposes, unable to articulate a theory or an account of textual production that allows him any independence. As these 'preoccupations with failure and dependency,' to return to Dubrow's phrase, are sufficiently obvious, I shall not proceed through the sequence heartache by heartache; instead, I shall conclude my discussion of *Astrophil and Stella* by looking at the last sonnet.

On one level, sonnet 108 is familiar enough, balanced as it is between Astrophil's joy in Stella and his despair at the hopelessness of his love for her:

> When sorrow (using mine owne fier's might)
> Melts downe his lead into my boyling brest,
> Through that dark fornace to my hart opprest,
> There shines a joy from thee my only light.   (108.1–4)

As readers would expect, this joy does not last. Here, the short duration of Astrophil's joy is due to the intrusion of 'Most rude dispaire my daily unbidden guest' (108.7), but what most interests me here is the dominant image, which is of alchemy.[28] The first example of alchemy is the production of joy from the lead of sorrow; the second is given at the end of the sonnet:

> So strangely (alas) thy works in me prevaile,
> That in my woes for thee thou art my joy,
> And in my joyes for thee my only annoy.   (108.12–14)

As in the ending of sonnet 57, Stella turns pain into pleasure. Here, however, in a manner that is suitably sombre for the conclusion of the sequence, Stella also turns pleasure into pain.

I read the alchemical metaphor as Astrophil's attempt to find an alternative to the reproductive metaphor, which has so signally failed to help him. As sonnet 50 indicates, reproduction is controlled by Stella and is, after all, reproduction – specifically, the reproduction of his unhappiness and abjection. Alchemy, on the other hand, is intended to produce something entirely new and, in the example of turning lead to gold, which was the great hope held out by alchemists and to which Sidney alludes here, something that is not only new but far better, as well as something that is not abject. Of course, this is not the result of the alchemy in the last sonnet. In fact, it could be argued that the prime example of alchemy in this poem is Astrophil's use of the metaphor to turn alchemy into something bad. It is also significant that even here he is passive rather than active – he is neither the alchemist nor even the provider of the raw material (here, sorrow's lead), but rather is only the supplier of the 'fier' of his passion that will be used to turn lead into gold. Sorrow's alchemy is successful and does produce gold, but Astrophil's imprisonment in his own misery makes this result pointless. As he says, 'what doth *Phoebus'* gold that wretch availe, / Whom iron doores do keepe from use of day' (108.10–11). In these lines, and to some extent in the sonnet as a whole, Sidney gestures towards the identification of sexual and financial teleology that is one of Marlowe's chief subjects in *Hero and Leander*.

However, Sidney does not altogether abandon the reproductive metaphor in sonnet 108; instead, he uses it in a way that highlights Astrophil's predicament. After the reference to the light of joy in the fourth line, he says, 'thought of thee breeds my delight, / And my yong soule flutters to thee his nest' (108.5–6). But this use of the metaphor is bizarre in the extreme, although it could be argued that it is a logical development from sonnet 50. The thought of Stella is the active participant in this reproduction, and Stella, in being his nest, can also be seen as his mother. The result of the reproduction is Astrophil himself: he is the child rather than the parent. Furthermore, as he is instantly imprisoned by despair, who 'Clips streight my wings, streight wraps me in his night' (108.8), he remains a child trapped within himself and within his emotions. As I see it, the point of the reproductive metaphor is to give the poet a control over his poetry that is similar to – and, perhaps, derived from – a parent's control over a child and a man's control over a woman; or, to use an analogy that seems particularly apt for Sidney, a rider's control over a horse. But the 108 sonnets and 11 songs that comprise *Astrophil and Stella* have not succeeded in demonstrating this kind of control. Instead of using the reproductive metaphor to achieve mastery of his poems and of the woman he loves, Astrophil has managed only to render himself a dependent and helpless child. His metaphorical imprisonment within himself in the last poem of the sequence replaces the triumphant teleology that poetry is intended to achieve with a picture of poetry as a closed circuit that leads back only to the abject self.

II

In *Astrophil and Stella*, poetic success is to some extent tied to one man's romantic success, but of course, for Milton in *Paradise Lost* the stakes are much higher. Recklessly saying in the poem's first invocation that he seeks to 'justifie the wayes of God to men,' Milton begins his epic work by taking on a task that will be judged on theological as well as poetic grounds.[29] In a perceptive comparison of Milton's poetics with Sidney's *Defence of Poesie* (from which he quotes in the passage I shall cite), Kent R. Lehnhof points out that the task is made even more difficult, since 'for Milton, God's deity derives from his ability to create; consequently, God's deity is to a certain degree diminished when anyone other than God is able to summon "the vigor of his owne intention" and give rise to a new world "with the force of a divine breath." Within Milton's formulation of deity, then, the assertion of poetic identity operates at some level as a challenge to God the Father.'[30] Lehnhof's wording reminds us of the extent to which the reproductive metaphor is implicated in our thinking about God as creator. As we shall see, however, the connection between creation and reproduction in *Paradise Lost* is rather more complicated than a simple equation of fathering and creating would imply. Nevertheless, Lehnhof makes a valuable contribution to our understanding of Milton's poetic aims in his epic.

As will already be clear, the Milton I discuss in this section is not the utterly self-assured poet who is still the prevalent image of Milton, but rather a more tentative poet, trying to work out the relation between his poetics and his religious duty. In thinking about this Milton, I have learnt much from Peter C. Herman's focus on the importance of the word 'or' in *Paradise Lost*. As Herman remarks, 'although one must recognize the presence of a strong, totalizing impulse within this poem, a desire for unity and a movement toward organicism, we also need to recognize that his impulse is countered by an equally powerful counter-tendency toward undoing unity and toward unresolved choices leading to aporias.'[31] As I see it, much of this counter-tendency is expressed in the passages in which Milton, here as elsewhere an exceptionally self-conscious poet, talks specifically about his poetic aims and his textual production.[32] It is in these passages, and especially in the proems to Books I, III, VII, and IX, that we can most clearly see that, as Onno Oerlemans suggests, 'Milton does not have absolute control over his text, but is rather much more like Barthes's notion of the "scriptor," who is born simultaneously with the text.'[33] Oerlemans's comment is truer at some points in *Paradise Lost* than at others, of course. As Lehnhof points out, 'Again and again, Milton's rhetoric of bold poetic innovation mingles with the meek language of divine inspiration.'[34] The incertitude of the poem never quite becomes certitude, and one of the poem's important features is the movement between the two.

One of the useful aspects of seeing the poet who speaks in *Paradise Lost* as a scriptor whose existence is coterminous with the poem itself is that it allows us to focus on the narrator and to bypass the character-driven analysis against which Anne Ferry protested almost half a century ago when she argued that Miltonists had 'assumed that the meaning of the poem was to be found in our response to the characters in it as figures in a piece of dramatic literature.'[35] This approach would also allow us to avoid referring to the narrator of the poem as Milton and thus conflating the real man who wrote the poem with the figure who speaks in the poem. In this connection, a useful example is provided by Robert McMahon, whose book on Milton is called *The Two Poets of* Paradise Lost – two, because one is the real Milton and the other is the narrator (or, as McMahon calls him, the Bard). Unfortunately, both Ferry and McMahon seek to establish a narrator who is stable and coherent; for instance, Ferry says that the proems 'create and define a speaker whose identity and characteristic tone are sustained throughout the epic and control our interpretations of its meaning.'[36] In my analysis, I want to follow Ferry and McMahon in their focus on the narrator – and, specifically, on the meta-poetic matter of the poem – but also to keep in mind Herman's statement that 'the Miltonic "Or" ... inscribes incertitude at the heart of *Paradise Lost*.'[37] I would also locate this incertitude at the heart of the narrator.

We can see both certitude and incertitude in the first invocation. After Milton has given a brief summary of the poem's subject and summoned the 'Heav'nly Muse' (I.7), he explains why he needs the muse's help:

> I thence
> Invoke thy aid to my adventrous Song,
> That with no middle flight intends to soar
> Above th'*Aonian* Mount, while it pursues
> Things unattempted yet in Prose or Rime.   (I.12–16)

It is important to note that all the daring here is the doing of the personified song rather than of the singer. As well, when Milton uses the phrase 'with no middle flight,' he makes an allusion to Daedalus's warning to Icarus in the *Metamorphoses*: a middle flight is what he fruitlessly advises his son to take.[38] And when Milton says the poem will contain 'Things unattempted yet in Prose or Rime,' the claim is undermined because the line is a translation of Ariosto's claim in *Orlando Furioso* that his story is 'cosa non detta in prosa mai né in rima.'[39] Comparing Ariosto's original with Milton's version emphasizes the latter's incertitude: for 'detta' (said) Milton has 'unattempted,' a change that is further stressed, as it is the only polysyllabic word in the line. Ariosto presents his poem as something already finished; Milton presents his poem as a process about whose success he is still unsure.

One of the difficulties in writing about Milton's presentation of his textual production is that he is central to our sense of English poetry as a whole. What is more, the origin of his poetry is part of his greater concern with origins – perhaps most obviously in *Paradise Lost*, which deals, as I have remarked, with the origin of the universe and of human beings and of time itself. Milton's oeuvre as a whole seems to focus on origins, but as Bill Readings points out, it does so in a way that is not always straightforward: 'Milton's poetic work simultaneously inscribes and defers origin.'[40] Readings's statement suggests that the account of poetic aims and composition that opens Milton's great epic is not the whole story, that it does not inaugurate *Paradise Lost* once and for all. When we read it, we find instead that *Paradise Lost* is a poem that has to be begun again and again – a poem that is, in fact, still going on. Despite the thrilling grandeur of the invocation with which the poem opens, then, we might usefully consider it only as the invocation to Book I (or only to Books I and II) rather than to the poem as a whole. We soon find first that Book III requires its own invocation, and then that this invocation finds a response in Satan's speech to the sun in Book IV, which Walter Schindler has called an 'anti-invocation.'[41] Later on, of course, we find passages strongly resembling invocations at the beginnings of Books VII and IX. This poem that speaks of origins keeps returning to its own origins.

A possible reason for this return is that it mimics Milton's ideas about Christianity, which he famously saw as an active enterprise requiring vigilance and energy, and Protestantism as a form of Christianity that returned to the origins of the religion and bypassed the papistical deviation. Another possible reason is that it demonstrates his unease with the existing metaphors for textual production, and it is the second reason that will be the focus for my highly selective look at *Paradise Lost*. Like many of the other poets I discuss in this book, Milton uses the reproductive metaphor in ways that reveal an awareness of its potential for abjection and a desire to consider the ways in which this metaphor does or does not work for a male poet. I want to begin by looking at a famous anecdote from Milton's life, which was recorded by Cyriack Skinner in his early biography of the poet: 'The time friendly to the Muses fell to his Poetry. And hee waking early (as is the use of temperate men) had commonly a good Stock of Verse ready against his

Amanuensis came; which if it happend to bee later than ordinary, hee would complain, Saying, *hee wanted to bee milkd.'*[42] As was the case with Newcastle's metaphor of paper bodies, Milton transforms the reproductive metaphor.[43] Dairy cows are prized primarily for their milk production rather than for their fertility, after all, and Milton does not present his poems as his children but rather as something that will nourish other people. Furthermore, what will turn out to be typical of much of Milton's self-presentation in *Paradise Lost* is his passivity in this metaphor. Just as a cow cannot milk itself, so the poet cannot produce poetry without assistance. In context, this passivity is most obviously the result of Milton's blindness, but as we shall see, Milton presents his textual production as passive in *Paradise Lost* itself.

As I have suggested, Milton indicates his need for assistance very near the beginning of the first invocation. A few lines after the passage I quoted above, Milton calls on the Holy Spirit for help:

> Instruct me, for Thou know'st; Thou from the first
> Wast present, and with mighty wings outspread
> Dove-like satst brooding on the vast Abyss
> And mad'st it pregnant.   (I.19–22)

In its technical sense 'brooding' is what female birds do, but by the next line the Holy Spirit has become male and impregnates the abyss. As Oerlemans points out, these line show 'a mixing of sexual function as well as gender.'[44] The reproductive metaphor is used here not to describe textual production but rather the production of the entire universe, and the creator is at once the father and the mother in this metaphor – the active force that impregnates and the passive space that is impregnated or, at least, that nurtures the young. What will turn out to be paradigmatic for *Paradise Lost* as a whole in this metaphor is that Milton uses things and situations we know from our own life in order to present a situation that is ultimately unknowable for humans.

I think Milton expected the reader to draw the parallel between the coming together of the active force and the passive space that leads to creation on the one hand and the desired encounter between the muse and the poet on the other, but in case this parallel is not sufficiently clear, Milton returns to talking about himself directly following this metaphor: 'What in me is dark / Illumin, what is low raise and support' (I.22–3). As Angela Esterhammer remarks, 'The same Spirit that brooded on the abyss is to re-enact creation within the poet, making light out of darkness and raising and supporting the deep. Milton is quite literally casting himself in the role of the abyss.'[45] Qualifying our sense of Milton's poetic daring and his 'adventrous Song,' then, is his depiction of himself as the inert and dark and low emptiness. And as Gordon Teskey has recently suggested, Milton's description of chaos in the second book – 'The Womb of nature and perhaps her Grave' (II.911) – returns to this original abyss.[46] We could say that in these instances the reproductive metaphor is simultaneously a metaphor for textual production and a metaphor for the abyss: it is perhaps the abyss that is the real thing, and both childbirth and writing poems are merely imitations. Returning to the question of how this account of textual production situates the poet, we can see that, as is the case with many of the poets I discuss in this book, the abjection of the poet is seen as being to some extent a necessary precondition for poetic production.

Milton's ambivalence about creation in these passages is typical of *Paradise Lost* and of his uncertainties about his poetic project more generally. While the description of the abyss and of the abyss-like poet in the invocation suggests that what is dark and low can become bright and high, the possibility is still there that abjection will remain abjection. In Book I, this is most clearly illustrated in the account of the building of the devils' palace, Pandemonium, which I see as Milton's parody of his own account of creation.[47] The devils find ore underneath the plain of Hell; they purify the ore, and then pour it into moulds – 'and from the boyling cells / By strange conveyance fill'd each hollow nook' (I.706–7) – until 'out of the earth a Fabrick huge / Rose like an Exhalation' (I.710–11). Here again, as in alchemy and as in Virgil's and Montaigne's accounts of their textual production, what is low becomes high. That the building rises 'with the sound / Of Dulcet symphonies and voices sweet' (I.711–12) parallels the way in which Milton's darkness becomes the lightness of religious art, but insofar as the building rises 'like an Exhalation' from the bowels of hell, we could also see it as infernal flatulence. Milton's point, of course, is that the building is a spectacular work of architecture and that the music of devils surpasses human music in beauty, but he also wants to make it clear that Pandemonium is hellish. Thus, he tacitly admits that art, even if extremely pleasing on aesthetic grounds, may remain base and low and that humans are easily seduced by that which is pleasing or euphonious. To some extent, this is a familiar comment on the fallibility of the human senses, but I think Milton would extend this comment to his own poem, which he fears may be bad even if it is beautiful.

Perhaps, then, the abjection that is often presented as the origin of poetry cannot be transcended. I think that it is in order to emphasize this point that Milton uses the image of bees when he describes the assembly of the devils in their new palace (I.768–76). I see this as an allusion to the discussion of bees in the fourth book of the *Georgics*.[48] Milton's passage begins by making a parallel between apian and demonic behaviour at the level of the collective rather than the individual, a parallel that recalls Virgil's stress on apian politics and warfare. The comparison to bees is emphasized when the devils suddenly make themselves small. Although Milton drops the comparison to bees at this point and compares the now minuscule devils to 'smallest Dwarfs' (I.779), the 'Pigmean Race' (I.780), and 'Faerie Elves' (I.781), the persistence of the allusion to *Georgics* IV is signalled by Milton's introduction of the change by 'Behold a wonder!' (I.777), a phrase that translates the 'mirabile monstrum / aspiciunt' (they see an amazing wonder; IV.554–5) by which Virgil introduces the transformation of the cow's carcass into the hive of bees. As I suggested in the introduction, this is the point at which the abject putrefaction that is literally low because it is on the ground becomes the hive that is literally high; when Virgil compares himself lying under a tree singing his pastoral and georgic poems to conquering Augustus, he connects poetry and abjection and literal and metaphorical lowness. In his recension of the Virgilian passage, Milton seeks to associate abjection with demonic creation and to distinguish art that celebrates God from infernal art, but I feel that the danger for him is that the parallels with his own textual production as he has described it at the beginning of *Paradise Lost* are too close.

Of course, the use of *Georgics* IV here is only one of many instances of Milton's adaptation of Virgil throughout *Paradise Lost*. As Estelle Haan has recently noted, the part of the invocation to Book III in which Milton speaks of himself as having returned from Hell (III.13–21) is modelled on Aeneas's descent to the Underworld in Book VI of the *Aeneid*, although, as she points out, Milton's invocation 'inverts and transcends that Virgilian invocation to night and darkness.'[49] In fact, Milton began to use this passage earlier, as a version of the sibyl's famous warning to Aeneus before his descent,

> facilis descensus Auerno:
> noctes atque dies patet atri ianua Ditis;
> sed reuocare gradum superasque euadere ad auras,
> hoc opus, hic labor est

> The descent to Avernus is easy: night and day the doors of Hell are open;
> but to retrace your path and escape to the upper air, this is the feat, this the
> toil (VI.128–9),

has already appeared when Satan addresses the assembly of devils: 'long is the way / And hard, that out of Hell leads up to light' (II.432–3). Milton's allusion to Virgil in Book III, an allusion in which he actually compares himself to Aeneas rather than to Virgil and thus claims a heroic status for himself as poet, is thus also an allusion to himself, and through himself to Satan. We can thus read Milton's use of the passage in Book III as an attempt to make sublimity out of abjection, a task that the image of bees in Book I suggested was, at the least, dangerous.

Even at the beginning of the invocation to Book III Milton seems unsure of his ability to write the poem he intends to write; indeed, for all its grandeur the passage is curiously tentative:[50]

> Hail holy Light, ofspring of Heav'n first-born,
> Or of th' Eternal Coeternal beam
> May I express thee unblam'd?   (III.1–3)

Milton's uncertainty here – his 'Or' – is not only a theological question but also a matter of poetic concern, given his fears about poetic creation as an infringement on God's being.[51] The nature of the concern is given in the next line, in which Milton, as always considering the Latin meanings of English words, means both 'may I speak of holy light without blame' and 'may I emit holy light without blame.'[52] In singing of light, Milton fears that he may be imitating (and thus sacrilegiously parodying) yet another of God's attributes. We can also see these fears in his presentation of himself as flying 'now with bolder wing, / Escap't the *Stygian* Pool' (III.13–14), a description that recalls the passage that concludes Book II, in which Satan, having escaped Hell, journeys towards Earth. The first eight lines of the invocation, in which Milton has attempted to define 'holy Light' break down in to a series of questions. As Herman points out, 'we are never given the answer to these questions or to any of the other choices in this extraordinarily resonant invocation.'[53] Milton does not work through his uncertainties but rather presents them to his readers.

One way to summarize the effect of Milton's difficulties with expression in both senses (including his use of his own poetry and the poetry of other poets) is to say that he is forced to acknowledge that language, the very stuff of which *Paradise Lost* is made (and, in particular, the poetic language of himself and his great predecessor Virgil) is irremediably tainted. This would obviously be a problem for any poet, but it is particularly serious for Milton, as his blindness makes him especially dependent on language. His presentation of the privative effects of his blindness is heart-rendingly moving, but he proceeds towards imagining it as an opportunity. Although 'ever-during dark' (III.45) envelops him and although he speaks of being

> from the chearful wayes of men
> Cut off, and for the Book of knowledge fair
> Presented with a Universal blanc
> Of Nature's works to mee expung'd and ras'd,
> And wisdom at one entrance quite shut out,   (III.46–50)

he turns this blindness to the things of the earth into an invitation: 'So much the rather thou Celestial Light / Shine inward' (III.51–2).[54] As Elizabeth M.A. Hodgson suggests in her perceptive analysis of the importance of grief to Milton's poetics in *Paradise Lost*, 'grief here seems a necessary element of that prophetic power.'[55] His grief for his blindness turns into the ability to see it as a way to escape the corruptions of human language.

What Milton seeks here is to become himself a source of light – in other words, to 'express [light] unblam'd.' He continues his appeal to Celestial Light by saying:

> the mind through all her powers
> Irradiate, there plant eyes, all mist from thence
> Purge and disperse, that I may see and tell
> Of things invisible to mortal sight.   (III.52–5)

Oerlemans argues that 'the magnificent trope of inward light is a refinement of the mind as passive receptacle that Milton describes in the first invocation,' but this is perhaps unduly optimistic.[56] To see this image as a refinement of the first is to see the proems as a narrative with forward movement, whereas I see this image as an example of what Rumrich calls 'the strikingly recursive association of creativity with the womb of darkness.'[57] What is more, this recursiveness is not even merely repetition but, in my view, repetition with a downward trend. In the first invocation, although Milton presented himself as dark and low, his song, at least, was adventurous. In the invocation to Book III, he is still dark and low, but now his song may be even sacrilegiously adventurous. Thus, it could be argued that what we have is not progression or even a return, but rather a retreat. In any case, I think the important point here is not only that Milton has come to see himself as passive and abject, but that now, like Virgil, he sees passivity and abjection as necessary for textual production.

In the final two proems, Milton is, if anything, increasingly passive. In the invocation that begins Book VII, he calls on Urania, one of the nine muses, to help him. Most Miltonists assume that Urania is the 'Heav'nly Muse' of I.6, but this is not clear to me – or, in fact, to Milton. Even here, for instance, after calling on her by name he says 'by that name / If rightly thou art call'd' (VII.1–2), and he ends the invocation by contrasting the classical Urania with an unspecified Christian power: 'So fail not thou, who thee implores: / For thou art Heav'nlie, shee an empty dream' (VII.38–9). Milton's doubts are clearly part of his larger problems with the conventional machinery and subject matter of the epic poem, but they are also part of his larger discomfort with his own poetic audacity.[58] Yet although Milton expresses this discomfort at the beginning and ending of the invocation to Book VII, the middle of this invocation reveals his inability to do without the classical machinery. When he asks Urania for help to guide him back down from heaven, for instance, he refers to two examples from classical mythology. The first is the story of the final days of Bellerophon, who was thrown from Pegasus after attempting to reach heaven and was condemned to wander the Aleian plain, blind and insane. Of course, both Bellerophon's disastrous descent from heaven and his blindness make this an apt classical precedent for Milton, but I think that we are intended to find the classical example jarring, coming as it does only a few lines after Milton's disclaiming of the truth of classical mythology.

The second classical example is the story of the death of Orpheus. Significantly, this is preceded by a brief autobiographical passage:

> I sing with mortal voice, unchang'd
> To hoarce or mute, though fall'n on evil dayes,
> On evil dayes though fall'n, and evil tongues.   (VII.24–6)

The use of chiasmus – repetition with a difference – underlines the fact that this section of the invocation to Book VII is a version of the passage on his blindness in Book III. In the earlier passage, Milton's blindness is relieved by the possibility that he will become a source of holy light; here, however, he goes on to say: '[I am] not alone, while thou / Visit'st my slumbers Nightly' (VII.28–9). In both III and VII, then, the sorrows and dangers of Milton's real-life situation are alleviated by his special relation to holiness. The crucial difference between the passages is that, while in the first he imagines becoming filled with light in some unspecified way, here the consolation and inspiration come from the direct intervention of a superior being. Milton underlines this fact by ending this section of the invocation with a direct appeal: 'still govern thou my Song, / Urania' (VII.30–1). In contrast to the passage in Book III announcing an inward shining that he himself will transmit – as he says, he will use this light to 'see and tell / Of things invisible to mortal sight' – Milton now calls upon the goddess by her name to take an active role in the poem.

As I suggested earlier, insofar as there is a development from Book III to Book VII, it is in the direction of greater passivity and submission. What is more, this submission is to female figures: both Urania and the unspecified Christian deity who is the true muse. Milton addresses his dependence on female figures by turning to his second classical example, the story of Orpheus.[59] He begins by asking Urania to 'drive farr off the barbarous dissonance / Of Bacchus and his revellers' (VII.32–3). The reference is obviously to the Maenads; he goes on to specify which of the stories involving the Maenads he means: 'that wild Rout that tore the Thracian Bard / In Rhodope' (VII.34–5). The reference to Orpheus increases our sense of the dangers of women, as, although many people were apparently killed by the Maenads just because they were in the wrong place at the wrong time, they actually planned to kill Orpheus. In Ovid's version this was because after his failure to bring Eurydice back to the human world he had given up the love of women for the love of boys and was consequently seen as an enemy to women in general.[60] Milton thus refers to a legend that presents women as especially violent and vengeful and hostile to men, and he underlines this point at the end of the passage when he says, 'nor could the Muse defend / Her Son' (VII.37–8): the power of mortal women is greater even than the power of Calliope, the goddess whose special function is to inspire epic poets.

Milton's point is that his Urania is more powerful than imaginary classical goddesses, but the emphasis on the dangers posed by women (even to great poets) increases our sense of Urania's power and Milton's powerlessness. Furthermore, threatened by women, protected by another woman, he cuts a noticeably unheroic figure. The extended passage in the invocation to Book IX, in which Milton tries to redefine heroism (IX.13–41), is in part prompted by his awareness of this fact. He begins by stating that the subject of his story is more heroic than the events narrated in the *Iliad*, the *Odyssey*, or the *Aeneid*, but he then tacitly admits that his superior subject is not enough for poetic success by inserting a qualification:

> If answerable style I can obtain
> Of my Celestial Patroness, who degnes
> Her nightly visitation unimplor'd,
> And dictates to me slumbering, or inspires
> Easie my unpremeditated Verse.   (IX.20–4)

With its reference to the nightly visits of his muse, this passage recalls VII.28–9; the crucial changes are 'unimplor'd' and 'dictates.' While the passage inspires envy, as most people would like to wake up and find that they had written a great poem, Milton's poetic achievements turn out to be unwilled and beyond his control. Once again, he is passive, a receptacle to be filled with poetry.

After these lines he returns to his argument that the subject matter associated with epics and romances has nothing to do with true heroism and he ends this last of his invocations by asserting his true heroic status as the chronicler of true heroism:

> Mee of these [i.e., martial or chivalric subjects]
> Nor skill'd nor studious, higher Argument
> Remains, sufficient of itself to raise
> That name.   (IX.41–4)

The raising of the name alludes to Virgil's 'temptanda uia est, qua me quoque possim / tollere humo uictorque uirum uolitare per ora' (a way must be found by which I too may raise myself from the ground and fly as a victor through the mouths of men; *Georgics* III.8–9). Coming immediately after his dismissal of Virgil's subject matter, Milton's allusion should be seen as a claim that he will surpass Virgil's achievements, but the contrast between Virgil's use of a first-person pronoun and a first-person verb form as well as the highly marked alliteration with his own name ('uia' in line 8 and three of the words in line 9 alliterate with Virgil) and Milton's reliance on the 'higher Argument' rather than his own talent to make him famous as well as his use of 'That name' rather than 'My name' immediately undercut that claim.

The claim is further undercut by the fact that just after theses lines Milton turns to considering the things that could prevent his poetic success:

> unless an age too late, or cold
> Climate, or Years damp my intended wing
> Deprest, and much they may, if all be mine,
> Not Hers who brings it nightly to my Ear.   (IX.44–7)

Here, Milton passively submits himself to a higher authority. On one level this is the completely proper humility of a Christian, especially one writing a poem about such a sacred matter. As well, Milton's stress on his own obedience contrasts effectively with *Paradise Lost*'s narration 'Of Mans First Disobedience' (I.1), just as the nightly visits of his heavenly muse contrast effectively (and enviably) with the suspension of sociability between humans and celestial beings that he announced a few lines earlier:

> No more of talk where God or Angel Guest
> With Man, as with his Friend, familiar us'd
> To sit indulgent.   (IX.1–3)

In this invocation, then, Milton could be said to return to the proper behaviour of a Christian and to atone in his own person for the actions of Adam and Eve.

That, at least, is one way to understand Milton's presentation of himself throughout the invocations to *Paradise Lost*, particularly in Books VII and IX, and my argument is certainly not that such an understanding is mistaken. Nevertheless, this is only one way to understand it. While much in Milton's meta-poetics, as in his poetry in general, is distinctive, I feel that we can profitably compare his accounts of his textual production with the others I have looked at throughout this book, particularly with those of Virgil and Montaigne, which present textual production as something that is associated with the body, that is largely unwilled, and that is in many respects unpleasant or undignified for the writer. Although Milton is generally regarded as the most self-confident of poets – and frequently, in fact, as the most self-confident of humans – I think that his poetics, at least in *Paradise Lost*, is really to some extent a poetics of abjection. The reproductive metaphor is a part of this abjection, but it is not the whole thing: Milton imagines himself as to some extent feminine, a receptacle to be filled, but as we have seen, to be filled by female figures rather than male ones. Poetry is the result not of the exercise of the active will but rather of self-abnegation. Like Virgil – idle in the shade and tacitly comparing himself to the rotting carcasses of cows and, like Montaigne, submitting himself in his rural retirement to the sexual assaults of his imagination, which he imagines as a horse – over the course of the four invocations in *Paradise Lost* Milton demonstrates his awareness that textual production comes from abjection. Perhaps the composition of a text implies the decomposition of the writer.

III

While Milton's stated intention is to present a biblical story in a way that will be clear to all, Bunyan's is to tell an allegorical story that will demand some interpretation. In Milton, the allegory is often in the service of narrative clarity, as, for instance, when he recounts the war in heaven in terms of human wars or when he compares God to the sun. In Bunyan, allegory is the basic mode of the book and the reader is expected to do the sort of translation into everyday terms that Milton performs for his readers. Bunyan's decision to write allegorically has been the subject of much of the critical commentary on *The Pilgrim's Progress* and of almost all the commentary on 'The Author's Apology for his Book.' This poem seems straightforward, indeed often naively so, but as Barbara A. Johnson remarks in one of only a very few analyses devoted to the apology, it is, in fact, 'one of the most puzzling statements ever offered for a work of fiction.'[61] For one thing, while much of the poem is taken up with Bunyan's defence of allegory, parts of it (the parts with which I shall be concerned here) emphasize textual production in a way that is at odds with the book's famous opening – still, I think, the best first sentence of any novel in English: 'As I walk'd through the wilderness of this world, I lighted on a certain place, where was a Denn; And I laid me down in that place to sleep: And as I slept I dreamed a Dream.'[62] In contrast, as Johnson points out, in the poem Bunyan 'must call attention to the book's status as a made thing, rather than gloss over it.'[63]

Another way to put this is to say that while the prose presents us with a dream whose interpretation will occasion no great hermeneutic anguish, the poem presents us with a text that had to be written down and that concentrates on the author's use of a famous literary method. In this respect, 'The Author's Apology for his Book' is not so much like the preamble to a sermon as it is like the preface to a play. Like these prefaces – for instance, the preface to *The Two Noble Kinsmen*, which I discussed in chapter 1 – the poem makes us think about what it takes to produce a narrative before it invites us to suspend our disbelief. As a result, by the time we read that the narrator has 'dreamed a Dream' and realize that the book we are about to read is that dream, we already know we have entered the world of fiction. Dreaming, that is, is an allegory for textual production, and it is notable that in the poem as well Bunyan chooses to present that kind of production as something that is largely unwilled:

> When at the first I took my Pen in hand,
> Thus for to write; I did not understand
> That I at all should make a little Book
> In such a mode; Nay, I had undertook
> To make another.[64]   (1.1–5)

Here, sitting down to write a certain kind of book produces a different kind of book in a way that corresponds to an allegorical reading's production of a text other than what is written: the story of Christian becomes our story. From the beginning of the poem, Bunyan stresses the similarity between the producer and the consumer of the text.

The other book was apparently to have been a more conventional account of '*the Way / And Race of Saints in this our Gospel-Day*' (1.7–8), but this plan was put aside when, as Bunyan tells us in one of the most significant lines in the poem, he '*Fell suddenly into an Allegory*' (1.9).[65] Discussing this passage in terms of Bunyan's retreat from intentionality, Johnson remarks, 'We notice also that he is falling into verse.'[66] It is certainly true that in this early section of 'The Author's Apology for his Book' Bunyan presents himself as unable not to write the book we are holding, but it is especially significant that he is also unable not to write in verse. Although the quality of the poetry is not particularly high, Bunyan's use of verse permits him tacitly to claim a literary status for his work. This claim is bolstered by its similarity to another and much more famous claim about being unable not to write poetry: Sidney's misquotation or adaptation of Ovid in *The Defence of Poesie*: '*Quicquid conabor dicere, Versus erit*' (whatever I shall write will be verse; 37).[67]

Ovid's original is 'sponte sua carmen numeros veniebat ad aptos, / et quod temptabam scribere versus erat' (my song came of its own will in fitting numbers, and what I tried to write was poetry).[68] Sidney's point is that people in his day write everything in verse without writing properly, while Ovid is making a point about his upbringing. I think it is impossible either to prove or to disprove that Bunyan had read either Sidney or Ovid, but with its insistence on the moral profitability of fiction *The Defence of Poesie* is certainly an obvious precedent for Bunyan in this prefatory material.

Bunyan's emphasis on the unwilled nature of the text's composition might seem to militate against any claim to literary status, but once he has fallen into his allegory, he begins to use familiar literary metaphors to describe the composition of *The Pilgrim's Progress*. He begins by saying that falling into allegory led to

> *more than twenty things, which I set down;*
> *This done, I twenty more had in my Crown,*
> *And they again began to multiply,*
> *Like sparks that from the coals of Fire do flie.*
> *Nay then, thought I, if that you breed so fast,*
> *I'll put you by your selves, lest you at last*
> *Should prove* ad infinitum, *and eat out*
> *The Book that I already am about.*   (1.11–18)

One of the metaphors here is that of the *furor poeticus* or poetic rage, the possession by a god that leads to the poem. Accounts of poetic rage are often accompanied by imagery of fire, as is the case here.

The other metaphor Bunyan uses to present his composition is, of course, the reproductive metaphor. I see this both in his use of 'multiply,' with its echo of the famous injunction 'Be fruitful, and multiply' (Genesis 1:28) and, more obviously, in the reference to the breeding of the fancies in his brain. However, Bunyan's use of the metaphor is unusual. For one thing, when he presents himself as saying to the ideas *'I'll put you by your selves,'* he appears as an editor rather than a writer, or – in the terms of the reproductive metaphor – as a guardian rather than a parent. In this respect, the passage resembles the Duchess of Newcastle's assigning of autonomy to her texts (paper bodies), which I discussed at the beginning of my introduction. In a superb article on Bunyan and textuality, Sylvia Brown argues that 'Bunyan understood texts (or at least the only texts that mattered) as reproductive agents ...

They were autonomous, they acted on human subjects rather than being produced by them, and they were fertile – equally capable of producing more texts as well as readers formed in the image of the text.'[69] This textual autonomy, which Brown sees as typical of much seventeenth-century Puritan writing, is what is most striking about Bunyan's preface, in which the human author provides only the (paper) form of the text: it is not his own creation.

In some ways the most noteworthy aspect of the passage is that the ideas do not appear to be welcome. In their frantic proliferation and their apparently insatiable hunger they evoke an infestation of parasites who will consume their host – and as Brown remarks, this host is 'not Bunyan, but another book, the one Bunyan was originally writing.'[70] The author is at first only the spectator of these textual conflicts. It is partly for this reason that I feel that Bunyan's reproductive metaphor ultimately seems less like Newcastle's and more like Montaigne's. In this connection, I am thinking specifically of Montaigne's description in 'Of Idlenesse' of being raped by his own spirit: 'playing the skittish and loose-broken jade, he takes a hundred times more cariere and libertie unto himselfe, than hee did for others, and begets in me so many extravagant *Chimeraes*, and fantasticall monsters, so orderlesse, and without any reason, one hudling upon an other, that at-leasure to view the foolishnesse and monstrous strangenesse of them, I have begun to keep a register of them.'[71] There are obviously many differences between the two, as Bunyan is careful not to denigrate the resulting text and his language is not sexual, but there are also the important similarities that, while both Bunyan and Montaigne resolve to put their fancies in textual order, this may well be the only order they can hope to attain and that they present their textual production as reaction rather than as action.

What is particularly important to me in the resemblance between Bunyan's and Montaigne's metaphorical presentations of textual production as reproduction is that both presentations are unpleasant. For Montaigne, writing a book is like being raped and then giving birth to a multitude of bizarre offspring; for Bunyan, the ideas for *The Pilgrim's Progress* sprang unbidden to his brain, where they bred rapidly and threatened to drive out everything else. Of course, the unpleasantness is largely humorous in both cases, but it is still significant that both authors choose to develop the reproductive metaphor in such a way as to stress abjection. Whereas for Virgil the abjection of the cow's carcass is sublimated into the useful bees that produce honey (and thus, metaphorically, poetry), for Montaigne and for Bunyan the abjection apparently cannot be separated from the resulting text, however much Bunyan's swarming ideas may recall Virgil's bees. Perhaps it is for this reason that Bunyan emphasizes the transition from the reproductive metaphor to a more literal account of what it means to write and publish a book when he relates his friends' reactions to his manuscript: *'some said, let them live; some, let them die: / Some said,* John, *print it; others said, Not so'* (2.8–9). In the first line, his ideas are living things; in the second, they have become a singular manuscript; in both cases and in the lines as a whole the emphasis is on Bunyan's command.

Up to this point, I have emphasized the abjection in Bunyan's account of his textual production, but the account as whole is more obviously marked by happiness. For one thing, his composition appears to have been quick and painless:

> *For having now my Method by the end;*
> *Still as I pull'd, it came; and so I penn'd*
> *It down, until it came at last to be*
> *For length and breadth the bigness which you see.*   (2.1–4)

The ease and inevitability of this process have been a source of envy to other writers for more than 300 years. More immediately important to me is the crucial shift from private to public. He first says that he wrote *'mine own self to gratifie'* (1.24) and then corrects that to say that he wrote *'to divert my self in doing this, / From worser thoughts, which make me do amiss'* (1.27–8). The shift from pleasure alone to pleasure mixed with profit is obviously important as well, but the profit is as private as the pleasure. In the passage I quoted at the beginning of this paragraph, Bunyan uses the image of weaving (specifically, converting the flax on the distaff into thread), a process in which a pre-existing material modified by many hands is turned into something useful, as opposed, for instance, to scribbling down the thoughts that come to one's own mind.[72] Weaving, that is, is inescapably communal (however solitary the labour of the individual spinner may be), and Bunyan's use of the second-person pronoun in this passage – the first direct address to the readers in the poem – underscores his turning outwards to the world.[73]

After the defence of allegory that takes up most of 'The Author's Apology for his Book' (by my count, 132 of the poem's 236 lines), Bunyan begins the final section of his poem by saying to the reader *'I'le shew the profit of my Book'* (6.20). His stress on the edifying nature of the book is certainly not unexpected, but I think that his way of doing so is. For Bunyan, reading the book is a process that must be as active as writing it, and perhaps even as active as Christian's own journey: Christian stands in for the reader as a reader, not just a Christian. One of the ways in which he makes this point is to return to the reproductive metaphor: '*This Book will make a Travailer of thee*' (6.33). To be a 'Travailer' is simultaneously to be a traveller, a worker, and a woman in labour. As Michael Davies points out in his excellent analysis of the poem, Bunyan is still in control here: the book will have the desired effect only 'if one is willing to be ruled by its "Counsel," from which point alone (as the word "Travailer" and the other birthing puns of the apology suggest) can the labour for a new life take effect.'[74] The reproductive metaphor applies no longer to the spontaneous generation of Bunyan's ideas, the ideas that become *The Pilgrim's Progress*, but to the reader, and the metaphorical child is no longer the book but the reader himself or herself in the new life that to a devout Christian like Bunyan is not metaphorical but real – really real.

However great Bunyan's control, then, he intends reading *The Pilgrim's Progress* to be a process in which both he and the reader are engaged. The book is not sent from the author to the reader but rather is shared, and this mutuality – almost unknown in literary uses of the reproductive metaphor – is what concludes the poem:

> *Would'st read thy self, and read thou know'st not what*
> *And yet know whether thou art blest or not,*
> *By reading the same lines? O then come hither,*
> *And lay my Book, thy Head and Heart together.*   (7.22–5)

As Tamsin Spargo points out, 'it is the effects of the text on an individual subject which are offered as the ultimate "profit" of the book. The reader is enlisted as an essential component of the active progress of the text which can only be complete when "*my Book, thy Head and Heart*" are combined in the process of attentive reading.'[75] In his prologue, Bunyan is able to use both the intimacy and the teleology of the reproductive metaphor in a way that stresses individual pleasure and profit, that focuses on reading and change rather than on consumption and stasis, and that concludes with a textual embrace. Nor does this closeness end with the preface: as Stanley Fish remarks, within *The Pilgrim's Progress* itself 'the narrator … is not our guide, but our fellow': the meeting of the text and the reader in the preface initiates a relationship.[76]

The best recent analysis of the role of prefaces (and 'postfaces' and much else beside) is by Gérard Genette, who says in *Paratexts* that 'authorial practice ... consists of forcing on the reader an indigenous theory defined by the author's *intention*, which is presented as the most reliable interpretive key; and in this respect the preface clearly constitutes one of the instruments of authorial control.'[77] Both Bunyan's emphasis on the spontaneous and largely unwilled nature of his textual production and his emphasis on the reader as active would appear to lessen his authorial control, but this control is to some extent reasserted in 'The Conclusion,' the short poem at the end of the first part of *The Pilgrim's Progress*. Indeed, a certain vacillation about the question of authorial control informs the opening lines of the poem:

> *Now Reader, I have told my Dream to thee;*
> *See if thou canst Interpret it to me;*
> *Or to thy self, or Neighbour.*   (1–3)

Bunyan begins by presenting a personal relationship between himself and the reader; by the second line the relationship appears not so much like a friendship as like the relationship between a teacher and a student. After this, Bunyan changes to imagining the reader as someone who will use the book either for personal reflection or for informal preaching – in other words, in ways that no longer involve Bunyan himself.

Still, Bunyan does seek to retain some control over the text, and he does so by warning the reader to '*take heed / Of mis-interpreting*' (3–4) and to '*be not extream, / In playing with the* out-side *of my Dream*' (7–8). The 'out-side' is the text itself; using metaphors, Bunyan cautions the reader against being fixated on metaphors:

> *Put by the Curtains, look within my Vail;*
> *Turn up my Metaphors and do not fail:*
> *There, if thou seekest them, such things to find*
> *As will be helpful to an honest mind.*   (13–16)

While 'The Author's Apology for his Book' ends with the reader's embrace of the text, 'The Conclusion' is concerned with what will happen when that embrace is over and the reader turns once again to the world. Bunyan exemplifies this shift by transforming his own image of the text as the outside when he advises the reader to keep the gold of his text and throw away the dross: '*What if my Gold be wrapped up in Ore? / None throws away the Apple for the Core'* (19–20). In the first of these lines, the text is the outside of the thing that is really valuable; in the second, the text is the inside of the valued object. In making this move from text as outside to text as inside, the poem provides, as Fish suggests, 'an authoritative description of the "dynamics of the narrative" which are finally the dynamics of the reading process.'[78] It is the reader who controls this process by the internalization of the text and, crucially, of the moral teachings it contains.

At the very end of 'The Conclusion,' Bunyan turns to another metaphor for textual production – one that also serves to reassert his control of the text – when he says that if the reader discards everything '*I know not but 'twill make me Dream again'* (22). He returns to the narrative's initial image of textual production as a dream, as something spontaneous and not under the control of the writer himself – something analogous, that is, to the accidental apple tree that may result from our throwing the apple's core away. This may make textual production seem rather like reproduction as we understand it, but it is very different from the deliberate harnessing of the powers of the body that the reproductive metaphor is intended to evoke. I would add that the metaphor of the apple can also be seen to provide a version of the reproductive metaphor, one that is also a partial defence of his text. Although the core of the apple is not edible, it is vitally important in containing the seeds by which the tree propagates itself: the apple sustains us here and now; the apple tree will sustain us indefinitely. This is, in a sense, the reproductive metaphor, but in this case it is not the author who reproduces but rather the text, and what is reproduced is not more texts but a different kind of reader. As was the case with the text by Newcastle that I cited in the introduction, the text comes from a body and itself is a body. For Bunyan, however, the body is made not of paper but of wood: the substance from which paper is made.

IV

In focusing on 'The Author's Apology to his Book' rather than on *The Pilgrim's Progress* itself, I have privileged Bunyan's paratext rather than his text, not because I feel the introductory poem is necessarily better or more interesting than the prose narrative it precedes (although I would like to see it considered as an indispensable part of the novel as a whole), but because to some extent my interest throughout this book has been in paratexts: with the prefaces to *The Roaring Girl* and *The Two Noble*

Kinsmen, with Daniel's first book of poetry as a preface to his plans for a poetic career, and, in this chapter, with Sidney's and Milton's inclusion of what is in many respects paratextual material throughout their poems. In the book as a whole, my argument could be characterized as the claim that the use of the reproductive metaphor is always in some sense a paratext. This term was first used by Genette in the book I have just cited in my discussion of *The Pilgrim's Progress*, and I shall quote his definition. Paratexts, he says, 'surround and extend [the text], precisely in order to *present* it, in the usual sense of this verb but also in the strongest sense: to *make present*, to ensure the text's presence in the world, its "reception" and consumption in the form (nowadays, at least) of a book.'[79] As his use of the verb 'surround' in this passage suggests, Genette's concern in the examples he discusses in this book is chiefly with the elements that could be said to lie outside what we would think of as the text itself: titles, dedications, prefaces, binding, and so on. Nevertheless, he also discusses elements within the text – illustrations and chapter headings, for example – and he looks at all the ways in which we receive texts. The original French title of the books is *Seuils* (thresholds), and I think that we should see paratexts as thresholds in that they determine (or seek to determine) our ingress into the interpretation of a text, rather than only into the text itself. As Michael Saenger suggests in his analysis of the front matter of Renaissance printed books, these pages 'can be seen as a particularly articulate contemporary sliding edge between the text and the world.'[80]

The reproductive metaphor functions as a paratext – a sliding edge – in that it provides a narrative of textual origins that corresponds to the prevailing narrative about the management of the origins of the person. We are thus implicitly assured that the text we are about to read will not challenge the regulation of profit and loss in every aspect of human behaviour that governs our lives; in other words, it serves as our guarantee that the book we are about to read may be safely consumed. Like a literal threshold, the reproductive metaphor is intended to provide a safe way into a space that will also be a safe way out of that space. As the space in question is textual, we could say that the paratext, in a larger sense, is designed to enable the movement of bodies throughout both textual and extra-textual worlds, and these last pages of my book themselves are a threshold through which readers leave the book. What I have tried to do throughout this book is to suggest that it is important to interrogate the ways in which the paratextual function of the reproductive metaphor, whether intentionally or not, seeks to permit certain kinds of movement and interdict others. In metaphorically presenting texts as entities that are produced in socially legible ways, the reproductive metaphor restricts their freedom. It also restricts our freedom: not just in how we interpret texts, but also in imposing on all our activities – textual and sexual – a method of proceeding in which it is only the successful and useful ending that matters.

Throughout this book I have focused on what I have seen as the particular solutions to this problem that Renaissance writers used: concentrating on the work required for this sort of ending, for instance, or separating the pleasures of language from language's ability to achieve concrete results. My introduction suggested other solutions, however, and I would like to return to these now at the very end of my book. If, as the Duchess of Newcastle suggests, books are paper bodies in their manuscript state before publication, then we could understand the metaphorical reproduction associated with textual production as not ours but theirs. This move would be part of understanding texts as living things ('artificial, artful, alive,' as I wrote in the introduction), as organisms that change and respond to stimuli in the same way as the creations of A-Life. Like these creations, texts begin as artefacts, but they gradually acquire a certain amount of autonomy and change in ways that are not entirely predictable. In this theory of textual production, the focus would be neither on the family as a private unit nor on the family as a microcosm of the state but rather on textuality as a succession of encounters of various sorts between texts and readers and also between texts and other texts. This free-floating and atopic series of frequently unplanned and impermanent encounters and pleasures is an analogue for the idea of sexuality as something unmoored from service to reproduction. For both paper bodies and flesh bodies, reproduction, as metaphor or as biological fact, would be only one possible outcome among a sea of pleasures.

Notes

Preface

1 Bersani, 'Is the Rectum a Grave?' 206. Bersani's extended discussion of this point can be found on 206–10.
2 Ibid., 218. Bersani had already discussed this idea in *The Freudian Body*, which had appeared in the previous year.
3 Bersani, 'Is the Rectum a Grave?' 222.
4 Miller, 'Anal Rope,' 117, 118, 119.
5 Edelman has continued this kind of analysis in his recent book *No Future*. I return to this title in my introduction.
6 I make use of Stockton's book at a number of points in this volume. See also Sally R. Munt's recent *Queer Attachments*.
7 In this aspect of my book I endorse Carla Freccero's recent statement in *Queer / Early / Modern* that 'all textuality, when subjected to close reading, can be said to be queer' (9).
8 Edelman, *No Future*, 4

Introduction: The Work of Art in the Age of Human Reproduction

1 Cavendish, *Paper Bodies*, 10. For a good discussion of the duchess's attitude towards her publications, see Salzman, 'Early Modern (Aristocratic) Women,' 289–91.
2 Cavendish, *Paper Bodies*, 11.
3 For a brief discussion of a similar passage in *Two Gentlemen of Verona*, see Guy-Bray, 'Shakespeare,' 15.
4 Sedgwick, *Epistemology of the Closet*, 3.

5 Spencer, *Literary Relations*, 230. For Spencer's excellent discussion of the reproductive metaphor and of ideas about the family in the period covered by her book, see 1–17. For a discussion of the reproductive metaphor in this period, see Stephanson, *Yard of Wit*, especially 97–115, and Castle, '"Lab'ring Bards."' For the argument that poetic influence should be read through sexuality rather than always through reproductive metaphors, see Guy-Bray, *Loving in Verse*.

6 Feinberg, *Stone Butch Blues* (1993).

7 Interestingly, in the ten-year anniversary edition Feinberg drops this passage, although she writes in the preface ('A Decade Later: Thanks') of a character coming not from 'the womb of creativity' but rather from 'the immersion pool of memory' and in the 'Afterword' of 'characters I birthed.' Her use of the metaphor in the 2003 edition is noticeably more conventional than her original use.

8 Friedman, 'Creativity and the Childbirth Metaphor,' 58. Friedman's article contains a useful summary and many good analyses of contemporary poetry. Perhaps the first extended discussion of the reproductive metaphor from a feminist point of view is in Gilbert and Gubar, *The Madwoman in the Attic*, 3–44.

9 Dienstfrey and Hillman, *Grand Permission*, xiv.

10 Hellwarth, 'Afterword,' 395.

11 For a similar confusion of the meaning of 'literal' and 'metaphorical,' see D. Cheney, 'Mysterious Genesis of *Paradise Lost*,' 57. At the beginning of his perceptive discussion of Milton's first invocation, Cheney says that 'any ... product of mental labour ... naturally lends itself to procreative metaphors'; a little later in the paragraph he writes that this product grows 'figuratively in the mind, or more literally in the computer's womb.' The confusion of tenor and vehicle is typical of many discussions of the reproductive metaphor. Interestingly, the stress on the passivity of the authorial role resembles the self-presentation of Milton, as I shall show in the last chapter of this book.

12 Foucault, 'What Is an Author?' 107.

13 I would argue that this point is demonstrated by the fact that even when Foucault wishes to rethink history, the term he comes up with is 'genealogy.' See, most obviously, his 'Nietzsche, Genealogy, History.'

14 De Grazia, 'Imprints,' 83. The article as a whole is an excellent discussion of Renaissance ideas about reproduction in both senses of the word. It is reprinted as the first article in *Printing and Parenting in Early Modern England*.

15 Roof, 'In Locus Parentis,' 377.

16 There is, of course, a vast body of literature on Renaissance reproduction, so my discussion will be not only brief but selective: I have no intention of attempting to summarize the entire scholarly debate. Probably the most thorough recent treatment of the subject is in Laqueur, *Making Sex*. For his discussion of the Renaissance, see chapters three and four (63–148). For more on the subject, see the bibliographies in the works I do cite. For a interesting sociological look at the ways in which reproduction is and has been socialized, see Robertson, *Beyond the Family*. For two good discussions of reproduction and the family in the Renaissance that are very different from mine, see Krier, *Birth Passages*, and Witmore, *Pretty Creatures*.

17 Keller, *Generating*, 191n1. However,Keller does use the term 'reproduction' in her subtitle. Her book as a whole provides a valuable summary of Renaissance knowledge of and discourses on reproduction and embryology. See also Fissell, *Vernacular Bodies* (especially chap. 2, 'The Womb Goes Bad,' 53–89) and, for Italy, Finucci, *Manly Masquerade*, 2–29.

18 *Finucci, Manly Masquerade*, 35.

19 Ibid., 77. For Finucci's discussion of these subjects as a whole, see 38–78.

20 Browne, *Religio Medici*, in *Major Works*, 148–9.

21 Swann, '"Procreate like Trees,"' 139.

22 For a fascinating discussion of the Renaissance discourse on monstrous births, see Crawford, *Marvelous Protestantism*.

23 For an interesting discussion of the reproduction of texts in English humanism, one that makes the claim that the printing press does not change textual production so much as it makes concrete what was already conceptual in fifteenth-century practice, see Wakelin, *Humanism, Reading, and English Literature*, especially chapter 5, 126–59.

24 Foucault, *History of Sexuality*, 136, 139. For a similar argument, see Bataille, *Erotism*, especially 49 and 105.

25 Glimp, *Increase and Multiply*, xii–xiii. For Glimp's discussion of Foucault and bio-politics, see xv–xix. See also Foucault, *Discipline and Punish*, especially 220–1, and, for the increasing importance of the nuclear family to church and state, see MacCulloch, *Reformation*, 647–62.

26 Glimp, *Increase and Multiply*, xx–xxi.

27 Lerer, 'The Courtly Body,' 80.

28 Orgel, 'Marginal Maternity,' 289. For two interesting recent discussions of Renaissance attitudes towards literary copying, see Eden, *Friends Hold All Things*, and Bjørnstad, *Borrowed Feathers*. In her discussion of Shakespeare's sonnets in *Reading Shakespeare's Will*, Lisa Freinkel makes a similar distinction to Orgel's when she contrasts 'endless and exhaustive copying' and '*succession*' (197); see 159–236 for her discussion of the sonnets as a whole.

29 For a similar argument, see Pierre Bourdieu's preface to the 1990 edition of his and Jean-Claude Passeron's *Reproduction in Education, Society*, especially vii–viii, and Haraway, 'Promise of Monsters,' 69.

30 Hayles, *How We Became Posthuman*, 2–3. See also Hayles's brief look at discussions of her work in 'Refiguring the Posthuman.' For a discussion of gender as prosthesis in the English Renaissance, see Fisher, *Materializing Gender*, 1–35.

31 Hayles, *How We Became Posthuman*, 22.

32 Deleuze and Guattari, *Anti-Oedipus*, 17, 20.

33 For a good discussion of Deleuze from the point of view of queer theory, see Cohen and Ramlow, 'Pink Vectors of Deleuze.'

34 H. Turner, *Shakespeare's Double Helix*, 17.

35 Ibid., 52.

36 Barkan, *Nature's Work of Art*, 114.

37 Hobbes, *Leviathan*, 9.

38 Ibid., 151.

39 In a recent book, Su Fang Ng has helpfully pointed out that although the familial metaphor was widespread in Renaissance England, the meaning of the family itself was not as fixed as has generally been assumed. For her discussion of Hobbes's opening analogy, see *Literature and the Politics of the Family*, 91–5. For Ng's useful discussion of Hobbes as a whole (a discussion that includes a very good summary of other recent work on *Leviathian*), see chapter 3, 76–102.

40 Smith, *Conceived by Liberty*, 222.

41 Whitelaw, *Metacreation*, 38. Whitelaw is writing specifically of the work of the American Steven Rooke, but the comment applies to Artificial Life in general.

42 Ibid., 140.

43 For a discussion of the issues raised here that also takes into account classical philosophy and the visual culture of Renaissance Italy, see Berger, 'Second-World Prosthetics.' For an analysis of the rhetoric of reproduction in genetics and popular discourse about genetics, see Roof, *Reproduction of Reproduction*.

44 Whitelaw, *Metacreation*, 3.

45 Terranova, 'Digital Darwin,' 81.

46 Helmreich, *Silicon Second Nature*, vii.

47 See ibid., 39–40.

48 Ibid, 146. Later, he points out that this is true even with things such as bit strings, in which reproduction occurs without sexual difference. See also 147.

49 I have already cited three of the essays in this collection: Hellwarth, 'Afterword,' Orgel, 'Marginal Maternity,' and Roof, 'In Locus Parentis.'

50 Maus, 'A Womb of His Own,' 89.

51 Brooks, 'Introduction,' 1.

52 Maguire, 'Alice Walker,' 344.

53 See Kirk, 'Women Academics.'

54 Maguire, 'Alice Walker,' 344.

55 Of all the contributors to *Printing and Parenting in Early Modern England,* it is Maria Teresa Prendergast who engages most with these questions. See 'Promiscuous Textualities.'

56 Butler, 'Kinship,' 40. For a somewhat different view of queer families, see Ahmed, *Queer Phenomenology,* especially 154–5.

57 Butler, 'Kinship,' 35.

58 Ibid., 18.

59 Benjamin, 'Work of Art,' 224.

60 Benjamin, 'Author as Producer,' 222.

61 Edelman, *No Future,* 9.

62 Ibid., 2.

63 Berlant and Warner, 'Sex in Public,' 194.

64 Edelman, *No Future,* 60. For another look at heterosexuality as repetitive, see Ahmed, *Queer Phenomenology,* 192n17.

65 In this connection, I would also like to cite Herbert Marcuse's *Eros and Civilization,* which envisions a state of affairs that would 'make the human body an instrument of pleasure rather than labor' (xv). See especially 49–51 on perversions.

66 Vaneigem, *Book of Pleasures,* 9.

67 Ibid., 70.

68 Ibid., 23, 24.

69 See Freud, 'Fixations of Preliminary Sexual Aims,' in *On Sexuality,* 68–73.

70 MacKendrick, *Counterpleasures,* 12. For MacKendrick's excellent review of protests against thinking of sexuality in terms of use and narrative, see 1–21.

71 Ibid., 19.

72 Ibid., 31.

73 Vaneigem, *Book of Pleasures,* 48.

74 Ibid., 23.

75 MacKendrick, *Counterpleasures,* 110.

76 The article as a whole offers a subtle and valuable intervention in the debate about male use of the reproductive metaphor.

77 Plato, *Symposium*, in *Opera*, 209. Unless otherwise stated, all translations in this book are my own.
78 Plato, *Phaidrus*, in *Opera*, 227d.
79 Ibid., 228b.
80 Ibid., 257b.
81 What is more, as Socrates, here and elsewhere in Plato, is so obviously the one who is going to have been right all along, it could be argued that the very obviousness of this particular *telos* vitiates the extent to which we can understand the *Phaidrus* as a teleological narrative.
82 Halpern, *Poetics of Primitive Accumulation*, 28. See 19–21 for Halpern's treatment of the centrality of rhetoric to humanist education. To some extent, the 'active embrace of ideology' that he sees as typical of the Renaissance is anticipated in Ancient Greek itself, as the word meaning 'I obey' ($\pi\varepsilon\iota\theta o\mu\alpha\iota$) is the middle form of the verb that in its active form ($\pi\varepsilon\iota\theta\omega$) means 'I persuade.' For speakers of Ancient Greek, then, to say that one obeys is also to say that one has been persuaded, rather than just to say that one has given in to authority.
83 Ibid., 53. For Halpern's discussion of the vexed relationship between poetry and rhetoric, see 45–60.
84 Ibid., 53.
85 Ibid., 57.
86 Žižek, *Parallax View*, 158.
87 Barthes, *Roland Barthes*, 139.
88 Barthes, *Pleasure of the Text*, 23.
89 Ibid., 40. I think it is necessary to acknowledge that Barthes himself tended to feel that there was no escape from these institutions. Although he suggested that in modernity perversion 'shields bliss from the finality of reproduction,' he glumly concluded that 'even so, modernity can do nothing: the exchange recuperates everything' (24). In *Reading Shakespeare's Will*, Lisa Freinkel sees the world in which Shakespeare's sonnets take place as one 'that is caught up ... in an increasingly exhaustive and thus exhausted repetition' (194). For her, the young man's reproduction of himself would provide a way out of this world. As should be clear by now, I see reproduction as more likely to continue this kind of repetition.
90 Barthes's discussion of the neutral is indebted to the concept of the neutral in semiotics. See, for instance, Marin, *Utopics*, and, for a good demonstration of the role of the concept, his 'Frontiers of Utopia.'
91 Barthes, *The Neutral*, 43.
92 Ibid., 53.
93 Ibid., 68.

94 Hammill, 'Are We Being Homosexual Yet?' 81.
95 Barthes, *The Neutral*, 162.
96 Adorno, 'Lyric Poetry and Society,' 58. For a more general defence of the political content of art, see Marcuse, *Aesthetic Dimension*.
97 Longenbach, *Resistance to Poetry*, 56.
98 Berger, 'Second-World Prosthetics,' 100.
99 Liddell and Short define the noun as meaning 'a maid, maiden, virgin, girl' and the adjective as meaning 'maiden, virgin, chaste'; they also list the use of the word to mean 'an unmarried man,' but that usage is found only in New Testament Greek. In any case, as the marital status of the male poet is not the question here, the term is still inappropriate.
100 See above, notes 19 and 21. For a reading of Norbert Wieners's influential *Cybernetics* as to some extent premised on a vision of asexual reproduction, see Hayles, *How We Became Posthuman*, 109.
101 Virgil, *Georgics* III.8–9, in *Opera*. Subsequent references to the works of Virgil will appear in parentheses in the text.
102 In my discussion of the *Georgics* I am indebted to R.D. Williams's notes to his edition. See Virgil, *Eclogues and Georgics*.
103 For a discussion of the beginning of the first eclogue, see Guy-Bray, *Homoerotic Space*, 38–40.
104 Swann, '"Procreate like Trees,"' 144. For Swann's discussion of Renaissance English ideas about generation, see 140–1.
105 See above, note 28.
106 The standard discussion of abjection is Kristeva, *Powers of Horror*. For instance, Kristeva remarks that the abject is 'something rejected from which one does not part' and something that is 'radically separate, loathsome. Not me ... [but] not nothing either' (4, 2).
107 For Sedgwick, see 'Shame, Theatricality, and Queer Performativity.' For Bersani, see 'Is the Rectum a Grave?' and *Homos*. See also Rambuss, 'After Male Sex,' for a recent look at sex and abjection.
108 Montaigne was particularly fond of Virgil's writing. In his essay 'Of Bookes,' Montaigne writes that he considers the *Georgics* 'to be the most accomplished peece of worke of Poesie' (II.X.227). Unless otherwise stated, all quotations from Montaigne are from the 1632 edition of John Florio's translation.
109 For Regosin's summary of Montaigne's uses of the reproductive metaphor, see *Montaigne's Unruly Brood*, 1–9; for his discussion of 'De l'Oysiveté' and of the monstrous, see 154–61.
110 Ibid., 207.
111 Ibid., 196.

112 Montaigne, *Les Essais*, 54.
113 Florio has increased the abjection of Montaigne's simile in a particularly unpleasant way by using 'manured' to translate the original 'embe-songner,' which simply means to be busied or occupied with something and implies the satisfaction of a need ('besoin').
114 For other examples of Montaigne's presentation of his method of composition as disorderly, see I.XXV.71 (in which he compares himself to bees) and I.XXVII.89–90. For a discussion of a similar association in the *Faerie Queene*, see Barkan, *Nature's Work of Art*, 162–72, especially 166.
115 Stockton, *Beautiful Bottom, Beautiful Shame*, 8. For Stockton's excellent summary of recent writing on shame and queer theory, see 8–23.
116 For an interesting discussion of Montaigne's attitude to writing, see O'Neill, *Essaying Montaigne*, especially chapter 2, 33–50.
117 See above, note 106.
118 Masten, *Textual Intercourse*, 4.
119 My focus throughout this book on the reproductive metaphor means that I do not discuss other metaphors for textual production that were used in the Renaissance. For a brilliant analysis of one of these metaphors, see Quint, *Origin and Originality*. For an excellent discussion of sodomy and textual production with reference to Shakespeare's sonnets, see Halpern, *Shakespeare's Perfume*.

1. Marriages

1 Vaneigem, *Book of Pleasures*, 23.
2 Kipnis, 'Adultery,' 291.
3 See H. Turner, *English Renaissance Stage*.
4 Lyly, *The Woman in the Moone*, Prologue, 17. Subsequent references to Lyly's plays will appear in the text. Unless otherwise stated, all references are to the *Complete Works*. For a discussion of the play's focus on art, see Lancashire, 'John Lyly and Pastoral Entertainment,' 39–40.
5 Nunokawa, *Tame Passions of Wilde*, 45.
6 Bourdieu, *Field of Cultural Production*, 31.
7 Barthes, *The Neutral*, 68.
8 For a discussion of the date of the play, see Leah Scragg's introduction to her edition, 3–9.
9 Vanhoutte, 'Strange Hatred of Marriage,' 98. Vanhoutte concentrates on the court plays and does not mention *The Woman in the Moone*.

10 For discussions of the lesbian eroticism of *Gallathea*, see Jankowski, '"Where there can be no cause of affection,"' and Traub, *Renaissance of Lesbianism*, 327–9.
11 Vanhoutte, 'Strange Hatred of Marriage,' 111.
12 Ovid, *Metamorphoses*, IX.794.
13 It may be significant that while Venus in *Gallathea* proclaims that nothing is 'vnpossible' to her, in *Endimion* Cynthia says only that she 'will trie.' As a result, even the activity of the goddess appears more like labour.
14 Houppert, *John Lyly*, 128.
15 For a critique of this opinion with reference to another of Lyly's texts, see Guy-Bray, 'Same Difference.'
16 Hunter, *John Lyly*, 243.
17 Houppert, *John Lyly*, 125.
18 Ibid., 213.
19 Lancashire, 'John Lyly and Pastoral Entertainment,' 25.
20 For a discussion of this change with specific reference to Renaissance pastoral, see Guy-Bray, *Homoerotic Space*, 132–75.
21 I shall return to this point in my discussion of *Hero and Leander* in chapter 2.
22 'Subtexts of *The Roaring Girl*,' 13.
23 For a good discussion of the real Moll (Mary Frith) and the criminal context of the play, see McManus, '*The Roaring Girle* and the London Underworld.'
24 Stockton, *Beautiful Bottom, Beautiful Shame*, 49.
25 For the view that Moll represents a real force for change in the play, see, for example, P. Cheney, 'Moll Cutpurse as Hermaphrodite,' Krantz, 'Sexual Identities of Moll Cutpurse,' and Kermode, 'Destination Doomsday.' For the view that the play ultimately contains any threat of subversion from Moll, see Baston, 'Rehabilitating Moll's Subversion,' and Eastwood, 'Controversy and the Single Woman.' Most critics take a stand on one side or the other of this debate, but see Rose, 'Women in Men's Clothing,' for an argument in favour of ambiguity.
26 Forman, 'Marked Angels,' 1542. For a similar argument, see Deborah Jacobs's important article, 'Critical Imperialism and Renaissance Drama.'
27 Mikalachki, 'Gender, Cant, and Cross-Talking,' 125.
28 Forman, 'Marked Angels,' 1531.
29 Harris, *Sick Economies*, 182.
30 Middleton and Dekker, *The Roaring Girl*, 4.80–1. Subsequent references will appear in the text.

31 For an excellent discussion of clothing in the play that includes the 'fashion of play-making' see Menon, *Wanton Words*, 54–64.

32 For the standard discussion of the constitutive nature of clothes in the period, see Jones and Stallybrass, *Renaissance Clothing*. An interesting recent discussion is Bailey, *Flaunting*.

33 Mulholland, note ad loc.

34 Garber, 'Logic of the Transvestite,' 229. Garber's discussion of Mary can be found on 227–30.

35 For a discussion of this scene in the context of a discussion of homeroticism in the play, see Howard, 'Sex and Social Conflict,' 174–5.

36 For an interesting discussion of female solidarity in the context of popular jest books, see Brown, *Better a Shrew*, 118–49. For Brown's brief discussion of *The Roaring Girl*, see 79.

37 For an article that concentrates on this subplot, see DiGangi, 'Sexual Slander and Working Women.'

38 Howard, 'Sex and Social Conflict,' 176.

39 Ibid., 170.

40 Harris, *Sick Economies*, 177.

41 Moll's emphasis on her money is echoed in Laxton's intrigue with Mistress Gallipot, in which what is at stake is not so much sex as the £30 that he tries to get from her. Here, as well, the relationship inverts the traditional model of the man as provider.

42 For a discussion of this scene in the context of Jacobean ideas about androgyny, see Helms, 'Roaring Girls and Silent Women,' 64–5.

43 Orgel, 'Subtexts of *The Roaring Girl*,' 22.

44 Baston,'Rehabilitating Moll's Subversion,' 331.

45 Taylor, '"Teach Me This Pedlar's French,"' 111.

46 Foucault, *History of Sexuality*, 100–1.

47 Bourdieu and Passeron, *Reproduction*, 116.

48 To say nothing of Sir Fopling Flutter, Lady Wishfort, the Duke of Omnium, and so on – examples could be multiplied almost indefinitely from most periods of English literature.

49 Howard, 'Sex and Social Conflict,' 186.

50 Forman, 'Marked Angels,' 1556.

51 H. Turner, *English Renaissance Stage*, 26.

52 Ibid., 27.

53 Menon, *Wanton Words*, 64.

54 Readers desperate to follow the debate over who wrote what in *The Two Noble Kinsmen* are referred to any edition of the play; excellent (and more general) considerations of what Renaissance dramatic authorship means

are Stallybrass, 'Shakespeare, the Individual, and Text' and de Grazia and Stallybrass, 'Materiality of the Shakespearean Text.' For excellent discussions of the play's style, see Lief and Radel, 'Linguistic Subversion,' and Magnusson, 'Collapse of Shakespeare's High Style.'

55 For a discussion of this subject, see Guy-Bray, *Loving in Verse*, 3–10.

56 The prologue has attracted a great deal of commentary; one of the best discussions is Frey, 'Collaborating with Shakespeare,' 32–4.

57 *The Two Noble Kinsmen*, Prologue, 1–2. Subsequent references will appear in the text. In quoting from other works by Shakespeare I shall use the Riverside edition; in the case of *The Two Noble Kinsmen*, however, Lois Potter offers much better readings of the play's many difficult passages. Her readings are informed by Jeffrey Masten's groundbreaking work in *Textual Intercourse*.

58 Green, '"A mad woman?"' 123.

59 Weller, '*The Two Noble Kinsmen*,' 104.

60 Masten, *Textual Intercourse*, 56–7.

61 Frey, 'Collaborating with Shakespeare,' 36, 40.

62 For a discussion of collaboration with reference to the morris dance, see Iyengar, 'Moorish Dancing,' especially 86.

63 Hedrick, '"Be Rough with Me,"' 63.

64 For good general discussions of Emilia, see Kehler, 'Shakespeare's Emilias,' 166–9, Mallette, 'Same-Sex Erotic Friendship,' 32–7, Traub, *Renaissance of Lesbianism*, 72–5, and Shannon, *Sovereign Amity*, 96–122.

65 For a good discussion of what is at stake in naming and not naming female homoeroticism in Renaissance texts, see Andreadis, *Sappho in Early Modern England*, especially 19–24 for the 'erotics of unnaming' and the 'lesbian ellipsis.'

66 The single best discussion of this speech is perhaps Shannon, *Sovereign Amity*, 115–17.

67 Bizarrely, these lines are not generally seen as sexual: for instance, Lois Potter glosses 'their needs / The one of th'other' as 'i.e., in their military roles.' Perhaps 'military roles' is a euphemism with which I am unfamiliar. I would have thought that the physical imagery of 'intertangled roots of love' was sufficiently clear. For a brief discussion of the passage, see Abrams, 'Gender Confusion and Sexual Politics,' 72. For a discussion of Emilia's presentation of Theseus and Pirithous as 'at once sexualized and virginal,' see Masten, *Textual Intercourse*, 50.

68 See Shakespeare and Fletcher, *Two Noble Kinsmen*, Potter's introduction, 55–6.

69 The standard account of 'lesbian elegy' in Renaissance literature is Holstun, '"Will you rend our ancient love asunder?"'

70 Fisher, 'Queer Money,' 15.
71 For a discussion of the meaning of this kind of cousinhood (cognatic rather than agnatic), see Stewart, '"Near Akin,"' especially 64.
72 See Potter, note ad loc.
73 Hedrick, '"Be Rough with Me,"' 70.
74 Despite some resistance on the part of conservative critics, the sexual nature of the conversation between Emilia and her woman is now generally accepted. For discussions, see, among others, Abrams, 'Gender Confusion and Sexual Politics,' which I believe was the first article to make the claim, and Shannon, *Sovereign Amity*, 118–20.
75 Shannon, *Sovereign Amity*, 119.
76 For a reading of the scene as erotic, see Mallette, 'Same-Sex Erotic Friendship'; for a reading that connects the arming scene to the theme of collaboration, see Hedrick, '"Be Rough with Me,"' 165–7.
77 Hedrick, '"Be Rough with Me,"' 69.
78 The best general discussion of the significance of Amazons in Renaissance literature is K. Schwarz, *Tough Love*.
79 Chaucer, *The Knight's Tale*, in *The Riverside Chaucer*, 866.
80 Here I gratefully acknowledge and profit from the insights of my former student Leslie Henderson, who always insisted on the importance of Pirithous.
81 Frey, 'Collaborating with Shakespeare,' 38.
82 R. Ann Thompson has convincingly argued that the plot is derived from that other story of love between male cousins, *The Arcadia*; see 'Jailer's Daughters.'
83 Hadorn, 'Problem of Chivalry,' 53.
84 For an excellent discussion of the importance of the Jailer's Daughter, one that makes specific reference to the theme of the collaboration between Shakespeare and Fletcher, see Green, '"A mad woman?"'
85 Clark, *Plays of Beaumont and Fletcher*, 135.
86 In her analysis of madness in Renaissance literature, Carol Thomas Neely has a very good discussion of the Jailer's Daughter; see *Distracted Subjects*, 83–91.
87 Masten, *Textual Intercourse*, 60.
88 Bruster, 'The Jailer's Daughter,' 282.
89 Lief and Radel, 'Linguistic Subversion,' 421–4.
90 Neely, *Distracted Subjects*, 91.
91 Berggren, '"For what we lack, / We laugh,"' 9. Berggren cites Palamon's prayer to Venus and Arcite's prayer to Mars, V.i.19–28, V.iii.101, and V.iii.137–8.
92 Mallette, 'Same-Sex Erotic Friendships,' 47.

2. Seductions

1 Brown, *Redefining Elizabethan Literature*, 4 and 48. For Brown's general characterization of literature in this decade see especially the introduction (1–52) and the third chapter, 'Literature as Fetish' (102–78).

2 For the standard account of Daniel's use of French poetry see Rees, *Samuel Daniel*, 22–9.

3 This strain of criticism was inaugurated by Arthur F. Marotti in '"Love is Not Love."' For a more recent discussion see Warley, *Sonnet Sequences*.

4 Brown, *Redefining Elizabethan Literature*, 103.

5 The word *silicem* is the accusative singular of *silex*, which means any hard rock but especially flint. If we take Ovid to be referring specifically to flint, the metamorphosis is doubly apposite, as the fire that can be produced from flint would be the equivalent, in the metaphor, of the lusts inspired by the *Propoetidae* as prostitutes.

6 A. Green, 'Gay but Not Queer,' 522.

7 For a good criticism of analyses that focus on the poem's characters, see Altieri, '*Hero and Leander*.'

8 Keach, *Elizabethan Erotic Narratives*, 100.

9 Fineman, *Shakespeare's Perjured Eye*, 7.

10 Walker, *Rhetoric and Poetics*, 9, 7.

11 Longenbach, *Resistance to Poetry*, 4.

12 Walker, *Rhetoric and Poetics*, 236. For a discussion of humanist views on rhetoric, see Halpern, *Poetics of Primitive Accumulation*, especially 19–21 and 45–60.

13 For discussions of defences of poetry in the Renaissance, see Ferguson, *Trials of Desire* (especially 139–42 on Sidney and persuasion), and Matz, *Defending Literature*. See also H. Turner, *The English Renaissance Stage*, chap. 3, 82–113 (especially 88–9 and 111–13) for a discussion of Sidney's views on the uses of poetry.

14 Daniel, *Poems and a Defence of Ryme*, 9. Subsequent references to Daniel's work will appear in the text.

15 Saunders, 'Stigma of Print,' 141. Michael Saenger has recently suggested that this stigma may emerge from the way in which published collections of sermons were marketed; see *Commodification of Textual Engagements*, 30.

16 *Manuscript, Print*, 233, 314.

17 Ibid., 314.

18 For discussions of Daniel's relations to his patrons, see Bergeron, 'Women as Patrons,' 287–90; Lamb, 'Countess of Pembroke's Patronage,'

167–8, 178–9; Brennan, *Literary Patronage*, 75–6; and Quinn, 'Fulke Greville's Friendly Patronage.'

19 Warley, *Sonnet Sequences*, 98.
20 For a summary of the scanty facts about Daniel's early life, see Seronsy, *Samuel Daniel*, 13–23. For a discussion of the difficulties of getting an accurate picture of the social hierarchy of Renaissance England (especially as it concerns poets), see May, *Elizabethan Courtier Poets* 9–40, especially 23–6.
21 Rees, *Samuel Daniel*, 13.
22 Roche, *Petrarch*, 362.
23 Spiller, *Development of the Sonnet*, 139.
24 Svensson, *Silent Art*, 66.
25 For an excellent account of Daniel's views on print and on the difficulties of editing his poems, see Pincher, 'Editing Daniel.' For an interesting argument that the dominant images in the sequence have to do with vision and the construction of the self, see Ettari, '"That Mirrour Faire."'
26 Wall, *Imprint of Gender*, 43–4.
27 Spiller, *Development of the Sonnet*, 138.
28 Hedley, *Power in Verse*, 100.
29 This comment is true of only the original (1592) version, as Daniel added sonnets in later editions.
30 Neely, 'Structure of Sonnet Sequences,' 378.
31 For a discussion of this poem, see Guy-Bray, 'Daniel, Ovid.'
32 For a good discussion of what is at stake in attempts to classify the poem, see Darcy, '"Under my hands."'
33 For Marlowe's use of Musaeus and for an interesting account of Renaissance humanism, see Boutcher, '"Who taught thee Rhetoricke."' For a discussion of Marlowe's Ovidianism, see Orlandi, 'Ovid True and False,' and Macfie, 'Marlowe's Ghost-Writing.'
34 See *Leandro*, 1119–567 in Boscán, *Obras Poéticas de Juan Boscán.*
35 Boutcher, '"Who taught thee Rhetoricke,"' 42; see 42–5 for Boutcher's discussion of Boscán's digression.
36 Duncan, '"Headdie Ryots" as Reformations,' 25.
37 Marlowe, *Complete Works*, Vol. II, 430. Subsequent references to Marlowe's works will appear in the text.
38 Campbell, '"Desunt Nonnulla,"' 249.
39 Ibid., 266. Campbell's discussion of the poem's narration is on 263–7.
40 Haber, '"True-loves blood,"' 374.
41 Ibid., 378.
42 Bredbeck, *Sodomy and Interpretation*, 110.

43 Ellis, *Sexuality and Citizenship*, 94. For Ellis's excellent discussion of the poem, see 94–108.
44 Brown, *Redefining Elizabethan Literature*, 106.
45 Ellis, *Sexuality and Citizenship*, 96. For Ellis's analysis of the differences between Sestos and Abydos, see 96–8.
46 Foucault, *Order of Things*, xvii.
47 Summers, '"Hero and Leander,"' 141.
48 Adamson, 'Marlowe, *Hero and Leander*,' 67.
49 Marlowe famously expanded Virgil's brief mention – 'rapti Ganymedis honores' (the honours of abducted Ganymede; *Aeneid* I.28) – into the opening scene of *Dido Queene of Carthage*.
50 For an especially good discussion of homoeroticism in the poem see Summers, '"Hero and Leander."'
51 Bredbeck, *Sodomy and Interpretation*, 133.
52 Homes, 'Identity and Dissidence,' 167. Holmes's article contains an intriguing discussion of the productive dissidence of homoerotic desire in *Hero and Leander*.
53 Haber, '"True-loves blood,"' 375.
54 Tromly, *Playing with Desire*, 163.
55 Carlson, 'Clothing Naked Desire,' 36. For Carlson's interesting discussion of the veil as a whole, see 36–8.
56 Harry Levin notes that Pelops was 'compared to Ganymede in Pindar's first Olympian ode.' The mention of Pelops may thus be another illustration of the point that however beautiful a man may be, only Ganymede can become immortal; see *The Overreacher*, 165.
57 One relatively early example is Turner, 'Pastoral and Hermaphrodite.'
58 Bredbeck, *Sodomy and Interpretation*, 113.
59 Logan, '"Perspective in *Hero and Leander*,' 282.
60 Summers, '"Hero and Leander,"' 133. See also the discussion in Bredbeck, *Sodomy and Interpretation*, especially 124.
61 Godshalk, '*Hero and Leander*,' 298.
62 Haber, '"True-loves blood,"' 383. See 382–4 for Haber's discussion of the order of these lines.
63 D. Miller, 'Death of the Modern,' 775. See also Macfie, 'Ghostly Metamorphoses,' 178–83. Similarly, William Kerrigan and Gordon Braden see 'one of the worlds of unknown joy' as the world of seventeenth-century English poetry about consummated love; see 'Milton's Coy Eve,' 28.
64 For the argument that the 1598 volume as a whole is unified, see Shelburne, 'Principled Satire'; for the argument that *The Metamorphosis of Pigmalions Image* is intended to teach us how to read satire, see Buckridge,

'True Reading.' Keach's discussion includes a useful summary of criticism of the poem to that point (1977); see *Elizabethan Erotic Narratives*, 134–61.

65 Ellis, *Sexuality and Citizenship*, 154.

66 Enterline, *Rhetoric of the Body*, 129. For Enterline's discussion as a whole, see 125–51.

67 Perhaps more than most other poets of his time, Marston makes it difficult to be certain of his attitude towards his works. For the argument that this difficulty is also true of his plays, see Brown, 'Disgusting John Marston.'

68 Keach, *Elizabethan Erotic Narratives*, 136. For an interesting discussion of (chiefly nineteenth-century) renditions of the story, see J.H. Miller, *Versions of Pygmalion*.

69 See Braden, *English Renaissance Poetry*, 137–41.

70 Enterline, *Rhetoric of the Body*, 126.

71 Marston, *Poems of John Marston*, 49. Subsequent reference to Marston's works are to this edition and will appear in the text. Quotations from *The Metamorphosis of Pigmalions Image* will be identified by stanza and line number.

72 It has often been noted that Marston is inconsistent in his references to the statue's material. Although it is usually ivory, he sometimes refers to it as marble or, more generically, as stone. I would say that he uses the metaphorical connotation of stone to indicate the proverbial hardness of the woman who refuses to have sex with a poet. For the suggestion that the poem is an extended pun on this metaphor, see Horne, 'Voices of Alienation.'

73 I assume that, in making Paphos a son, Marston was following the lead of Arthur Golding, who says in his translation that Galatea 'was delivered of a son that Paphos hight' (X.323). The name only occurs in the *Metamorphoses* in the accusative form 'Paphon' (X.297), which looks like a standard Greek masculine accusative. The gender of the child is made clear only in the pronominal phrase 'de qua' (from whom [feminine]; X.297) and, as Arnold Davenport points out, 'some mss. of Ovid support Marston' in that they read 'de *quo*' (from whom [masculine]; see note ad loc.). I do not think that the change is significant.

74 Brown, *Redefining Elizabethan Literature*, 146.

75 Ibid., 137. For a discussion of another version of the Pygmalion story that focuses on masturbation, see Guy-Bray, 'Beddoes, Pygmalion.'

76 Enterline, *Rhetoric of the Body*, 132.

77 Enterline also sees this metamorphosis as tumescence; see *Rhetoric of the Body*, 148.

78 Keach points out that 'the modern meanings of "image" and "imagery" were just evolving during the sixteenth century, but they were available to

Marston, along with the literal meanings referring to carved statues';
Elizabethan Erotic Narratives, 139.

79 MacKendrick, *Counterpleasures*, 19.

80 Enterline, *Rhetoric of the Body*, 143.

3. Beginnings

1 Sidney, *Defence of Poesie*, in *Prose Works*, 3: 7. Subsequent references will appear in the text.

2 See Marotti, 'Love is Not love,' to which I have already referred (at the beginning of chapter 2).

3 For a discussion of the importance of class to *Astrophil and Stella*, see Warley, *Sonnet Sequences*, 72–100; for a discussion of the importance of Sidney's biography to *Astrophil and Stella*, see Quilligan, 'Sidney and His Queen,' 184–92.

4 Two particularly cogent objections to the tyranny of historicism in discussions of *Astrophil and Stella* are Minogue, 'A Woman's Touch,' and Hull, 'All my deed but copying is.' On the other hand, for an essay that shows how to use historicism, see Hulse, 'Stella's Wit.'

5 For a discussion of the relation between sexual and poetic communication in Renaissance literature, see de Grazia, 'Lost Potential,' especially 32–3, and Campbell, 'Unending Desire.'

6 Ferry, *'Inward' Language*, 149. For a good recent discussion of the poems as a sequence, see Kambaskovic-Sawers, '"Never was I the golden cloud,"' 648–55.

7 See Prendergast, 'Unauthorized Orpheus.'

8 Sidney, *Astrophil and Stella*, in *Poems of Sir Philip Sidney*, 1.1–4. Subsequent references will appear in the text.

9 And, as Warley has recently suggested, it also means obliged; see *Sonnet Sequences*, 77.

10 Prendergast, 'Unauthorized Orpheus,' 20.

11 Ferry, *'Inward' Language*, 129.

12 Bates, 'Astrophil and the Manic Wit,' 10.

13 Levao, *Renaissance Minds*, 159.

14 Dubrow, *Echoes of Desire*, 102–3.

15 Levao, *Renaissance Minds*, 160.

16 Barkan, *Nature's Work of Art*, 182. For Barkan's description of the sequence as a whole, see 181–3.

17 Dubrow, *Echoes of Desire*, 103.

18 Kalstone, *Sidney's Poetry*, 125–6, 129. For Kalstone's superb analysis of *Astrophil and Stella*, see 124–30.

19 Fumerton, '"Secret Arts,"' 121.
20 Gil, *Before Intimacy*, 39. For Gil's illuminating discussion of *Astrophil and Stella*, see 27–39.
21 We could make a similar comparison between the discussion of controlling a horse that opens the *Defence of Poesie* and Astrophil's statement, 'I on my horse, and *Love* on me doth trie / Our horsmanships' (49.1–2). Here as well, the comparison is to Astrophil's disadvantage.
22 Prendergast, 'Unauthorized Orpheus,' 26. For an analysis of Stella's role with regard to the songs, see Almasy, 'Stella and Songs.'
23 Fienberg, 'Emergence of Stella,' 7.
24 J.T. Miller, '"Love doth hold my hand,"' 546.
25 Bates, 'Astrophil and the Manic Wit,' 9.
26 Fienberg, 'Emergence of Stella,' 11.
27 Dubrow, *Echoes of Desire*, 109.
28 For a good (and very brief) discussion of this, see Cain, 'Sidney's Astrophil and Stella.'
29 Milton, *Paradise Lost*, I.26. Subsequent references will appear in the text.
30 Lehnhof, 'Concept of Creation,' 33.
31 Herman, *Destabilizing Milton*, 43.
32 For an interesting discussion of Milton's uncertainties about rhetoric in *Paradise Lost*, especially with reference to classical literature, see Pavlock, *Eros, Imitation*, 187–218.
33 Oerlemans, 'Will to Knowledge,' 4. The reference to Barthes is to his *Image, Music, Text*.
34 Lehnhof, 'Concept of Creation,' 34. For a discussion of Milton's uncertainties in the four proems, see Adelman, 'Creation and the Place of the Poet,' and Cooley, 'Reformed Eloquence.'
35 Ferry, *Milton's Epic Voice*, 15.
36 Ibid., 22.
37 Herman, *Destabilizing Milton*, 57.
38 See Low, '"No middle flight."' The reference is to *Metamorphoses* VIII.203–4.
39 A thing never said in prose or rhyme; *Orlando Furioso*, 1.2.2. Milton would have read the original; for purposes of comparison, here is the sixteenth-century translation by Sir John Harington, which he would also have known: 'A tale in prose ne verse yet song or sayd.'
40 Readings, '"An age too late,"' 456. For a similar statement about how the poem has difficulty in reaching its goal, see Parker, *Inescapable Romance*, 158.
41 Schindler, *Voice and Crisis*, 50. For a discussion of the connections between the passages, see Schwarz, *Remembering and Repeating*, 107–9.

42 Cited by Lewalski in *Life of John Milton*, 448.
43 For a discussion of Milton's transformations of the family, see Murphy, 'Milton's "Birth Abortive."'
44 Oerlemans, 'Will to Knowledge,' 6.
45 Esterhammer, 'Creation, Subjectivity,' 270.
46 Teskey, *Delirious Milton*, 77. Teskey also draws our attention to Milton's second return to this passage in the account of the creation (VII.234–7). See also Rumrich, *Milton Unbound*, 94–117.
47 For a discussion of Pandemonium, see Theis, 'Milton's Principles of Architecture,' 109–11.
48 For a discussion of Milton's use of bees, see Moeck, 'Bees in My Bonnet'; for a discussion of Milton's use of the *Georgics*, see Pellicer, 'Virgil's *Georgics* II.' Neither of these excellent articles sees a Miltonic allusion to *Georgics* IV in this passage.
49 Haan, '"Both English and Latin,"' 700. For Haan's discussion of the invocation to Book III as a whole, see 696–700.
50 For discussions of this tentativeness, see Lord, 'Milton's Dialogue with Omniscience,' 45–7.
51 There have been many studies of the nature of light in this invocation. A good recent one is Mattison, *Milton's Uncertain Eden*, 107–14.
52 As I have pointed out, Sidney makes this play on words in the fiftieth sonnet of *Astrophil and Stella*. Another example of Milton's exploitation of the ambiguity can be found in Book X when he tells us that God 'on the Son / Blaz'd forth unclouded Deitie; he full / Resplendent all his Father manifest / Express'd' (X.64–7).
53 Herman, *Destabilizing Milton*, 46.
54 Milton's enjambment of 'Cut off' shows that despite his blindness he was able to visualize the look of his poetry on the page. For an excellent discussion of Milton's use of lineation in *Paradise Lost*, see Burnett, '"Sense variously drawn out."'
55 Hodgson, 'Mourning Eve, Mourning Milton,' 14.
56 Oerlemans, 'Will to Knowledge,' 9.
57 Rumrich, *Milton Unbound*, 101.
58 For an interesting discussion of Milton's use of Urania, see Shoulson, 'Embrace of the Fig Tree,' 878–9. This article also has a good analysis of the biblical backgrounds to *Paradise Lost*.
59 For an interesting discussion of the gender dynamics of Milton's presentation of himself as a poet see Halley, 'Female Autonomy.' However, Halley overestimates Milton's own autonomy in these sections of *Paradise Lost*.
60 See Ovid, *Metamorphoses* XI.1–43.
61 Johnson, 'Falling into Allegory,' 113.

62 Bunyan, *Pilgrim's Progress*, 8. Subsequent references will appear in the text. For a discussion of the biblical allusions in this sentence – allusions that equate Bunyan with Jacob – see Lynch, *John Bunyan*, 89.

63 Johnson, 'Falling into Allegory,' 132.

64 I cite 'The Author's Apology for his Book' by page and line number. I reproduce the italics in which the poem has always been printed, as these italics have the useful effect of underlining the difference between the poem and the prose.

65 For the argument that the fall here should be taken as indicating the fall of man, see Machosky, 'Trope and Truth.'

66 Johnson, 'Falling into Allegory,' 115.

67 In the list of 'Faults escaped, thus corrected' appended to one of the 1595 editions of Sidney's work, 'conabor' (I shall endeavour) is changed to 'conabar' (I endeavoured). 'Conor' and 'tempto' are synonymous, but I would say that the former suggests that the attempt is harder to make. It is not clear to me whether Sidney was presumably quoting from memory or whether he wished to produce a new version of the passage that would be more suitable for his own purposes.

68 Ovid, *Tristium Liber IV*, 10.25–6.

69 Brown, 'Reproductive Word,' 24.

70 Ibid., 29.

71 Montaigne, I.VIII.15, in *Essays Written in French*.

72 See the note ad loc. Weaving is a well-established metaphor for writing. An especially good discussion of Renaissance uses of this metaphor is Stephens, *Limits of Eroticism*, 102–40, especially 102–9.

73 For a reading of these lines, see De Marco, 'Structural "Pliability,"' 36–7. De Marco sees the image (wrongly, I think) as referring to 'a perfectly natural process of midwifery'; it is interesting that here a critic imports the reproductive metaphor when the author did not. Also, of course, it is symptomatic of the general tendency to misuse terms such as 'natural' and 'real' that De Marco describes as natural something as artificial as midwifery, the trained intervention in a biological process.

74 Davies, *Graceful Reading*, 190. For Davies's discussion of the poem, see 192–201.

75 Spargo, *Writing of John Bunyan*, 115.

76 Fish, *Self-Consuming Artifacts*, 263.

77 Genette, *Paratexts*, 222.

78 Fish, *Self-Consuming Artifacts*, 263.

79 Genette, *Paratexts*, 1.

80 Saenger, *Commodification of Textual Engagements*, 3. For Saenger's discussion of the reproductive metaphor, see 110–16.

Works Cited

Abrams, Richard. 'Gender Confusion and Sexual Politics in *The Two Noble Kinsmen*.' In *Themes in Drama VII: Drama, Sex and Politics*, ed. James Redmond. 69–76. Cambridge: Cambridge University Press, 1985.

Adamson, Jane. 'Marlowe, *Hero and Leander*, and the Art of Leaping in Verse.' *Critical Review* 17 (1974): 59–81.

Adelman, Janet. 'Creation and the Place of the Poet in *Paradise Lost*.' In *The Author in His Work: Essays on a Problem in Criticism*, ed. Louis L. Martz and Aubrey Williams. 51–69. New Haven, CT: Yale University Press, 1978.

Adorno, Theodor. 'Lyric Poetry and Society.' *Telos* 20 (Summer 1974): 56–71.

Ahmed, Sara. *Queer Phenomenology: Orientations, Objects, Others*. Durham, NC: Duke University Press, 2006.

Almasy, Rudolph. 'Stella and Songs: Questions about the Composition of "Astrophil and Stella."' *South Atlantic Review* 58.4 (1993): 1–17.

Altieri, Joanne. '*Hero and Leander*: Sensible Myth and Lyric Subjectivity.' *John Donne Journal* 8 (1989): 151–66.

Andreadis, Harriette. *Sappho in Early Modern England: Female Same-Sex Literary Erotics, 1550–1714*. Chicago: University of Chicago Press, 2001.

Ariosto, Ludovico. *Orlando Furioso*. Edited by Marco Dorigatti and Gerarda Stimato. Ferrara: Leo S. Olschki, 2006.

– *Orlando Furioso in English Heroical Verse*. Translated by J. Harington. London: Richard Field, 1591.

Bailey, Amanda. *Flaunting: Style and the Subversive Male Body in Renaissance England*. Toronto: University of Toronto Press, 2007.

Barkan, Leonard. *Nature's Work of Art: The Human Body as Image of the World*. New Haven, CT: Yale University Press, 1975.

Barthes, Roland. *The Pleasure of the Text*. Translated by R. Miller. New York: Hill and Wang, 1975.

- *Roland Barthes by Roland Barthes.* Translated by R. Howard. New York: Hill and Wang, 1977.
- *The Neutral.* Translated by R.E. Kraus and D. Hollier. New York: Columbia University Press, 2005.
- Baston, Jane. 'Rehabilitating Moll's Subversion in *The Roaring Girl.' Studies in English Literature* 37 (1997): 317–35.
- Bataille, Georges. *Erotism: Death and Sensuality.* Trans. M. Dalwood. San Francisco: City Lights, 1986.
- Bates, Catherine. 'Astrophil and the Manic Wit of the Abject Male.' *SEL* 41 (2001): 1–24.
- Benjamin, Walter. 'The Work of Art in the Age of Mechanical Reproduction.' In *Illuminations,* ed. Hannah Arendt. Trans. H. Zohn. 217–52. New York: Schocken, 1969.
- 'The Author as Producer.' In *Reflections: Essays, Aphorisms, Autobiographical Writing,* ed. Peter Demetz. Trans. E. Jephcott. 220–38. New York: Harcourt Brace Jovanovich, 1978.
- Berger, Harry, Jr. 'Second-World Prosthetics: Supplying Deficiencies of Nature in Renaissance Italy.' In *Early Modern Visual Culture: Representation, Race, and Empire in Renaissance England,* ed. Peter Erickson and Clark Hulse. 98–147. Philadelphia: University of Pennsylvania Press, 2000.
- Bergeron, David M. 'Women as Patrons of English Drama.' In *Patronage in the Renaissance,* ed. Guy Fitch Lytle and Stephen Orgel. 274–90. Princeton, NJ: Princeton University Press, 1981.
- Berggren, Paula S. '"For what we lack, / We laugh": Incompletion and *The Two Noble Kinsmen.' Modern Language Studies* 14.4 (1984): 3–17.
- Berlant, Lauren, and Michael Warner. 'Sex in Public.' In *Publics and Counterpublics,* ed. Michael Warner. 187–208. New York: Zone, 2002.
- Bersani, Leo. *The Freudian Body: Psychoanalysis and Art.* New York: Columbia University Press, 1986.
- 'Is the Rectum a Grave?' *October* 43 (Winter 1987): 197–222.
- *Homos.* Cambridge, MA: Harvard University Press, 1995.
- Bjørnstad, Hall, ed. *Borrowed Feathers: Plagiarism and the Limits of Imitation in Early Modern England.* Oslo: Unipub, 2008.
- Boscán, Juan. *Obras Poéticas de Juan Boscán.* Ed. Martín de Riquer, Antonio Comas, and Joaquín Malas. Vol. 1. Barcelona: University of Barcelona Press, 1957.
- Bourdieu, Pierre. *The Field of Cultural Production: Essays on Art and Literature.* Ed. Randal Johnson. Trans. R. Nice et al. New York: Columbia University Press, 1993.
- Bourdieu, Pierre, and Jean-Claude Passeron. *Reproduction in Education, Society and Culture.* Trans. R. Nice. London: Sage, 1990.

Boutcher, Warren. '"Who taught thee Rhetoricke to deceive a maid?"': Christopher Marlowe's *Hero and Leander*, Juan Boscán's *Leandro*, and Renaissance Vernacular Humanism.' *Comparative Literature* 52.1 (2000): 11–52.

Braden, Gordon. *The Classics and English Renaissance Poetry: Three Case Studies.* New Haven, CT: Yale University Press, 1978.

Bredbeck, Gregory. *Sodomy and Interpretation: Marlowe to Milton.* Ithaca, NY: Cornell University Press, 1991.

Brennan, Michael. *Literary Patronage in the English Renaissance.* London: Routledge, 1988.

Brooks, Douglas A. 'Introduction.' In *Printing and Parenting in Early Modern England*, ed. Douglas A. Brooks. 1–25. Aldershot, UK: Ashgate, 2005.

Brown, Georgia. *Redefining Elizabethan Literature.* Cambridge: Cambridge University Press, 2004.

– 'Disgusting John Marston: Sensationalism and the Limits of Post-Modern Marston.' *Nordic Journal of English Studies* 4:2 (2005): 121–41.

Brown, Pamela Allen. *Better a Shrew than a Sheep: Women, Drama, and the Culture of Jest in Early Modern England.* Ithaca, NY: Cornell University Press, 2003.

Brown, Sylvia. 'The Reproductive Word: Gender and Textuality in the Writings of John Bunyan.' *Bunyan Studies* 11 (2004): 23–45.

Browne, Sir Thomas. *The Major Works.* Edited by C.A. Patrides. Harmondsworth, UK: Penguin, 1977.

Bruster, Douglas. 'The Jailer's Daughter and the Politics of Madwomen's Language.' *Shakespeare Quarterly* 46 (1995): 277–300.

Buckridge, Patrick. 'True Reading and How to Get It: John Marston's Primer for Satire.' *Southern Review* 23 (1990): 58–67.

Bunyan, John. *The Pilgrim's Progress.* Edited by James Blanton Wharey. Rev. Roger Sharrock. Oxford: Clarendon, 1960.

Burnett, Archie. '"Sense variously drawn out": The Line in *Paradise Lost*.' *Literary Imagination* 5 (2003): 69–92.

Butler, Judith. *Gender Trouble: Feminism and the Subversion of Identity.* New York: Routledge, 1990.

– 'Is Kinship Always Already Heterosexual?' *Differences* 13.1 (2002): 14–44.

Cain, Jeffrey P. 'Sidney's Astrophil and Stella, Sonnet 108.' *Explicator* 52.1 (1993): 12–16.

Campbell, Marion. '"Desunt Nonnulla": The Construction of Marlowe's *Hero and Leander* as an Unfinished Poem.' *ELH* 51 (1984): 241–68.

– 'Unending Desire: Sidney's Reinvention of Petrarchan Form in *Astrophil and Stella*.' In *Sir Philip Sidney and the Interpretation of Renaissance Culture:*

The Poet in His Time and in Ours, ed. Gary F. Waller and Michael D. Moore. 84–94. London: Croom Helm, 1984.

Carlson, Cindy L. 'Clothing Naked Desire in Marlowe's *Hero and Leander*.' In *Gender Reconstructions: Pornography and Perversions in Literature and Culture*, ed. Cindy L. Carlson, Robert L. Mazzola, and Susan M. Bernardo. 25–41. Aldershot, UK: Ashgate, 2002.

Castle, Terry. '"Lab'ring Bards": Birth *Topoi* and English Poetics 1660–1820.' *Journal of English and Germanic Philology* 78 (1979): 193–208.

Chaucer, Geoffrey. *The Riverside Chaucer*. Edited by Larry D. Benson. Boston: Houghton Mifflin, 1987.

Cheney, Donald. 'The Mysterious Genesis of *Paradise Lost*.' *Connotations* 9 (1999–2000): 57–70.

Cheney, Patrick. 'Moll Cutpurse as Hermaphrodite in Dekker and Middleton's *The Roaring Girl*.' *Renaissance and Reformation* 7 (1983): 120–34.

Clark, Sandra. *The Plays of Beaumont and Fletcher: Sexual Themes and Dramatic Representations*. New York: Harvester Wheatsheaf, 1994.

Cohen, Jeffrey J., and Todd R. Ramlow. 'Pink Vectors of Deleuze: Queer Theory and Inhumanism.' *Rhizomes* 11.12 (2005–6).

Cooley, Ronald W. 'Reformed Eloquence: Inability, Questioning, and Correction in *Paradise Lost*.' *University of Toronto Quarterly* 62 (1992–3): 232–55.

Crawford, Julie. *Marvelous Protestantism: Monstrous Births in Post-Reformation England*. Baltimore: Johns Hopkins University Press, 2005.

Daniel, Samuel. *Poems and a Defence of Ryme*. Ed. Arthur Colby Sprague. Chicago: University of Chicago Press, 1930.

Darcy, Robert. '"Under my hands ... a double duty": Printing and Pressing Marlowe's *Hero and Leander*.' *Journal for Early Modern Cultural Studies* 2.2 (2002): 26–56.

Davies, Michael. *Graceful Reading: Theology and Narrative in the Works of John Bunyan*. Oxford: Oxford University Press, 2002.

de Grazia, Margreta. 'Lost Potential in Grammar and Nature: Sidney's *Astrophil and Stella*.' *SEL* 21 (1981): 21–35.

– 'Imprints: Shakespeare, Gutenberg and Descartes.' In *Alternative Shakespeares*, Vol. 2, ed. Terence Hawkes. 63–94. London: Routledge, 1996.

de Grazia, Margreta, and Peter Stallybrass. 'The Materiality of the Shakespearean Text.' *Shakespeare Quarterly* 44 (1993): 255–83.

Deleuze, Gilles, and Félix Guattari. *Anti-Oedipus: Capitalism and Schizophrenia*. Trans. R. Hurley, M. Seem, and H.R. Lane. New York: Viking, 1977.

De Marco, Nick. 'Structural "Pliability" and Narratological "Diffidence" in *The Pilgrim's Progress*.' *Bunyan Studies* 8 (1998): 36–53.

Dienstfrey, Patricia, and Brenda Hillman, ed. *The Grand Permission: New Writings on Poetics and Motherhood*. Middletown, CT: Wesleyan University Press, 2003.

DiGangi, Mario. 'Sexual Slander and Working Women in *The Roaring Girl*.' *Renaissance Drama* n.s. 32 (2003): 147–76.

Dubrow, Heather. *Echoes of Desire: English Petrarchism and its Counterdiscourses*. Ithaca, NY: Cornell University Press, 1995.

Duncan, Helga. '"Headdie Ryots as Reformations: Marlowe's Libertine Poetics.' *Early Modern Literary Studies* 12.2 (2006): 1.1–38.

Eastwood, Adrienne L. 'Controversy and the Single Woman in "The Maid's Tragedy" and "The Roaring Girl."' *Rocky Mountain Review of Language and Literature* 58:2 (2004): 7–27.

Edelman, Lee. *Homographesis: Essays in Gay Literary and Cultural Theory*. New York: Routledge, 1994.

– *No Future: Queer Theory and the Death Drive*. Durham, NC: Duke University Press, 2004.

Eden, Kathy. *Friends Hold All Things in Common: Tradition, Intellectual Property, and the "Adages" of Erasmus*. New Haven, CT: Yale University Press, 2001.

Ellis, Jim. *Sexuality and Citizenship: Metamorphoses in Elizabethan Erotic Verse*. Toronto: University of Toronto Press, 2003.

Enterline, Lynn. *The Rhetoric of the Body from Ovid to Shakespeare*. Cambridge: Cambridge University Press, 2000.

Esterhammer, Angela. 'Creation, Subjectivity, and Linguistic Structure in *Paradise Lost*: Milton with Saussure and Benveniste.' *English Studies in Canada* 20 (1994): 267–82.

Ettari, Gary. '"That Mirrour Faire": Samuel Daniel and the Collapse of the Subject.' *Publications of the Arkansas Philological Association* 33:2 (2007): 1–22.

Feinberg, Leslie. *Stone Butch Blues: A Novel*. Ithaca, NY: Firebrand Books, 1993.

– *Stone Butch Blues: A Novel*. Rev. 10th Anniversary ed. New York: Alyson Books, 2003.

Ferguson, Margaret W. *Trials of Desire: Renaissance Defenses of Poetry*. New Haven, CT: Yale University Press, 1983.

Ferry, Anne. *Milton's Epic Voice: The Narrator in* Paradise Lost. Cambridge, MA: Harvard University Press, 1963.

– *The "Inward" Language: Sonnets of Wyatt, Sidney, Shakespeare, Donne*. Chicago: University of Chicago Press, 1983.

Fienberg, Nona. 'The Emergence of Stella in *Astrophil and Stella*.' *SEL* 25 (1985): 5–19.

Fineman, Joel. *Shakespeare's Perjured Eye: The Invention of Poetic Subjectivity in the Sonnets*. Berkeley: University of California Press, 1986.

Finucci, Valeria. *The Manly Masquerade: Masculinity, Paternity, and Castration in the Italian Renaissance*. Durham, NC: Duke University Press, 2003.

Fish, Stanley E. *Self-Consuming Artifacts: The Experience of Seventeenth-Century Literature*. Berkeley: University of California Press, 1972.

Fisher, Will. 'Queer Money.' *ELH* 66 (1999): 1–23.

– *Materializing Gender in Early Modern English Literature and Culture*. Cambridge: Cambridge University Press, 2006.

Fissell, Mary E. *Vernacular Bodies: The Politics of Reproduction in Early Modern England*. Oxford: Oxford University Press, 2004.

Forman, Valerie. 'Marked Angels: Counterfeits, Commodities, and *The Roaring Girl*.' *Renaissance Quarterly* 54 (2001): 1531–60.

Foucault, Michel. 'Nietzsche, Genealogy, History.' In *Language, Counter-Memory, Practice: Selected Essays and Interviews*, ed. Donald F. Bouchard. Trans. D.F. Bouchard and S. Simon. 139–64. Ithaca, NY: Cornell University Press, 1977.

– *Discipline and Punish: The Birth of the Prison*. Trans. A. Sheridan. New York: Vintage, 1979.

– *The History of Sexuality*. Trans. R. Hurley. New York: Vintage, 1980.

– 'What Is an Author?' In *The Foucault Reader*, ed. Paul Robinson. Trans. J.V. Harari. 101–20. New York: Pantheon, 1984.

– *The Order of Things: An Archaeology of the Human Sciences*. London: Routledge, 1989.

Freccero, Carla. *Queer / Early / Modern*. Durham, NC: Duke University Press, 2006.

Freinkel, Lisa. *Reading Shakespeare's Will: The Theology of Figure from Augustine to the Sonnets*. New York: Columbia University Press, 2002.

Freud, Sigmund. *On Sexuality: Three Essays on the Theory of Sexuality and Other Works*. Edited by Angela Richards. Trans. J. Strachey. Harmondsworth: Penguin, 1977.

Frey, Charles H. 'Collaborating with Shakespeare: after the Final Play.' In *Shakespeare, Fletcher and* The Two Noble Kinsmen, ed. Charles H. Frey. 31–44. Columbia: University of Missouri Press, 1989.

Friedman, Susan Stanford. 'Creativity and the Childbirth Metaphor: Gender Differences in Literary Discourse.' *Feminist Studies* 13 (1987): 49–82.

Fumerton, Patricia. '"Secret Arts": Elizabethan Miniatures and Sonnets.' In *Representing the English Renaissance*, ed. Stephen Greenblatt. 93–133. Berkeley: University of California Press, 1988.

Garber, Marjorie. 'The Logic of the Transvestite: *The Roaring Girl* (1608).' In *Staging the Renaissance: Reinterpretations of Elizabethan and Jacobean Drama*, ed. David Scott Kastan and Peter Stallybrass. 221–34. New York: Routledge, 1991.

Genette, Gérard. *Paratexts: Thresholds of Interpretation*. Trans. J.E. Lewin. Cambridge: Cambridge University Press, 1997.

Gil, Daniel Juan. *Before Intimacy: Asocial Sexuality in Early Modern England*. Minneapolis: University of Minnesota Press, 2006.

Gilbert, Sandra, and Susan Gubar. *The Madwoman in the Attic: The Woman Writer and the Nineteenth-Century Literary Imagination*. New Haven, CT: Yale University Press, 1979.

Glimp, David. *Increase and Multiply: Governing Cultural Reproduction in Early Modern England*. Minneapolis: University of Minnesota Press, 2003.

Godshalk, W.L. 'Hero and Leander: The Sense of an Ending.' In '*A Poet and a filthy Play-maker': New Essays on Christopher Marlowe*, ed. Kenneth Friedenreich, Roma Gill, and Constance B. Kuriyama. 293–314. New York: AMS, 1988.

Green, Adam Isaiah. 'Gay but Not Queer: Toward a Post-Queer Study of Sexuality.' *Theory and Society* 31 (2002): 521–45.

Green, Susan. '"A mad woman? We are made, boys": The Jailer's Daughter in *The Two Noble Kinsmen*.' In *Shakespeare, Fletcher, and* The Two Noble Kinsmen, ed. Charles H. Frey. 121–32. Columbia: University of Missouri Press, 1989.

Guy-Bray, Stephen. 'Beddoes, Pygmalion, and the Art of Onanism.' *Nineteenth-Century Literature* 52 (1997–98): 446–70.

– *Homoerotic Space: The Poetics of Loss in Renaissance Literature*. Toronto: University of Toronto Press, 2002.

– *Loving in Verse: Poetic Influence as Erotic*. Toronto: University of Toronto Press, 2006.

– 'Shakespeare and the Invention of the Heterosexual.' *Early Modern Literary Studies* 13.2 (2007): 12.1–28.

– 'Rosamond's Complaint: Daniel, Ovid, and the Purpose of Poetry.' *Renaissance Studies* 22 (2008): 338–50.

Haan, Estelle. '"Both English and Latin": Milton's Bilingual Muse.' *Renaissance Studies* 21 (2007): 679–700.

Haber, Judith. '"True loves-blood": Narrative and Desire in *Hero and Leander*.' *English Literary Renaissance* 28 (1998): 372–86.

Hadorn, Peter T. '*The Two Noble Kinsmen* and the Problem of Chivalry.' *Studies in Medievalism* 4 (1992): 45–57.

Halley, Janet. 'Female Autonomy in Milton's Sexual Poetics.' In *Milton and the Idea of Woman*, ed. Julia M. Walker. 230–53. Urbana: University of Illinois Press, 1988.

Halperin, David M., and Valerie Traub, eds. *Gay Shame*. Chicago: University of Chicago Press, 2008.

Halpern, Richard. *The Poetics of Primitive Accumulation: English Renaissance Culture and the Genealogy of Capital*. Ithaca, NY: Cornell University Press, 1991.

– *Shakespeare's Perfume: Sodomy and Sublimity in the Sonnets, Wilde, Freud, and Lacan*. Philadelphia: University of Pennsylvania Press, 2002.

Hammill, Graham. 'Are We Being Homosexual Yet?' *Umbr(a)* (2002): 71–85.

Haraway, Donna. 'The Promise of Monsters.' In *The Haraway Reader*. 63–124. London: Routledge, 2004.

Harris, Jonathan Gil. *Sick Economies: Drama, Mercantilism, and Disease in Shakespeare's England*. Philadelphia: University of Pennsylvania Press, 2004.

Hayles, N. Katherine. *How We Became Posthuman: Virtual Bodies in Cybernetics, Literature, and Informatics*. Chicago: University of Chicago Press, 1999.

– 'Refiguring the Posthuman.' *Comparative Literature Studies* 41 (2004): 311–16.

Hedley, Jane. *Power in Verse: Metaphor and Metonymy in the Renaissance Lyric*. University Park: Pennsylvania State University Press, 1988.

Hedrick, Donald. '"Be Rough with Me": The Collaborative Arenas of *The Two Noble Kinsmen*.' In *Shakespeare, Fletcher and* The Two Noble Kinsmen, ed. Charles H. Frey. 45–77. Columbia: University of Missouri Press, 1989.

Hellwarth, Jennifer Wynne. 'Afterword.' In *Printing and Parenting in Early Modern England*, ed. Douglas A. Brooks. 395–401. Aldershot, UK: Ashgate, 2005.

Helmreich, Stefan. *Silicon Second Nature: Culturing Artificial Life in a Digital World*. Berkeley: University of California Press, 1998.

Helms, Lorraine. 'Roaring Girls and Silent Women: The Politics of Androgyny on the Jacobean Stage.' In *Themes in Drama 11: Women in Theatre*, ed. James Redmond. 59–73. Cambridge: Cambridge University Press, 1989.

Herman, Peter C. *Destabilizing Milton: "Paradise Lost" and the Poetics of Incertitude*. New York: Palgrave Macmillan, 2005.

Hobbes, Thomas. *Leviathan*. Edited by A.P. Martinich. Peterborough, ON: Broadview, 2002.

Hodgson, Elizabeth M.A. 'Mourning Eve, Mourning Milton in *Paradise Lost*.' *Early Modern Literary Studies* 11.1 (2005): 6.1–32.

Holmes, M. Morgan. 'Identity and the Dissidence It Makes: Homoerotic Nonsense in Kit Marlowe's *Hero and Leander*.' *English Studies in Canada* 21 (1995): 151–69.

Holstun, James. '"Will you rend our ancient love asunder?": Lesbian Elegy in Donne, Marvell, and Milton.' *ELH* 54 (1987): 835–67.

Horne, R.C. 'Voices of Alienation: The Moral Significance of Marston's Satiric Strategy.' *Modern Language Review* 81 (1986): 18–33.

Houppert, Joseph W. *John Lyly*. Boston: Twayne, 1975.

Howard, Jean. 'Sex and Social Conflict: The Erotics of *The Roaring Girl.*' In *Erotic Politics: Desire on the Renaissance Stage*, ed. Susan Zimmerman. 170–90. New York: Palgrave, 1992.

Hull, Elizabeth. 'All my deed but copying is: The Erotics of Identity in *Astrophil and Stella.*' *Texas Studies in Literature and Language* 38 (1996): 175–90.

Hulse, Clark. 'Stella's Wit: Penelope Rich as Reader of Sidney's Sonnets.' In *Rewriting the Renaissance: The Discourse of Sexual Defference in Early Modern Europe*, ed. Margaret W. Ferguson, Maureen Quilligan, Nancy J. Vickers, and Catharine R. Stimpson. 272–86. Chicago: University of Chicago Press, 1986.

Hunter, G.K. *John Lyly: The Humanist as Courtier*. London: Routledge and Kegan Paul, 1962.

Iyengar, Sujata. 'Moorish Dancing in *The Two Noble Kinsmen.*' *Medieval and Renaissance Drama in England* 20 (2007): 85–107.

Jacobs, Deborah. 'Critical Imperialism and Renaissance Drama: The Case of *The Roaring Girl.*' In *Feminism, Bakhtin, and the Dialogic*, ed. Dale M. Bauer and Susan Jaret McKinstry. 73–84. Albany: State University of New York Press, 1991.

Jankowski, Theodora A. '"Where there can be no cause of affection": Redefining Virgins, Their Desires, and their Pleasures in John Lyly's *Gallathea.*' In *Feminist Readings of Early Modern Culture: Emerging Subjects*, ed. Valerie Traub, M. Lindsay Kaplan, and Dympna Callaghan. 253–74. Cambridge: Cambridge University Press, 1996.

Johnson, Barbara A. 'Falling into Allegory: The "Apology" to *The Pilgrim's Progress* and Bunyan's Scriptural Methodology.' In *Bunyan in Our Time*, ed. Robert G. Collmer. 113–37. Kent, OH: Kent State University Press, 1989.

Jones, Ann Rosalind, and Peter Stallybrass. *Renaissance Clothing and the Materials of Memory*. Cambridge: Cambridge University Press, 2000.

Kalstone, David. *Sidney's Poetry: Contexts and Interpretations*. Cambridge, MA: Harvard University Press, 1965.

Kambasković-Sawers, Danijela. '"Never was I the golden cloud": Ovidian Myth, Ambiguous Speaker and the Narrative in the Sonnet Sequences by Petrarch, Sidney, and Spenser.' *Renaissance Studies* 21 (2007): 637–61.

Keach, William. *Elizabethan Erotic Narratives: Irony and Pathos in the Ovidian Poetry of Shakespeare, Marlowe, and Their Contemporaries*. New Brunswick, NJ: Rutgers University Press, 1977.

Kehler, Dorothea. 'Shakespeare's Emilias and the Politics of Celibacy.' In *In Another Country: Feminist Perspectives on Renaissance Drama*, ed. Dorothea Kehler and Susan Baker. 157–78. Metuchen, NJ: Scarecrow Press, 1991.

Keller, Eve. *Generating Bodies and Gendered Selves: The Rhetoric of Reproduction in Early Modern England*. Seattle: University of Washington Press, 2007.

Kermode, Lloyd Edward. 'Destination Doomsday: Desires for Change and Changeable Desires in *The Roaring Girl*.' *English Literary Renaissance* 27 (1997): 421–42.

Kerrigan, William, and Gordon Braden. 'Milton's Coy Eve: *Paradise Lost* and Renaissance Love Poetry.' *ELH* 53 (1986): 27–51.

Kipnis, Laura. 'Adultery.' *Critical Inquiry* 24 (1998): 289–327.

Kirk, Elizabeth. 'Women Academics at Royal Holloway and Bedford Colleges, 1939–69.' *Historical Research* 76:191 (2003): 128–50.

Krantz, Susan E. 'The Sexual Identities of Moll Cutpurse in Dekker and Middleton's *The Roaring Girl* and in London.' *Renaissance and Reformation* 19 (1995): 5–20.

Krier, Theresa M. *Birth Passages: Maternity and Nostalgia, Antiquity to Shakespeare*. Ithaca, NY: Cornell University Press, 2001.

Kristeva, Julia. *Powers of Horror: An Essay on Abjection*. Trans. L. Roudiez. New York: Columbia University Press, 1982.

Lamb, Mary Ellen. 'The Countess of Pembroke's Patronage.' *English Literary Renaissance* 12 (1982): 162–79.

Lancashire, Anne. 'John Lyly and Pastoral Entertainment.' In *The Elizabethan Theatre VIII*, ed. G.R. Hibbard. 22–50. Port Credit, ON: P.D. Meany, 1982.

Laqueur, Thomas. *Making Sex: Body and Gender from the Greeks to Freud*. Cambridge, MA: Harvard University Press, 1990.

Lehnhof, Kent R. '*Paradise Lost* and the Concept of Creation.' *South Central Review* 21.2 (2004): 15–41.

Lerer, Seth. 'The Courtly Body and Late Medieval Literary Culture.' In *The Book and the Body*, ed. Dolores Warwick Frese and Katherine O'Brien O'Keeffe. 78–115. Notre Dame, IN: University of Notre Dame Press, 1997.

Levao, Ronald. *Renaissance Minds and their Fictions: Cusanus, Sidney, and Shakespeare*. Berkeley: University of California Press, 1985.

Levin, Harry. *The Overreacher: A Study of Christopher Marlowe*. London: Faber and Faber, 1954.

Lewalski, Barbara K. *The Life of John Milton: A Critical Biography*. Oxford: Blackwell, 2000.

Lief, Madelon, and Nicholas F. Radel. 'Linguistic Subversion and the Artifice of Rhetoric in *The Two Noble Kinsmen*.' *Shakespeare Quarterly* 38 (1987): 405–25.

Logan, Robert A. 'Perspective in Marlowe's *Hero and Leander*: Engaging our Detachment.' In *'A Poet and a filthy Play-maker': New Essays on Christopher Marlowe*, ed. Kenneth Friedenreich, Roma Gill, and Constance B. Kuriyama. 279–91. New York: AMS, 1988.

Longenbach, James. *The Resistance to Poetry*. Chicago: University of Chicago Press, 2004.

Lord, George de F. 'Milton's Dialogue with Omniscience in *Paradise Lost*.' In *The Author in His Work: Essays on a Problem in Criticism*, ed. Louis L. Martz and Aubrey Williams. 31–50. New Haven, CT: Yale University Press, 1978.

Love, Heather. *Feeling Backward: Loss and the Politics of Queer History*. Cambridge, MA: Harvard University Press, 2007.

Low, Anthony. '"No middle flight": *Paradise Lost*, I.14.' *Milton Newsletter* 3 (1969): 1–4.

Lyly, John. *The Complete Works of John Lyly*. Edited by R. Warwick Bond. 3 vols. Oxford: Clarendon Press, 1902.

– *The Woman in the Moon*. Edited by Leah Scragg. Manchester: Manchester University Press, 2006.

Lynch, Beth. *John Bunyan and the Language of Conviction*. Woodbridge, UK: D.S. Brewer, 2004.

MacCulloch, Diarmaid. *Reformation: Europe's House Divided, 1490–1700*. London: Allen Lane, 2003.

Macfie, Pamela Royston. 'Ghostly Metamorphoses: Chapman, Marlowe, and Ovid's Philomela.' *John Donne Journal* 18 (1999): 177–93.

– 'Marlowe's Ghost-Writing of Ovid's *Heroides*.' In *Renaissance Papers 2001*, ed. M. Thomas Hester. 57–72. Rochester, NY: Camden House, 2001.

Machosky, Brenda. 'Trope and Truth in *The Pilgrim's Progress*.' *Studies in English Literature* 47 (2007): 179–98.

MacKendrick, Karmen. *Counterpleasures*. Albany: State University Press of New York, 1999.

Magnusson, Lynne. 'The Collapse of Shakespeare's High Style in *The Two Noble Kinsmen*.' *English Studies in Canada* 13 (1987): 375–90.

Maguire, Laurie. 'How Many Children Had Alice Walker?' In *Printing and Parenting in Early Modern England*, ed. Douglas A. Brooks. 327–50. Aldershot, UK: Ashgate, 2005.

Mallette, Richard. 'Same-Sex Erotic Friendship in *The Two Noble Kinsmen*.' *Renaissance Drama* 26 (1995): 29–52.

Marcuse, Herbert. *Eros and Civilization: A Philosophical Inquiry into Freud*. Boston: Beacon Press, 1966.

– *The Aesthetic Dimension: Toward a Critique of Marxist Aesthetics*. Boston: Beacon Press, 1978.

Marin, Louis. *Utopics: Spatial Play*. Trans. R.A. Vollrath. London: Macmillan, 1984.

– 'Frontiers of Utopia: Past and Present.' *Critical Inquiry* 19 (1993): 307–420.

Marlowe, Christopher. *The Complete Works of Christopher Marlowe*. Edited by Fredson Bowers. Vol. 2. Cambridge: Cambridge University Press, 1981.

Marotti, Arthur F. '"Love is Not Love": Elizabethan Sonnet Sequences and the Social Order.' *ELH* 49 (1982): 396–428.
– *Manuscript, Print, and the English Renaissance Lyric*. Ithaca, NY: Cornell University Press, 1995.
Marston, John. *The Poems of John Marston*. Edited by Arnold Davenport. Liverpool: University of Liverpool Press, 1961.
Masten, Jeffrey. *Textual Intercourse: Collaboration, Authorship and Sexualities in Renaissance Drama*. Cambridge: Cambridge University Press, 1997.
Mattison, Andrew. *Milton's Uncertain Eden: Understanding Place in* Paradise Lost. New York: Routledge, 2007.
Matz, Robert. *Defending Literature in Early Modern England: Renaissance Literary Theory in Social Context*. Cambridge: Cambridge University Press, 2000.
Maus, Katharine Eisaman. 'A Womb of His Own: Male Renaissance Poets in the Female Body.' In *Printing and Parenting in Early Modern England*, ed. Douglas A. Brooks. 89–108. Aldershot, UK: Ashgate, 2005.
May, Steven. *The Elizabethan Courtier Poets: The Poems and Their Contexts*. Columbia: University of Missouri Press, 1995.
McMahon, Robert. *The Two Poets of* Paradise Lost. Baton Rouge: Louisiana State University Press, 1998.
McManus, Clare. 'The Roaring Girl and the London Underworld.' In *Early Modern English Drama: A Critical Companion*, ed. Garrett A. Sullivan, Jr, Patrick Cheney, and Andrew Hadfield. 213–24. New York: Oxford University Press, 2006.
Menon, Madhavi. *Wanton Words: Rhetoric and Sexuality in English Renaissance Drama*. Toronto: University of Toronto Press, 2004.
– *Unhistorical Shakespeare: Queer Theory in Shakespearean Literature and Film*. New York: Palgrave Macmillan, 2008.
Middleton, Thomas, and Thomas Dekker. *The Roaring Girl*. Edited by Coppélia Kahn. In *Thomas Middleton: The Collected Works*. Edited by Gary Taylor and John Lavagnino. Oxford: Clarendon Press, 2007.
Mikalachki, Jodi. 'Gender, Cant, and Cross-Talking in *The Roaring Girl*.' *Renaissance Drama* n.s. 15 (1994): 119–43.
Miller, D.A. 'Anal Rope.' *Representations* 32 (Autumn 1990): 114–33.
Miller, David Lee. 'The Death of the Modern: Gender and Desire in Marlowe's "Hero and Leander."' *South Atlantic Quarterly* 88 (1989): 757–87.
Miller, J. Hillis. *Versions of Pygmalion*. Cambridge, MA: Harvard University Press, 1990.
Miller, Jacqueline T. '"Love doth hold my hand": Writing and Wooing in the Sonnets of Sidney and Spenser.' *ELH* 46 (1979): 541–58.

Milton, John. *The Complete Poetry of John Milton*. Edited by John T. Shawcross. New York: Doubleday, 1971.

Minogue, Sally. 'A Woman's Touch: Astrophil, Stella, and "Queen Vertue's Court."' *ELH* 63 (1996): 555–70.

Moeck, William. 'Bees in My Bonnet: Milton's Epic Simile and Intertextuality.' *Milton Quarterly* 32.4 (1998): 122–35.

Montaigne, Michel de. *Essays Written in French*. Translated by J. Florio. London, 1632.

– *Les Essais*. Edited by Jean Balsamo, Michel Magnien, and Catherine Magnien-Simonin. Paris: Gallimard, 2007.

Munt, Sally R. *Queer Attachments: The Cultural Politics of Shame*. Aldershot, UK: Ashgate, 2007.

Murphy, Erin. 'Milton's "Birth Abortive": Remaking Family at the End of *Paradise Lost*.' *Milton Studies* 43 (2004): 145–70.

Neely, Carol Thomas. 'The Structure of English Renaissance Sonnet Sequences.' *ELH* 45 (1978): 359–89.

– *Distracted Subjects: Madness and Gender in Shakespeare and Early Modern Culture*. Ithaca, NY: Cornell University Press, 2004.

Newcastle, Margaret Cavendish, Duchess of. *Paper Bodies: A Margaret Cavendish Reader*. Edited by Sylvia Bowerbank and Sara Mendelson. Peterborough, ON: Broadview, 2000.

Ng, Su Fang. *Literature and the Politics of the Family in Seventeenth-Century England*. Cambridge: Cambridge University Press, 2007.

Nunokawa, Jeff. *Tame Passions of Desire: The Styles of Manageable Desire*. Princeton: Princeton University Press, 2003.

Oerlemans, Onno. 'The Will to Knowledge and the Process of Narrative in *Paradise Lost*.' *English Studies in Canada* 16 (1990): 1–15.

O'Neill, John. *Essaying Montaigne: A Study of the Renaissance Institution of Writing and Reading*. Liverpool: Liverpool University Press, 2001.

Orgel, Stephen. 'The subtexts of *The Roaring Girl*.' In *Erotic Politics: Desire on the Renaissance Stage*, ed. Susan Zimmerman. 12–26. New York: Palgrave, 1992.

– 'Marginal Maternity: Reading Lady Anne Clifford's *A Mirror for Magistrates*.' In *Printing and Parenting in Early Modern England*, ed. Douglas A. Brooks. 267–89. Aldershot, UK: Ashgate, 2005.

Orlandi, Mary-Kay Gamel. 'Ovid True and False in Renaissance Poetry.' *Pacific Coast Philology* 13 (1978): 60–70.

Ovid. *Tristium Liber IV*. Edited by Theodore de Jonge. Groningen, Netherlands: de Waal, 1951.

– *Ovid's Metamorphoses*. Edited by Madeleine. Forey. Translated by A. Golding. Baltimore: Johns Hopkins University Press, 2001.

– *Metamorphoses*. Edited by R.J. Tarrant. Oxford: Clarendon Press, 2004.

Parker, Patricia. *Inescapable Romance: Studies in the Poetics of a Mode*. Princeton, NJ: Princeton University Press, 1979.

Pavlock, Barbara. *Eros, Imitation, and the Epic Tradition*. Ithaca, NY: Cornell University Press, 1990.

Pellicer, Juan Christian. 'Virgil's *Georgics* II and *Paradise Lost*.' *Translation and Literature* 14 (2005): 129–47.

Pincher, John. 'Editing Daniel.' In *New Ways of Looking at Old Texts: Papers of the Renaissance English Text Society, 1985–1991*, ed. W. Speed Hill. 57–73. Binghamton, NY: Medieval and Renaissance Texts and Studies, 1993.

Plato. *Opera*. Edited by John Burnet. Oxford: Clarendon Press, 1901.

Prendergast, Maria Teresa (Micaela). 'The Unauthorized Orpheus of *Astrophil and Stella*.' *SEL* 35 (1995): 19–34.

– 'Promiscuous Textualities: The Nashe-Harvey Controversy and the Unnatural Productions of Print.' In *Printing and Parenting in Early Modern England*, ed. Douglas A. Brooks. 173–95. Aldershot, UK: Ashgate, 2005.

Quilligan, Maureen. 'Sidney and His Queen.' In *The Historical Renaissance: New Essays on Tudor and Stuart Literature and Culture*, ed. Heather Dubrow and Richard Strier. 171–96. Chicago: University of Chicago Press, 1988.

Quinn, Kelly A. 'Fulke Greville's Friendly Patronage.' *Studies in Philology* 103 (2006): 417–35.

Quint, David. *Origin and Originality in Renaissance Literature: Versions of the Source*. New Haven, CT: Yale University Press, 1983.

Rambuss, Rick. 'After Male Sex.' *South Atlantic Quarterly* 106 (2007): 577–88.

Readings, Bill. '"An age too late": Milton and the Time of Literary History.' *Exemplaria* 4 (1992): 455–68.

Rees, Joan. *Samuel Daniel*. Liverpool: Liverpool University Press, 1964.

Regosin, Richard L. *Montaigne's Unruly Brood: Textual Engendering and the Challenge to Paternal Authority*. Berkeley: University of California Press, 1996.

Robertson, A.F. *Beyond the Family: The Social Organization of Human Reproduction*. Berkeley: University of California Press, 1991.

Roche, Thomas P., Jr. *Petrarch and the English Sonnet Sequence*. New York: AMS, 1989.

Roof, Judith. *Reproduction of Reproduction: Imaging Symbolic Change*. New York: Routledge, 1996.

– 'In Locus Parentis.' In *Printing and Parenting in Early Modern England*, ed. Douglas A. Brooks. 371–94. Aldershot UK: Ashgate, 2005.

Rose, Mary Beth. 'Women in Men's Clothing: Apparel and Social Stability in *The Roaring Girl*.' *English Literary Renaissance* 14 (1984): 367–91.

Rumrich, John P. *Milton Unbound: Controversy and Reinterpretation*. Cambridge: Cambridge University Press, 1996.

Saenger, Michael. *The Commodification of Textual Engagements in the English Renaissance*. Aldershot, UK: Ashgate, 2006.

Salzman, Paul. 'Early Modern (Aristocratic) Women and Textual Property.' In *Women, Property, and the Letters of the Law in Early Modern England*, ed. Nancy E. Wright, Margaret W. Ferguson, and A.R. Buck. 281–95. Toronto: University of Toronto Press, 2004.

Saunders, J.W. 'The Stigma of Print: A Note on the Social Bases of Tudor Poetry.' *Essays in Criticism* 1 (1951): 139–64.

Schindler, Walter. *Voice and Crisis: Invocations in Milton's Poetry*. Hamden, CT: Archon Books, 1984.

Schwarz, Kathryn. *Tough Love: Amazon Encounters in the English Renaissance*. Durham, NC: Duke University Press, 2000.

Schwarz, Regina. *Remembering and Repeating: Biblical Creation in* Paradise Lost. Cambridge: Cambridge University Press, 1988.

Sedgwick, Eve Kosofsky. *Epistemology of the Closet*. New York: Harvester Wheatsheaf, 1991.

– 'Shame, Theatricality, and Queer Performativity: Henry James's *The Art of The Novel*.' In *Touching Feeling: Affect, Pedagogy, Performativity*, ed. Eve Kosofsky Sedgwick and Adam Frank. 35–65. Durham, NC: Duke University Press, 2003.

Seronsy, Cecil. *Samuel Daniel*. New York: Twayne, 1974.

Shakespeare, William. *The Riverside Shakespeare*. Edited by G. Blakemore Evans. Boston: Houghton Mifflin, 1974.

Shakespeare, William, and John Fletcher. *The Two Noble Kinsmen*. Edited by Lois Potter. Walton-on-Thames, UK: Thomas Nelson, 1997.

Shannon, Laurie. *Sovereign Amity: Figures of Friendship in Shakespearean Contexts*. Chicago: University of Chicago Press, 2002.

Shelburne, Steven R. 'Principled Satire: Decorum in John Marston's *The Metamorphosis of Pigmalions Image and Certaine Satyres*.' *Studies in Philology* 86 (1989): 198–218.

Shoulson, Jeffrey S. 'The Embrace of the Fig Tree: Sexuality and Creativity in Midrash and Milton.' *ELH* 67 (2000): 873–903.

Sidney, Sir Philip. *The Poems of Sir Philip Sidney*. Edited by William A. Ringler Jr. Oxford: Clarendon Press, 1962.

– *The Prose Works of Sir Philip Sidney*. Edited by Albert Feuillerat. Vol. 3. Cambridge: Cambridge University Press, 1962.

Smith, Stephanie A. *Conceived by Liberty: Maternal Figures and 19th-Century American Literature*. Ithaca: Cornell University Press, 1994.

Spargo, Tamsin. *The Writing of John Bunyan*. Aldershot, UK: Ashgate, 1997.

Spencer, Jane. *Literary Relations: Kinship and the Canon, 1660–1830*. Oxford: Oxford University Press, 2005.

Spiller, Michael R.G. *The Development of the Sonnet: An Introduction.* London: Routledge, 1992.

Stallybrass, Peter. 'Shakespeare, the Individual, and the Text.' In *Cultural Studies*, ed. Lawrence Grossberg, Cary Nelson, and Paula A. Treichler. 593–612. New York: Routledge, 1992.

Stephanson, Raymond. *The Yard of Wit: Male Creativity and Sexuality, 1650–1750.* Philadelphia: University of Pennsylvania Press, 2004.

Stephens, Dorothy. *The Limits of Eroticism in Post-Petrarchan Narrative: Conditional Pleasures from Spenser to Marvell.* Cambridge: Cambridge University Press, 1998.

Stewart, Alan. '"Near Akin": The Trials of Friendship in *The Two Noble Kinsmen*.' In *Shakespeare's Late Plays: New Readings*, ed. Jennifer Richards and James Knowles. 57–71. Edinburgh: Edinburgh University Press, 1999.

Stockton, Kathryn Bond. *Beautiful Bottom, Beautiful Shame: Where 'Black' Meets 'Queer'.* Durham, NC: Duke University Press, 2006.

Summers, Claude J. '"Hero and Leander": The Arbitrariness of Desire.' In *Constructing Christopher Marlowe*, ed. J.A. Downie and J.T. Parnell. 133–47. Cambridge: Cambridge University Press, 2000.

Svensson, Lars-Hakan. *Silent Art: Rhetorical and Thematic Patterns in Samuel Daniel's* Delia. Lund: CWK Gleerup, 1980.

Swann, Marjorie. '"Procreate like Trees": Generation and Society in Thomas Browne's *Religio Medici*.' In *Engaging with Nature: Essays on the Natural World in Medieval and Early Modern Europe*, ed. Barbara A. Hanawalt and Lisa J. Kiser. 137–54. Notre Dame, IN: University of Notre Dame Press, 2008.

Taylor, Miles. '"Teach Me This Pedlar's French": The Allure of Cant in *The Roaring Girl* and Dekker's Rogue Pamphlets.' *Renaissance and Reformation* n.s. 29.4 (2005): 107–24.

Teague, Frances. 'Early Modern Women and "the muses ffemall."' In '*The Muses Female Are': Martha Moulsworth and Other Women Writers of the English Renaissance*, ed. Robert C. Evans and Anne C. Little. 173–9. West Cornwall, CT: Locust Hill Press, 1995.

Terranova, Tiziana. 'Digital Darwin: Nature, Evolution, and Control in the Rhetoric of Electronic Communication.' *New Formations* 29 (Autumn 1996): 69–83.

Teskey, Gordon. *Delirious Milton: The Fate of the Poet in Modernity.* Cambridge, MA: Harvard University Press, 2006.

Theis, Jeffrey S. 'Milton's Principles of Architecture.' *English Literary Renaissance* 35 (2005): 102–22.

Thompson, R. Ann. 'Jailer's Daughters in *The Arcadia* and *The Two Noble Kinsmen*.' *Notes and Queries* 224 (1979): 140–1.

Traub, Valerie. 'Sex Without Issue: Sodomy, Reproduction, and Signification in Shakespeare's Sonnets.' In *Shakespeare's Sonnets: Critical Essays*, ed. James Schiffer. 431–52. New York: Garland, 1999.
– *The Renaissance of Lesbianism in Early Modern England*. Cambridge: Cambridge University Press, 2002.
Tromly, Fred. *Playing with Desire: Christopher Marlowe and the Art of Tantalization*. Toronto: University of Toronto Press, 1998.
Turner, Henry S. *The English Renaissance Stage: Geometry, Poetics, and the Practical Spatial Arts*. Oxford: Oxford University Press, 2006.
– *Shakespeare's Double Helix*. London: Continuum, 2007.
Turner, Myron. 'Pastoral and Hermaphrodite: A Study in the Naturalism of Marlowe's *Hero and Leander*.' *Texas Studies in Literature and Language* 17 (1975): 397–414.
Vaneigem, Raoul. *The Book of Pleasures*. Translated by J. Fullerton. London: Pending, 1983.
Vanhoutte, Jacqueline. 'A Strange Hatred of Marriage: John Lyly, Elizabeth I, and the Ends of Comedy.' In *The Single Woman in Medieval and Early Modern England: Her Life and Representation*, ed. Laurel Amtower and Dorothea Kehler. 97–115. Tempe: Arizona Center for Medieval and Renaissance Studies, 2003.
Virgil. *Opera*. Edited by R.A.B. Mynors. Oxford: Clarendon Press, 1969.
– *The Eclogues and Georgics*. Edited by R.D. Williams. New York: St Martin's Press, 1979.
Wakelin, Daniel. *Humanism, Reading, and English Literature, 1430–1530*. Oxford: Oxford University Press, 2007.
Walker, Jeffrey. *Rhetoric and Poetics in Antiquity*. Oxford: Oxford University Press, 2000.
Wall, Wendy. *The Imprint of Gender: Authorship and Publication in the English Renaissance*. Ithaca, NY: Cornell University Press, 1993.
Warley, Christopher. *Sonnet Sequences and Social Distinction in Renaissance England*. Cambridge: Cambridge University Press, 2005.
Weller, Barry. 'The Two Noble Kinsmen, the Friendship Tradition, and the Flight from Eros.' In *Shakespeare, Fletcher, and* The Two Noble Kinsmen, ed. Charles H. Frey. 93–108. Columbia: University of Missouri Press, 1989.
Whitelaw, Mitchell. *Metacreation: Art and Artificial Life*. Cambridge, MA: MIT Press, 2004.
Witmore, Michael. *Pretty Creatures: Children and Fiction in the English Renaissance*. Ithaca, NY: Cornell University Press, 2007.
Žižek, Slavoj. *The Parallax View*. Boston: MIT Press, 2006.

Index